For Henry and Ingrid Wuga, and my parents.

HOME LANDS

The history of a friendship

Withdrawn
from Stock

CHITRA RAMASWAMY

CANONGATE

This paperback edition published in Great Britain, the USA and
Canada in 2023 by Canongate Books

First published in Great Britain, the USA and Canada in 2022
by Canongate Books Ltd, 14 High Street, Edinburgh EH1 1TE

Distributed in the USA by Publishers Group
West and in Canada by Publishers Group Canada

canongate.co.uk

1

Copyright © Chitra Ramaswamy, 2022

Every effort has been made to trace copyright holders
and obtain their permission for the use of copyright material.
The publisher apologises for any errors or omissions and would
be grateful if notified of any corrections that should be
incorporated in future reprints or editions of this book.

For permission credits, please see p.351

The author gratefully acknowledges the support of
Creative Scotland towards the publication of this book.

The right of Chitra Ramaswamy to be identified as the
author of this work has been asserted by her in accordance
with the Copyright, Designs and Patents Act 1988

British Library Cataloguing-in-Publication Data
A catalogue record for this book is available on
request from the British Library

ISBN 978 1 83885 269 6

Typeset in Sabon LT Std by Palimpsest Book Production Ltd,
Falkirk, Stirlingshire

Printed and bound in Great Britain by Clays Ltd, Elcograf S.p.A.

It seems to me then as if all the moments of our life occupy the same space, as if future events already existed and were only waiting for us to find our way to them at last, just as when we have accepted an invitation we duly arrive in a certain house at a given time. And might it not be, continued Austerlitz, that we also have appointments to keep in the past . . .?

W. G. Sebald, *Austerlitz* (2001)

People are trapped in history and history is trapped in them.

James Baldwin, 'Stranger in the Village' (1953)

The world lies between people.

Hannah Arendt, *Men in Dark Times* (1968)

Prologue
'It's the truth!'

It is easy to know the beginnings of things but impossible, at the time, to see what exactly they begin. So I will start here, on a recent Friday afternoon in the latter days of February. The day before Henry Wuga's ninety-fifth birthday. A staging post in a lifetime we sometimes call the twilight years. If a pin were to be dropped on a map it would land on a lone and unexpected row of houses on the southern edge of Edinburgh. Reached by an easily missed turn off a ceaselessly busy A-road and hemmed in on the other side by the Pentland Hills, which over the centuries have acquired some of the stately character of the city they overlook, it's hard to conceive how this particular stretch of houses came to be built on the nub end of the hills. Not that long after Henry was born a thousand miles away in Nuremberg.

It's also impossible to imagine getting here on foot. As I cannot drive and am the daughter of lifelong non-drivers, my not driving has calcified over the years into a personality trait. Like my love of a good laugh, or Henry's notoriously sharp memory. The outcome is that I never know exactly how I get here. That is, until the car, driven by my very-much-a-driver partner Claire, pulls up outside the house where Gillian, the younger of Henry's two daughters, lives and we make the short steep climb to the front door. In years gone by, before age put an end to it, Henry and his wife Ingrid would already be waiting outside to greet us

1

by the time we turned onto the street. Framed by the door, side by side, waving and smiling. Dressed in the carefully chosen and cared for clothes of people who know how to live a good stylish life. A photograph come to life, the kind you might find jumbled up with old postcards in a 50p box in a flea market. At the door an affectionate but restrained hug would take place, the straight-backed kind reminiscent of so many fathers of a certain generation and their children. Then we would disappear into the house together.

On this occasion Henry is waiting for us in the conservatory, where a small afternoon tea has been laid out. The room looks directly onto the section of the Pentlands which is home to Europe's longest dry ski slope. Skiing always makes me think of Henry and Ingrid. When I first met them, they were still taking to the slopes, by this time in their late eighties.

Once, when Henry was in the spa town of Klosters, Switzerland, he found himself standing next to Prince Charles in the queue for the ski lift. 'I mean!' Henry laughed, though I was unsure whether his incredulity was about running into the Prince of Wales 1,200 metres above sea level or the fact that he was standing in a queue. Henry, of course, said 'Afternoon, sir', and the heir to the British throne asked him where he came from, that polite enquiry that chases so many of us around the world. Whether formed in the mouths of princes or plebs, it always serves as a reminder, no matter where we happen to be or how benign the intention, that the possibility of our belonging here, or indeed anywhere, is questionable. Henry's reply, in this case, was Glasgow. But where did he come from before that, the Prince probed, intrigued by Henry's strong German accent. This, too, is part of the script. And the older I get the more I realise that there is no answer to the question that really satisfies anyone. It seems that the further we journey from birth, the more difficult it becomes to know where we come from. 'Perhaps home is not a place,' wrote James Baldwin, 'but simply an irrevocable condition.'

Then came another question: what is this you're sitting on? 'I said "It's a ski bob, sir,"' says Henry. 'He said "I've never seen one."' And then the story becomes pure Henry Wuga. A haiku of this man's character demonstrating his respect, above all else, for things as they are. The facts. 'I said "I beg your pardon, sir, but I've seen a picture of you sitting on one."' And when the Wugas returned home from Switzerland Henry located the photograph of Prince Charles sitting on a ski bob, sent it to the palace, and got a reply in which the mistake was confirmed.

'It's the truth!' Henry concluded triumphantly.

The afternoon tea is set on the table. Tea, poured from a pot into thin cups with saucers, cake, homemade by Gillian, and fruit. Sitting there I recall a past visit not long after the conservatory was built when my son fell and split his lip on the cool, newly laid tiles. The blood oozed between his just-cut teeth, and my fluttering panic, still then shockingly unfamiliar to me as a new mother, burst open like a wound. Gillian's husband, who is a dentist but kindly assumed the role of doctor for the duration, picked him up, examined his dainty screaming mouth, and diagnosed him to be fine. There is nothing remarkable about this memory. My son fell in a hundred other places, especially around that time when he had a tragic habit of falling flat on his face as he was careering towards an object of desire. And yet this mundane scrap of family history flashes before my eyes whenever I sit in that sunny conservatory, making conversation, drinking tea and eating freshly washed and cut strawberries selected from a big bowl. The hardness of that floor will always make me wince. When I ask if anyone else remembers, the answer unsurprisingly is no. It is the memory of a mother, and mine alone.

Henry is recovering from a desperately needed and valiantly fought-for hip operation. He stands up to greet us and takes a few careful steps towards me, flashing his trademark grin, the one he switches on like a bulb for photographs. We all cheer. Ingrid, who is a few months younger than her husband, remains sitting on the sofa blinking amused eyes behind thick glasses. She keeps asking 'why are we here?' and 'when are we going home?'. Both excellent questions, the answers to which, in this moment, are 'because it's Henry's birthday weekend' and 'not today Mummy'. Ingrid has vascular dementia. Sometimes when I see her she remembers a little more, sometimes less. Wading into her deep past is more reliable than staying in the shallows, but there is nothing linear about the loss of memory. It seems to be as much about what endures as what falls away. And what remains, in Ingrid's case, is life distilled to its poetics. Humour, music, family, childhood, and beneath all this, like an anchor lodged in the seabed of her past, Henry.

Also present at this celebration of one man's life are my two children. My daughter runs around charming everyone with her irrepressible one-year-oldness, blowing kisses to a digger on the hills. My son, who is five, goes straight upstairs to play in a bed. He is autistic and not in general a fan of parties, however small, significant, or hard-won. This is all three. Only weeks earlier Hilary, Henry and Ingrid's older daughter, phoned to ask me if I would be willing to write Henry's obituary if the hip operation was unsuccessful.

Later, however, my son agrees to join us in the conservatory, scene of the split lip. He instantly spots the room divide between conservatory and lounge as not just a potential train track but an actual, literal train track. He drops to his knees with his head on the ground, as has been his favoured stance since he could command his body at all. He runs an imaginary train back and forth along the track.

He makes train noises. He demands a ticket. Henry watches with great interest. I watch Henry. Then he gets up slowly and shuffles over to my son. He stands there for a while, asking nothing of him, staying out of his space, intuitively doing all the things parents of autistic children desperately want others to do in their company. It occurs to me that all three of us are thinking about trains yet our trains of thought are running on completely separate tracks. Eventually I fish around for a 'ticket' in my pocket and come up with a loyalty card for a café near where we live on the opposite side of Edinburgh. I hand it to Henry. He hands it to my son.

We don't stay long. Parties are a tiring business for young and old. Before we leave I sit on the floor beside Henry. He tells me that for the first time in his life he feels his age. A dear friend of his died recently. He was only a year younger than Henry. Ninety-four. And his name, too, was Henry. Henry Rose. The Wugas and the Roses had been 'true friends' for decades. They used to go on family holidays to Cornwall together in the 1950s with their daughters, which touches me because when I was a little girl, three decades later, my mother and father took their daughters, my sister and I, to Cornwall on holiday too. Since Henry Rose's death, his daughters have begun uncovering 'the most remarkable facts' about his life, which, like so many, he never spoke about. Henry goes quiet. The conversation, through our silent but mutual agreement, is at its end.

A few weeks later I will get an email from Henry. My inbox, and heart, will be full of him by this point. I have been interviewing Henry for years, we have become friends, and in recent months the conversations have started increasing in length, scope, and urgency. I am still considering what to do with them, but it is becoming clearer by the day that something must be done. In the meantime, every exchange seems to spawn another. Every story constructs a bridge to another time.

'I feel a little apprehensive but honoured that you wish to write about my story,' writes Henry. 'I would be pleased to meet with you as often as you like. You will have access to all my documents, files, photos and my writings, journals etc.'

His email then turns to his dear friend Henry Rose.

'Lost his whole family,' Henry continues. 'He never talked about it. Some people simply draw the line . . . Then and Now.'

Henry, however, chose a different way. Or perhaps it would be truer to say that the path of his own past permitted him, like a right of way, to speak out. 'Maybe I talk too much,' is how he puts it, 'but I was safe in Britain and escaped the horrors of the Shoa.'

'Look forward to talking with you,' he concludes. 'Hope I can answer all your questions.'

'We were sailing near the wind.'

Henry is at his desk, busy with his files. The midday sun pours through the window, blotting out the view so it seems there is nothing beyond but an empty burnished light, the never-ending kind that suffuses dreams. And memories. On the desk are stacks of papers in an order that only their owner can fathom, photos in frames, post-cards, newspapers, a table lamp, telephone, vase of yellow roses, and Henry's glasses, which he has a habit of removing to allow closer examination of a document. To his right, his computer. On his other side, Ingrid, his wife of more than seventy years, dozing in an oversized leather recliner. Poised, I instinctively feel, to pipe up any second now.

'Look,' says Henry. 'This is what I wanted to show you. The National Archives said they couldn't reveal this to me for another twenty-five years. I said I'll be dead by then! They eventually sent it, as you can see.' Henry sweeps a shaking hand across a stack of files. On the top is a title page with the National Archives logo. On a little green square at the bottom of the page, just below a Home Office series number (HO405/60809), are the words 'closed until 2049'. The only handwriting on the page is this quartet of numbers: 2049. The future. A place where none of us can go. A topsy-turvy suspense, relating to the revelation of past events, hangs in the room like the dust motes spotlit by the sun.

This is where I picture Henry whenever he enters my

thoughts. In the sitting room of his and Ingrid's mid-century flat in Giffnock on the south side of Glasgow. The image is like a portrait stored in the attic of my mind. Like a painting by an Old Master, the paint all shiny and veined with cracks, where everything stands both for itself and something else. The little silver dishes of nuts and individually wrapped chocolates on the gleaming coffee table speak of hospitality and an old-fashioned and unmistakably European skein of formality that is as much about showing you care as the performance of ritual. The yellow roses in full bloom emanate an attendance to beauty, nature, and making things last. The family photos lining every wall and surface, in which the Wugas grin from behind sunglasses on a crystalline slope in the Italian Alps or their two daughters throw sideways glances in Sixties headscarves, chronicle both a family saga of love and survival across four generations, and a potted history of Europe in the twentieth century. And the vintage map framed in the hall invites the visitor to return to the precise spot in the southern German state of Bavaria where a Jewish baby boy called Heinz Martin Wuga was born in the freezing second month of 1924.

The purpose of today's visit, also attended by Hilary, who is visiting from London and has over recent years assumed the role of her parents' personal assistant, archivist, and occasional translator, is to go through a sheaf of A3 documents. A forty-nine-page record recently acquired by the Wugas from the National Archives following a Freedom of Information request. The contents of the file are conveyed on paper so thin it reminds me of the blue airmail letters that arrived from India throughout my childhood. Fringed with blue and red. Opened immediately. The contents so highly prized, in a beautiful curly script I could not read, on paper as fragile as my parents looked when they read them. Those letters from an amorphous group of people collectively known as *our family* frightened me. They turned my mother and father into strangers. And me into a foreigner in my own home.

Henry's documents have been held for years in a Seventies building in southwest London, the brutalist kind in front of which fountains eternally spring and doors relentlessly revolve. The National Archives, built on the site of a First World War hospital in Kew, opened just two years before I was born. It turns out that I spent my childhood sleeping next to this alternative history of Henry's life. A secret kept from him until now.

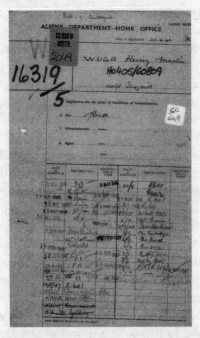

What's inside, relayed in the chilly and obfuscating language of officialdom, is both shocking and confirmation of what Henry has long suspected. That during and after the Second World War he was investigated by the Home Office and MI5, suspected of being a communist spy, and nearly refused naturalisation as a result. 'It was a hunch and that's all it ever was but we now have proof,' says Hilary. Henry is still working through the file, as if it is revision that requires learning before a citizenship test and not some long withheld palimpsest of his life. There are further documents in the record, which runs from 1 January 1946 to 31 December 1948, but the National Archives has withheld them under FOI and Data Protection legislation.

The reasons for MI5's suspicion are at once deeply personal and a blanket case of *what happened during the war*. It goes to the heart of Henry's formative experiences in Britain, particularly 'the first twenty-three months', as he describes them with typically stubborn specificity. An extraordinary period, with all the thundering pace, cliff-hangers, dizzying location changes and improbable characters of a spy thriller. When it began to occur to me slowly, like a sculpture emerging out of stone, that there might be more, perhaps even a book, in all this, it was to those twenty-three months that I kept returning. To what any journalist would call *a great story* in which Henry, then just sixteen years old, was brought before the High Court in Edinburgh, wrongly accused of corresponding with the enemy, labelled a dangerous enemy alien category A, and interned in six camps across Britain. But it is more than a great story. It is more than history. It is Henry's life, and like the endless passing of the present moment, the pages keep turning. The past is never still, and some of it remains forever closed to us.

In these pages Henry learns how closely he was tracked when he came to Britain in the spring of 1939. When he pulled into Liverpool Street Station on a Kindertransport, a British initiative that rescued almost 10,000 predominantly Jewish children in the nine months leading up to the war. From the moment he got off that train the fifteen-year-old boy became a German Jewish refugee. And it was for this reason, alighting into the red mist of panic and paranoia seizing wartime Britain, that he and thousands like him were watched. Suspected. Blamed. Rounded up. Interned. Deported.

In the file, there are reports supplied by a chief constable, the head chef of a restaurant, the painter David Sassoon, and a former headmaster at the Perthshire school where Henry was evacuated. There are school records in which Henry's high intelligence is framed as cause for suspicion. There's an official enquiry, made by MI5 to the CIA in August 1947, 'as to whether anything is known or recorded about him / her'. And a newspaper clipping of a notice, placed in the Glasgow *Evening Citizen* in September 1947, informing the public that 'Heinz Martin Wuga of 329 Maxwell Road, Glasgow, is applying to the Home Secretary for Naturalisation and that any person who knows any reason why Naturalisation should not be granted should send a written and signed statement of the facts to the Under-Secretary of State, Aliens Department, Home Office, London.'

'But you were just a child refugee!'

'All I can say, Chitra,' says Henry, 'is to go to all this trouble during wartime they must have suspected me of bad correspondence.'

'You were not much more than a child,' says Hilary.

'I know,' says Henry. 'That's the difficulty. Children can be used for all sorts of things.'

'What was that?' asks Ingrid. She is awake, and for all we know has been listening the entire time.

'They were worried that when Daddy was writing to Oma he was corresponding as a spy,' says Hilary loudly.

Ingrid is incensed. 'He was not passing on any messages!'

The most explosive report is the one filed by the chief constable of Glasgow claiming Henry 'was a communist sympathiser, but not a member of the Communist Party in the United Kingdom.' The report continues: 'There does

11

not, however, appear to be definite confirmation that he has Communist inclinations.' It was this suspicion that almost jeopardised Henry and Ingrid's naturalisation.

'Oh my God, I'm amazed,' says Henry. 'We were sailing near the wind.'

Hilary rolls her eyes. She addresses her father directly. Puts her hand to her heart. 'Yes, Daddy, but how did you *feel*?' She pummels her chest lightly. Henry does not reply. He is engrossed in the files again, his glasses dispatched to the desk with their arms outstretched. Eventually Hilary turns to me, and with a child's exasperation whispers of her father, 'He just moves on!'

'Henry!' Ingrid says. 'Henry!' She shouts again, louder this time, in her particular way of annunciating her husband's name. Rich, heavily accented, shot through with the memory of the banter that not so long ago would have followed in a torrent of mischief and affection. She points at the papers strewn everywhere. 'What is that?'

'What is that?' repeats Henry, laughing. 'It's our history!'

Then Ingrid turns to me. Her eyes narrow. 'What is it you want you know?' she asks. Her question is genuine. She cannot remember why I am here.

I am thrown.

Anything you want to tell me, I say.

Then, because this seems general to the point of meaningless, I add, 'About you and your family.'

'I can't remember how quickly my parents came here,' Ingrid says.

She turns to Henry.

'They came one week before war broke out,' Henry replies. 'They applied to be domestic servants. You could get in that way.'

'If you were prepared to do housework,' adds Ingrid. Then a memory returns suddenly, as effortlessly as a sketch flowing from an artist's pencil. 'Some of my parents' friends said "We have staff here. I'm not going to be staff somewhere else." They were too proud. My parents said "We can't afford to be proud and toffee-nosed."' She looks at me, lifts her chin, and flicks her nose lightly. '"If we can get to Britain by being a butler and maid we will do it." Take your cap off, and get on with it.'

We pause to savour this beautifully preserved vignette. Every object in the room, the flowers, documents, and map of Nuremberg in the hall, seems to beat with the story's pulse, the way a sore knee throbs in tandem with the heart after a fall.

'It wasn't her parents' friends,' says Hilary after a while. 'It was her uncles and aunts.'

'Right,' says Henry. 'And they didn't get out.'

Ingrid's words halt as abruptly as they came. The sun continues to flood the room with diaphanous northern light. Many years ago, when I was a less experienced journalist and not so much myself, I might have filled this eternity up. Poured my words into it like sand into an egg timer. Now I know better. Time is teaching me. I say nothing.

Finally it is Hilary who speaks. 'She is very proud of her parents for doing that.'

'Rightly so,' says Henry.

Ingrid nods her head, tentatively, childlike, as if it is expected of her.

Henry receives this new information confirming that his suspected communist sympathies threatened his naturalisation in 2018, not long after a major scandal breaks in the country. Windrush. A word that previously evoked old black and white photos of the great bow of a ship docking in Tilbury in the early summer of 1948. The same stretch of Essex coast on which Henry first set foot when he arrived in Britain nine years earlier. The same ship that, before it was called the *Empire Windrush*, was seized by the Nazis and used to transport troops and Norwegian Jews to

Poland's concentration camps and, inevitably, Auschwitz. The same death camp where Ingrid's aunt, uncle and cousins, the ones who didn't get out, were sent.

Windrush, for most of my life, means BBC archive reports, delivered in *Brief Encounter*-ish clipped voices about the changing face of the nation. Windrush means people on the move, as they have always been, carrying belongings in suitcases and holding children with blank faces by the hand. Windrush means the official birth of post-war immigration to Britain, which also brings my parents, immigrants from another former British colony, to this small island a couple of decades later. Windrush is a ship carrying 1,027 passengers, the vast majority of whom are Commonwealth immigrants from the Caribbean. Windrush signifies the docking of a new era. Windrush means something fine, good, upstanding, British. It is the proud opening chapter of our story, for we are not taught that our history began long before 1948. That our people lived in Britain for centuries. That many on board the HMT *Empire Windrush* were Second World War veterans. That the people we call immigrants were, in fact, coming home. That our people are, in fact, your people.

In the summer of 2013, as I become a mother, the Conservative government launches Operation Vaken, a short-lived initiative employing vans to circle aimlessly around six London boroughs. The vans carry billboards decorated with images of handcuffs and words of warning.

'In the UK illegally? Go home or face arrest.'

At the same time, Home Office leaflets encouraging what is referred to as 'voluntary departure' are distributed, featuring bright pictures of planes, and inviting those returning home of their own accord to enjoy the key benefits, which are avoiding arrest and living in detention until documents are obtained, of leaving by so-called choice. 'They can leave the UK in a more dignified manner than if their removal is enforced,' the leaflet concludes. Earlier that year, in the hope that greater numbers of immigrants will 'self-deport', the Home Office sends texts to more than 170,000 people living in the UK, many of whom are living here legally. 'Message from the UK Border Agency:' the texts begin, 'you are required to leave the UK as you no longer have the right to remain.'

Four years later, when the Wugas are preparing their FOI request with the help of their local MP, it begins to surface that the British government has classified as illegal immigrants thousands of British Caribbean residents who arrived in the country between 1948 and 1973. 'Surface', though, is the wrong word. It has all been carried out in the cold light of day and is a matter of public record. As the then home secretary put it in 2012, in an interview with an increasingly right-wing broadsheet, it is a direct result of an explicit policy 'to create here in Britain a really hostile environment for illegal migration'. A home secretary who by the time the scandal fully breaks and becomes international news is our prime minister.

When Henry's file arrives in the post, Windrush no longer stands for history. It represents live, present and continuous scandal. The betrayal of hundreds, perhaps even thousands, of people born in the Caribbean and their descendants by their own government. British people. People who are wrongly detained, their very past existence denied. People who lose jobs, homes, access to benefits, and medical treatment. People who are deported. Taken from their homes to a country they left long ago, that they perhaps cannot remember at all. The knock at the door. The letter landing softly, the lightest of terrors, on the mat. The childhood fear come to life.

This breach of the trust each of us puts in our government every single day is a betrayal not just by the country to which people happened to migrate. It is a rejection by the mother country. For the Windrush generation, and my parents a few decades later, the passenger liner docking on the banks of the Thames or the plane thumping down on the smooth ribbon of runway at the newly named Heathrow Airport, is a form of homecoming. A return, as well as a flight. For us, the scandal induces only a terrible confirmation. The world is, after all, exactly as we experience it. As we have been taught to fear it, and never speak of it. Our footing never felt sure but after the Windrush scandal the earth cracks open beneath our feet. It seems not to close again. We begin to admit to ourselves that it was never secure in the first place. 'The chief constable [of Glasgow] reports that this applicant was interned from 1940 to 1941 as an enemy alien and that he was suspected of being Communistic in politics,' says Henry, reading aloud from the conclusion of the report by Glasgow's procurator fiscal. 'Accordingly we cannot regard him as being suitable for a grant of British nationality.'

Naturalisation, the admittance of a foreigner to the citizenship of a country, also describes the introduction of plants and animals to non-native regions. It is a term, like enemy alien, laden with judgement so established we have forgotten the weight of all that it carries. A word that hauls me back to Kew, where Henry's documents were held right next to the largest botanical gardens in the world. Kew Gardens, the bucolic scene of many happy childhood visits with my parents, when it cost a few pennies to go through the turnstiles into the carefully collected, cultivated and, though the word was never used, colonised paradise within. Like museums, the history of botanical gardens is entwined with imperialism. These are oases with which we all share history in profoundly different ways. And unsurprisingly, considering its position right up against the banks of the Thames, Kew Gardens was a target in the Second World War. During the Blitz, at the same time as Henry was interned on the Isle of Man, thirty high-explosive German bombs were dropped on the lawnmower-striped lawns and Victorian glasshouses of Kew. What happened to those prized organisms yanked from the earth of every continent in the British Empire, brought 'home' and *naturalised* over time? Were they protected? Hidden? Dug up and sent away for safekeeping?

My centre of the world, though I have not lived there for more than twenty years, continues to be a post-war block of council flats on the banks of the Thames. The place where my parents live. The building overlooks an arterial London road, never free of traffic, which in turn tracks the tidal river that brought the *Empire Windrush* to the country. This is where the Oxford and Cambridge Boat Race finishes each spring. It has the bleak and beautiful feel of a Dickensian ghost town, its past as a centre of industry – tapestry, pottery, a brewery, maltings, bottling plant and sugar refinery – outlined in the old warehouses and grand manor houses long since portioned up first into offices and then luxury apartments. The history is pure blue-plaqued Establishment. Thomas Cromwell once lived here. J. M. W. Turner painted the view up and down the river from a house known as The Limes where former residents included a family of Jewish merchant bankers who came from New York in 1754, and Lord Byron's widow.

Over the years the flats in my parents' block are bought over, one by one, until my mother and father are amongst the very few council tenants left in the building. The eerie petrol station over the road strung with giant cobwebs is knocked down. So too is the derelict pub beside it, where one easily imagined the ghosts of weavers congregating for an after-work pint. The narrow river path, oozing with ripe Thames mud and tide-propelled rubbish, is covered with a traditional cobbled path. An accessible ramp follows, and then come the runners, cyclists, dog walkers with Labradors and spaniels, and mothers jogging with buggies suspended on giant off-road wheels, their blonde ponytails swinging to the beat of gentrification. All of this happens stealthily until one day you find yourself looking at the same stretch of ancient riverside and can't remember what was once, surely not that long ago, there.

A few miles west along the river is Richmond, where I grew up, which continues to haunt me as only the places we belong to can. You would be hard-pressed to find a more quintessentially English backdrop for a formative story. I went to primary school atop Richmond Hill, which boasts a view of the land so emblematic it is the only outlook in England to be protected by an Act of Parliament. This magnificent scene of a water meadow drawing the eye down to the Thames vale, the snaking bend of the river, and beyond, the genial drama of the North Downs, has such harmonious composition it presents to the naked eye as a painting. But perhaps this is because it has been painted many times, most famously by Turner in 1809. Occasionally a view becomes so integral to a person's perspective that it's taken into the self like a visitor admitted to a house. I often dream about the view from Richmond Hill. It's as though the scene Sir Walter Scott described as 'a huge sea of verdure' is engraved on the backs of my eyelids. When I close my eyes, it's waiting for me. The sparkling river bend and the ancient water meadow spilling down to meet it. The thick furrow of trees in the middle distance. The land keening towards the horizon's rim. And the mixed emotional palate. The sense of pride, Britishness and otherness. A rush of belonging so furtive and uncontrollable it feels like shame.

In the end Henry applied for naturalisation in 1946. He shows me the first letter, received by the Home Office Aliens Dept on 24 April, in which he enclosed a preliminary fee of £1 alongside his application, and signed off 'yours respectfully, Heinz Martin Wuga'. By this point he had been living in the UK for seven years. He was twenty-two years old and married to Ingrid. And so they received naturalisation together the following year, none the wiser about how close they had sailed to the wind.

What would have happened if the application was refused?

'Who knows?' Henry says. 'I guess they could have deported me back to Germany.'

When I get home to Leith on the northern edge of Edinburgh, which clings to another river with a long and complicated history, I go on the website of the National Archives. I find the catalogue description of Henry's file, its legal status as a public record immediately followed by its closure status. The Home Office series to which Henry's records belong is the most detailed series on internees held by the National Archives. It relates specifically to foreign, mostly European nationals who applied for British citizenship after the war and permanently settled in the UK. Almost all these files were scheduled for destruction but in 1992 the Public Records Office learned that around 40 per cent of them had, in fact, survived. These were passed on to the National Archives. Amongst them was HO405/60809, a file about a German Jewish refugee called Heinz Martin Wuga.

I perform a search under 'Jewish refugees Second World War' and fall down another rabbit hole. In a section on 'immigration and immigrants' and a sub-section on 'First and Second World War Records', I find an entry on internment records regarding what's termed the 'Aliens Department internees index'. These detail a sub-series of index cards originally issued in September 1939, when war broke out and the first round of decisions on the internment of enemy aliens, as they were known, were considered by tribunals. Henry had, by this time, been in the UK for four months and was only fifteen. The following year, as the British public was gripped by panic in the midst of war and Winston Churchill was said to have issued an order to 'collar the lot!', larger numbers of people were interned, Henry amongst them.

The National Archives guide concludes: 'Those interned included Jewish refugees who had escaped Nazi persecution.'

The neutral, approaching ahistorical tone of this barely known fact upsets me. So, as readers tend to when we're unsettled, I go searching for another text. I pick up *The Emigrants*, W. G. Sebald's document of the lives of four Jewish refugees. The quartet of stories, which one always has to remind oneself are fictional, were allegedly inspired by Sebald's friendships with two elderly Jewish refugees, one of whom was his landlord in Manchester. My relationship with Sebald has blossomed in tandem with my friendship with Henry. Over the years this great German writer and academic, with whom I share precisely nothing in common, has somehow become a kind of guardian of my words relating to Henry. Sebald's last novel, *Austerlitz*, has become the place I go to when I am lost. The steadying view from the hill. I like to think Sebald would be amused by this because *Austerlitz* is a novel about dislocation.

I flick through my new Vintage edition of *The Emigrants*.

The book falls open on page twenty-seven.

The story of Paul Bereyter.

'There is mist that no eye can dispel,' begins the characteristically Sebaldian chapter inscription. And then come the long, sinewy sentences, propelling you in a direction you do not understand but must follow, like a stranger taking you by the hand in a dream. Paul Bereyter was the narrator's primary school teacher. In the very first sentence, which of course is lengthy, I read that he has 'put an end to his life'. The narrator finds this out in an obituary, which 'spoke merely of the dead man's services to education, his dedicated care for his pupils . . . his great love of music, his astonishing inventiveness', and so on. The narrator continues: 'Almost by way of an aside, the obituary added, with no further explanation, that during the Third Reich Paul Bereyter had been prevented from practising his chosen profession.' It is the tone of this report that devastates the narrator as much as the content. 'It was this curiously unconnected, inconsequential statement, as much as the violent manner of his death, which led me in the years that followed to think more and more about Paul Bereyter, until, in the end, I had to get beyond my own very fond memories of him and discover the story I did not know.'

'Within half an hour I became a dangerous enemy alien category A'

A letter drops on the mat of 169 Queen's Drive, Govanhill. The home of Mrs Etta Hurwich, her son Simon, and, for the past year, Henry. A main-door red sandstone tenement flat with three storeys and a basement. Ten soft stone steps lead to a heavy front door. Opposite is a neo-gothic parish church. The elegant green sweep of Queen's Park unfurls from the end of the street, and the latest episode of the serial that is Glasgow skies in summer plays out overhead. The letter may have disappeared down the bottomless well of history, but Henry can instantly summon its contents. Five miles away in Giffnock, he speaks them to me as they were once written for him.

'You must go to the High Court in Edinburgh.'

Henry is sixteen. He has been in Britain for just over a year. It is the third week of June in 1940. Wartime. The balance of power in Europe is being ripped up, country by country, day by day. A month ago, on the same day Winston Churchill became prime minister in Britain, the Wehrmacht invaded Luxembourg, the Netherlands and Belgium. Norway has just been seized by Nazi Germany. Less than a fortnight ago Italy declared war on France and Britain. The Fall of France, which will result in the French Army's defeat in six inconceivable weeks, is under way. More than 300,000 British and Allied soldiers have just been evacuated from the jetty and beaches of Dunkirk. Two months ago, a Nazi commandant arrived in the Upper Silesia region of occupied Poland with the order to establish a more extreme version of Dachau in the market town of Oświęcim, or, in German, Auschwitz.

In Nuremberg, Henry's parents continue to live in the family home. 'We are well,' writes his mother, Lore, in her most recent letter, sent on 20 March. 'Cheer up. One fine day we'll all be together again, that is our greatest wish.'

'You're on holiday now, always nice for you,' adds his father, Karl, in a few lines scrawled at the foot of the page, conveyed in a hand that eighty years later only Ingrid will be able to decipher. 'We didn't get to Graz for Whitsun. We are both well at the moment.'

The letters are a traffic of love in the midst of a war driven by hate. They shuttle back and forth via an uncle in Brussels and another in Paris. Then war breaks out, Belgium and France are invaded, and the correspondence between mother, father and son shrinks to the rare, desperately longed for and woefully outdated by the time it arrives Red Cross letter.

At 169 Queen's Drive in Glasgow, Henry's fate is being written for him.

He has only been home for a few days. He has been in Perthshire, where he was sent as soon as war broke out, one of 100,000 children evacuated from Glasgow in the space of just three days. At the same time, he and the rest of the 70,000 German and Austrian foreign nationals in Britain were classed as enemy aliens.

They are forbidden to possess cameras, maps, radios.

They are subject to a nightly curfew.

The police start coming to the door.

In Perthshire, Henry is sent first to the village of Guildtown where he is billeted on a farm run by a Mr William Lambie Douglas. Here, the city boy falls hard for country life. He attends the local village school and gets a week's holiday to plant potatoes in the earth, howking them up with groups of Irish men after the worst of the Scottish winter. He learns to tie bales of hay and makes friends with a horse called Clyde, who forms a habit of refusing to permit the fifteen-year-old refugee to leave his stable. He drinks his fill of fresh milk and cream and, in the midst of rationing, eats tinned peaches, rabbit, pheasant, chicken and eggs. The only outward sign of war in this lush old tree country is the drone of RAF Tiger Moths training at the nearby Scone airfield. This, and the scarcity of news from his parents. A single postcard from his mother reaches him here, forwarded on from 169 Queen's Drive in Glasgow. The original address has been crossed out, line by line, replaced by his temporary home on the farm.

'Thank you very much for your letter that arrived on Monday and the lovely poem,' writes Lore. 'We were sad not to get a photo of you, that would have been the right birthday present. We couldn't talk, that wasn't possible. We are well and think of you a lot.' Lore explains that her mother is in Heilbronn, where many of her family remain. 'I am worried about her and want to go and see her when possible,' she continues. The postcard closes with a maternal remonstration, the half-hearted kind that masks love. 'You must be thinking of us too. Did you get the chocolate? You didn't mention it. A kiss for you. Your Muma.'

By the end of September the Aliens Department of the Home Office has set up 120 internment tribunals all over the country, using emergency legislation passed on the eve of war. At these tribunals, presided over by government officials and local representatives, every UK registered enemy alien over the age of sixteen is assessed and divided into one of three categories. Category A means instant internment, B is exempt from internment but subject to restrictions, and C is exempt from both internment and restrictions. The process takes a few months. By the end of January 73,000 cases have been assessed. The majority of the 55,000 Jewish refugees in Britain due to Nazi persecution are placed in Category C, while 6,700 are classified as B, and just 560 as A. At just fifteen years old, none of this affects Henry.

Next, Henry is moved to a seventeenth-century estate in the village of Forgandenny run by the Glasgow Corporation. Around thirty boys and girls are evacuated to Rossie House overlooking the smooth caps of the Ochil Hills. Henry is the only foreigner but there is a Glaswegian Jewish boy called Max Barlasky, a future painter with whom Henry will become lifelong friends. The estate gamekeeper, Mr McCandlish, usually trailed by a pack of foxhounds, teaches Henry fly fishing on the River Earn. On Sundays when the rest of the children go to church Henry, a budding chef with a nine-month apprenticeship in a kosher hotel in Baden-Baden under his belt, is permitted into the kitchen of the old house to bake cakes for afternoon tea. 'Yes, there was a war on but we had a carefree time,' says Henry. 'All these months left a great impression on me, so many new experiences to absorb. I really loved it there.'

He starts attending Perth Academy, but is thrown out because 'they didn't like my English, didn't think it was good enough'. Finally he ends up in Balhousie, a boys' grammar school run by a headmaster, Mr Borthwick, who is particularly kind to the only foreigner amongst the pupils. He permits Henry to use German in his end of year exams and his English, nurtured by the kind attention of this man he will never forget and with whom he will continue to correspond for years, comes on in leaps and bounds. In the spring Henry is taught *Macbeth* and the door of his young mind swings open. 'Oh, it was fabulous,' Henry tells me with a sigh. 'I still know passages off by heart. "Out, out brief candle! / Life's but a walking shadow". It enthralled me.'

This is where Henry's sixteenth birthday passes. He is supposed to register at the local police station, as all enemy aliens are required to do, but Henry is young, he is busy, his life turns on a coin, and he is the only foreigner amongst locals. 'You're just a schoolboy,' says Henry. 'You are quite happy and then all of a sudden you have to register with the police? I think I didn't fully realise. All I can tell you . . .' He pauses, looking perplexed, as though he still feels he must explain himself. 'You're young, you're happy, you've got friends, you don't think you have to do this when you turn sixteen. It doesn't matter to you.'

Cycling to school one day, Henry is stopped at an army checkpoint by a young soldier. Road blocks have sprung up around Perthshire to prevent tanks from passing through its towns. The young soldier demands to see Henry's identity card and when he takes out his aliens' registration book and the soldier realises his nationality is German, he panics. The 'poor man nearly collapses and drops his gun', says Henry.

He calls first for the corporal and then the lieutenant.

'Let the laddie go to school,' is the lieutenant's immediate conclusion.

Henry, once again, is spared. He gets back on his bike, and pedals away.

The risk of German invasion grows. Britain is in a state of high alert. Stoked by anti-immigrant rhetoric in the right-wing press, the line begins to blur between German and Austrian refugees seeking safe haven and Nazi sympathisers and saboteurs hiding in plain sight. The British government interns a further 8,000 Germans and Austrians in south England, regardless of their classification. On 4 June Churchill delivers his 'we shall fight on the beaches' speech in the House of Commons. The next day, Henry sends his first Red Cross letter to his parents.

'Dear Parents!' he writes. 'Hope you are well. I am doing wonderfully. Chin up! Kisses, regards, your loving son.'

His mother replies on the flip side of the fragile paper, carefully staying within the allotted twenty-five words.

'Dear Heinz!' Lore writes. 'Your letter brought us endless joy. We are well too. All our love, regards, and many kisses. Write again soon, your mother.'

It will be another four months before this letter arrives at Rossie House on 4 October 1940.

Henry will no longer be there to receive it.

This is because Henry is forced to return to 169 Queen's Drive in June. Mussolini has declared war on Britain and France. Four thousand Italians, many of whom have resided in Britain for decades, have been rounded up and interned. And Henry has been 'kicked out' of Perthshire, which following the Dunkirk evacuation has become a protected area. 'The police came to Rossie House,' he says. 'They told me "You have to go back to Glasgow. You are an enemy alien, you are over sixteen, this is a protected area. I'm sorry but you have to go."' He will never know to what extent his not registering with the police, or the incident with the young soldier on the roadside, played a part. He knows only that he has to leave, which is fast becoming the story of his life.

During the next five days, the letter summoning Henry to the highest court in the land arrives. But over the years, Henry's mind will unconsciously stretch those handful of days into four months. By the time he sits down to write an astonishing seven-page essay about his first twenty-three months in the UK, sending it to me with perfect historical alignment in June of another year, 2018, he is convinced that he returned to Mrs Hurwich not in June 1940 but in March, just after his sixteenth birthday. 'No possibility to return to school,' he writes. 'Bought a bicycle for 15 shillings and explored the Clyde coastline. I love the outdoors.' Henry remembers the period in detail, writing about how one day he misread his map and ended up cycling an extra thirty miles home. He recalls joining the Hurwich family at Queen's Park Synagogue for Jewish festivals. A round of golf at Barassie Links on the west coast, followed by high tea at Ferrari's No 10 on Sauchiehall Street. 'How kind to be taken,' Henry writes. 'Glasgow middle class lifestyle I am learning!!'

When I show Henry the Red Cross letter he sent from Forgandenny on 5 June, revealing that all of this happened but at a slightly different time, he is shocked. 'Well, if that's the evidence, my thinking must be wrong,' he says. He looks crestfallen and I feel terrible. I have become the thoughtless biographer waving a letter in her subject's face to prove his lived experience is wrong.

'How you remember it is as valid as how it was,' I say. 'It was a long time ago. So much happened in such a short space of time. It doesn't matter.'

But of course it does. To Henry. He goes quiet and later, in the middle of another conversation, interjects. 'Can I just say that I'm upset. I really thought I was back in Glasgow in March. I thought I bought a bicycle . . . I'm sorry I can't be clear. I've told you what I know. I'm sorry if this disturbs the beginning of your book.'

20 June 1940. Henry takes a train fifty miles east to Edinburgh. He is accompanied by a lawyer from the refugee committee but when they arrive at the monumental building in the shadow of St Giles' Cathedral, the lawyer is not permitted to enter the court. Henry finds himself alone in a space that the passage of time has long since blanked out. He will recall nothing of the journey, the short steep walk from Waverley Station to the High Court which must make his young heart hammer in his chest, the building, nor the precise words and phrases used about him during the tribunal. The tribunals were not transcribed or officially documented but Henry will remember certain details. The name of the judge (Sir John Strachan). The presence of two assessors. His cherished letters lying in front of them. The pre-war correspondence between Henry and his parents, passing through Brussels and Paris, detailing the frustration of separation, and the nitty-gritty of pragmatism. Suffused with love and longing.

'It was overpowering,' says Henry. 'I was kind of . . . what's going to happen to me? I was frightened. I remember standing there being questioned. I remember looking the judge straight in the eye and him looking straight back at me. It was so immediate, so powerful. All of a sudden I realised . . . I am not free any longer.'

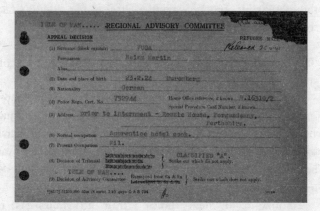

Reliving that day, as he will for the rest of his life, the events unfold at breakneck speed. Henry is cross-examined about his uncles in Brussels and Paris. He is astonished at how much these complete strangers in their flowing dark gowns of officialdom know about him. They have read his letters. They have made their decision. The tribunal is over before he knows it. Henry is charged with corresponding with the enemy.

'Within half an hour I went from being a friendly enemy alien due to religious persecution to a dangerous enemy alien category A,' says Henry. 'They didn't know what to do with me. Yes, it was frightening. Yes, it was traumatic. I was there all alone. But they had to do what they had to do. Remember, this was wartime. Corresponding with the enemy! They had no option but to arrest me.'

At this moment, Ingrid perks up. 'I'm upset,' she says.

About what?

'The weather.' She jerks her silver head towards the window. It is another June day in Glasgow, and it is raining. We laugh.

Back in 1940, Henry is handcuffed. He is taken to Waverley station by two police officers. 'They were reasonable people,' he says. 'I was not treated as an outcast.' He pauses. 'Well, I had not committed a crime.' The officers deposit Henry in a locked compartment on the train back to Glasgow. At the other end of the line, two detectives collect him at Queen Street Station and escort him to 169 Queen's Drive. He is given an hour to pack a small holdall, which he fills with clothes, and to make two phone calls, one to his cousin Grete Gummers, also in Glasgow, and the other to Mrs Hurwich, who is at work. Next he is taken to the Central Police Headquarters at 54 St Andrew's Square, where, this being what Henry calls 'a very civilised country' in comparison with the homeland he has fled, the sergeant refuses to put him in a cell.

'Cannae take him,' says Henry in his best German-inflected Scottish accent. 'Nae laddies under seventeen. He's just a boy.' He laughs. In his written account Henry concludes of the episode: 'They panicked. What to do with this Dangerous "Cat. A" boy? A stressful day, but I was well treated.'

What they do is take him to a remand home for juvenile offenders on St Vincent Street, a city centre thoroughfare where I will be based as a journalist when I first meet the Wugas. Henry is the oldest in the home. Most of the children are twelve or thirteen, held for 'stealing handbags and breaking windows', and due in court the following day. They crowd around Henry, intrigued by this German boy in their midst. 'What did ye dae?' they demand to know. 'When I told them "I didnae dae anythin", I was sidelined,' says Henry. 'Bottom of the pile.' His cigarettes are confiscated but he is invited by the manager of the remand home to his office for a smoke. Knowing the boys will ridicule him if he goes, Henry declines.

Two nights later he is transferred west across the city to Maryhill Barracks, a military complex constructed in the 1870s, and razed to the ground in the 1960s. The Barracks, as the housing scheme in its place is still known by the time I arrive in Glasgow in the 1990s, accommodated a thousand soldiers during the First World War. A history now resident in the tower blocks named after the infantrymen once based there and the original gate and wall built from local stone encircling the scheme. When Henry arrives, the Barracks are being used as a prisoner of war camp. Precisely one year later they will briefly hold Hitler's second-in-command, Rudolf Hess, when he parachutes into a field south of Glasgow on a so-called peace mission.

'It was horrendous,' says Henry. He is forced to share a cement air-raid bunker with German merchant seamen captured by the British Navy during the Icelandic blockade. For two weeks the Jewish refugee boy who is now known as a dangerous enemy alien category A must eat, sleep and live with twenty-five Nazi sympathisers. 'There were other prisoners there but I had no contact with them,' he says. 'There were anti-Semitic remarks, but a couple of senior ranking officers protected me. I wasn't physically abused, but it was horrible. It was depressing. We got to eat but it was not nice. How I got through that fortnight I don't know.'

'The problem, Daddy, is you blank bad things out in order to move on,' says Hilary. 'So unfortunately I don't think we can get to the truth of how you felt because . . . you've got to cope.'

'Look, I wasn't beaten up,' says Henry to his daughter. 'But mentally, yes, it was bad with these guys.'

Since the rounding up of thousands of Italians, many of them living in Scotland, the number of internees in Britain has soared. Even though temporary camps have sprung up across the country, on racecourses and in disused cotton mills, churches, housing estates, and a self-governing island in the middle of the Irish Sea, space is running out. And so, while Henry is locked in an underground bunker with twenty-five German sailors in Maryhill, more than 7,500 prisoners, many of them held in camps in Scotland, are shipped overseas on five vessels to Canada and Australia. One of these is a converted cruise ship called the *Arandora Star*.

'I was lucky to have missed that boat,' says Henry. 'I could have very easily been on the *Arandora Star*.'

In the early hours of 2 July 1940 the ship is torpedoed and sunk by a German submarine west of the Irish Atlantic coast. On board are 374 British seamen and soldiers, 712 Italians, 181 of whom had been in an internment camp in Edinburgh, and 438 Germans, both Nazi sympathisers and Jewish refugees. More than half of those on board the *Arandora Star* die. The impact of the torpedo instantly kills many below deck. Others are dragged underwater by the wire mesh or killed throwing themselves overboard. The survivors remain in the water for hours before they are rescued.

This well-publicised tragedy prompts a dramatic sea change in British public opinion. The internment of enemy aliens is no longer viewed as a vital military defence strategy. These Italian chefs and café owners, Jewish artists and academics fleeing persecution, many of whom will go on to fight with the Allied forces, are not, in fact, a threat to British security. It is a national disgrace. Or as Henry puts it more mildly, 'an unnecessary decision. We came here to flee from the Nazis and to help defeat them.' On 23 July, a letter co-signed by figures including E. M. Forster and Ralph Vaughan Williams runs in *The Times*. 'Jewish and other refugees from Nazi oppression should not be interned with Nazi sympathizers', it states. 'Could not the War Office make the distinction rapidly so as to avoid scenes of persecution such as have already been alleged?' Questions are raised in Parliament. A government White Paper allows interned German and Austrian refugees to bid for release. By August, 1,687 category C and B enemy aliens have been released, followed by 5,000 Germans, Austrians, and Italians in October, and a further 8,000 in December.

Meanwhile, Henry's internment continues apace. He and the twenty-five German sailors are taken by bus from Maryhill Barracks to a temporary holding camp on the western edge of Edinburgh's city centre: Donaldson's hospital and deaf school, where some of the Italians who boarded the *Arandora Star* were held just before Henry. To know Edinburgh intimately, to live in what Muriel Spark called 'the city of Calvinism, high teas, and loveless alliances' for any length of time, is to routinely pass by this palatial icon of the capital. Mostly encountered as it flashes by the window of a car or bus, Donaldson's is a microcosm of Edinburgh spirit: all elite northern restraint contained behind high wrought-iron gates. Parliament-esque in attitude, crowned with a flurry of mint-green cupolas, gothic turrets, and fronted with windows upon windows coolly surveying a sweeping and perpetually empty lawn. The building, constructed over a decade, was designed by star Edinburgh architect William Playfair and opened by Queen Victoria in 1851. And for the next 160 years, until the year I moved to Edinburgh from Glasgow, Donaldson's remained a deaf school. Then came a decade of emptiness, when the building was deemed no longer fit for purpose. The deaf school moved out, and nature and its bedfellow dry rot took up residence. In its latest chapter, Donaldson's has been purchased by a heritage property developer and converted into one of the most prestigious addresses in the city, boasting all the hallmarks of the twenty-first-century elite: optimised natural light, panoramic views, underground car parks, internet speeds up to 200mbps and a 'softened' courtyard planted with pleached trees.

Back in the summer of 1940, Donaldson's hospital is behind barbed wire and under armed guard. Henry and the German sailors sleep in separate dormitories. The conditions in this vast institution, empty save for the small band of men, are comparatively good after the misery of Maryhill Barracks. One day the camp commander arrives and tells them that up to 200 internees will be arriving within the next seventy-two hours. He asks a question. 'Anybody here who can cook?' Henry, the sole Jewish person in the camp, who has instinctively learned that making himself useful may protect him, raises his hand. 'I said yes, I can cook,' Henry laughs. 'I was put in charge of this huge kitchen, with huge equipment, huge boilers, and told to prepare a meal for all these men. My kitchen staff were the German sailors.' As they prepare the food there is an air raid. Tensions mount. One of the German sailors calls Henry 'a dirty Jew'. Another knocks the sailor out. 'Then we got a British corporal in the kitchen to keep the peace, we made the meal, and the people came,' says Henry. One of these people happens to be Ascher Wolff, Ingrid's father. The boy and his future father-in-law do not, as far as they know, cross paths.

Henry is told he is to be moved to another temporary holding camp in York. In the kitchens of Donaldson's, the corporal produces a list of rations for the train journey.

'Oatmeal, potatoes, beans, etc.,' says Henry, shaking his head. 'I said "We're going on a train! We can't cook this, there are no facilities. We need corned beef and bread."' In York, Henry is separated from the German sailors, taken to a racecourse, and housed below the stands. It is cold and cramped. Most of the other men are German Jewish refugees. A few days pass, during which there are constant roll calls to check prisoner numbers and lectures on sex, hygiene, and the 'dangers' of homosexuality. Henry suspects they are given bromide in their food.

And then he is moved again.

His next destination is a disused cotton mill in Bury, north of Manchester, which has become one of the largest internment camps in Britain. In the years and decades to come, Warth Mills will become known as the most brutal and hazardous internment camp in the country. 'It was the most horrendous experience of all the camps,' says Henry. 'It was frightening. It was crazy. We were just the German enemy [to them].' More than 2,000 men are crammed into this long Victorian building on the banks of the River Irwell. Henry joins a queue and at the front is strip-searched. He loses most of his belongings: a fountain pen, pocket knife and wristwatch he will never see again. He receives 'a fairly rough going over' by the guards. He is given a hessian sack to fill with straw and told to find a place on the floor, which is slippery with oil, to sleep. The toilets amount to sixty buckets in a yard. There are only eighteen water taps. The eating area is known as Starvation Hall, and the only readily available food item is tins of Carnation milk. For the rest of his life Henry will be unable to tolerate its 'sweet, sickly' taste. There is dust in the air and broken glass on the ground. At night, rats scurry across the greasy floors and rain courses through the smashed lights in the roof. There is a lot of sickness. Henry sees an Italian Catholic priest knocked down by falling machinery.

'Look, it was bad,' he says. 'We were treated as dirt. But

. . . the paranoia in this country. As far as these guards were concerned, "Here are the spies. We've got them!"' At night, the guards, who parade the camp with guns and bayonets, shout 'Halt, or I'll shoot' when the internees cross the yard. 'I recall one man pulling open his shirt and shouting "SHOOT",' says Henry. 'Someone described it as hell on earth. It was a very hard, tense and dangerous two weeks. It is a sad reflection on the government's panicky handling of the internment of friendly aliens when they knew who we were, and why we were in this country.'

In July, the same month Henry arrives at Warth Mills, an International Red Cross delegate reports on the camp, describing its 'dilapidated condition, lack of hygiene, absence of hot water and the fact that there were beds for only 30 sick people at a time whereas 250 needed treatment'. A Quaker relief worker who has visited concentration camps in Germany also files a damning report, describing Warth Mills as 'certainly worse than any I have seen'. He writes that several of the interned men 'said to me that the physical conditions in Dachau were better than in Bury. Having seen both, I agreed, but we also agreed, "Die Leute sind ganz anders, Gott sei dank!" ("The people are wholly different, thank God!").' The Ministry of Information reports two suicides at Warth Mills, which may well have occurred while Henry was interned there. 'The two men who succeeded in committing suicide had already been in Hitler's concentration camps,' writes the report's author Sir Walter Monckton. 'Against this they held out, but this camp has broken their spirit.'

A few months after Henry leaves Warth Mills it will become an official prisoner of war camp and in accordance with the 1929 Geneva Convention conditions will be improved. The following year, the camp commandant while Henry was at Warth Mills, Major Alfred James Braybrook, will be court-martialled for stealing 100 gold sovereigns, two typewriters, jewellery, 1,040 razor blades, and other articles belonging to enemy aliens, and sentenced to eighteen months' imprisonment.

In 'We Refugees', Hannah Arendt, who when the Nazis invaded France in 1940 was interned in Gurs in the Pyrenees with 6,000 other stateless Germans, wrote that history has created 'a new kind of human beings – the kind that are put in concentration camps by their foes and in internment camps by their friends'. And it is the kind of complicated history no one wants to remember. For most of his life Henry will not talk about Warth Mills to anyone. It will be described only as one of a handful of camps in which he was interned. He will not name it, to anyone. His daughters will only discover he was there at all when a project launches in 2018 to delve into the buried history of Warth Mills, now an industrial estate, and someone gets in touch with Henry.

'You are the last known survivor of Warth Mills,' they tell him.

Henry is ninety-four years old.

The project will run an exhibition at Bury's Fusilier Museum, to which Henry contributes pieces from his archive. His German Reisepass stamped with a red 'J' and fronted with the Nazi eagle clutching a swastika. One of the letters that passed through Brussels, neatly typed out by his mother and referred to during his High Court tribunal. A short film will be made about Henry's story in which he is videoed at home in Giffnock. Warth Mills 'filled me with horror', Henry says to the camera. 'That's how it was, we coped with it. I can understand, it was wartime. But to be a refugee and a foreigner it's quite horrible how people treat you. We were here to help this country, and we did.'

From Warth Mills, Henry is taken to an internment camp on an unfinished housing estate in Huyton, Merseyside: a few streets 'simply enclosed in barbed wire and hey presto! You have a camp.' Men and women sleep in the empty council houses and canvas tents on the road. On the other side of the high wire fence, local children pass by on their way to and from school.

Henry stays only two nights.

Then he is taken by ferry from Liverpool to the Isle of Man.

'A smooth three-hour crossing of the Irish Sea,' he says. 'Many camps were ready for us there. Whole sections of hotels and boarding houses surrounded by barbed wire.'

Once on the island Henry is escorted from Ramsey Pier to a railway station where a narrow-gauge train takes him to the western coast of the island. At the northern end of a long exposed promenade are nine red-brick Victorian houses and a hotel, the Creg Malin, which has been turned into the camp headquarters. Both sides of Marine Parade are sealed off by high barbed-wire fences. The prom overlooks the golden sands of Peel bay, a medieval castle ruin, and, interrupting the horizon in the far distance, Northern Ireland's Mountains of Mourne. It is a majestic, elemental and quintessentially British view. It also looks entirely unprotected. 'If Hitler won we were there, waiting to be taken,' Henry notes. 'It was fairly tough, but I was a boy, I could deal with it. To me, it was like a university.'

This is Peveril, the Isle of Man's most high-security camp where the vast majority of category-A enemy aliens are held. It is roughly a quarter full when Henry arrives, with around 250 internees in the houses along the prom and, as the camp expands during his time there, along Peveril Terrace and Mount Morrison. Local residents are given seven days to vacate their homes to make way for arriving internees and must leave behind everything but their personal belongings. And so the camp grows, even as the numbers of internees begin to dwindle. 'In this camp there is an exceptional amount of exercise space available,' the *Isle of Man Times* reports on 30 November 1940, during Henry's internment. '[A]ll the headland brows have been wired in and also the promenade and bowling green and tennis courts.' The report concludes that 'it is nothing short of a public scandal that all these houses have been requisitioned and not put to some use'. By February 1941, a headline in the *Isle of Man Times* runs: 'Three Empty Houses in the Peel Internment Camp'. Still, there is no suggestion that Henry will be released.

Behind the wire, many of Henry's fellow internees are also German and Austrian Jewish refugees. He recalls a few political prisoners (German officials including Franz von Papen's secretary), the future British Austrian mathematician Hermann Bondi, and one of the musicians who will form the Amadeus Quartet. Once again, he is the youngest by far. He shares a room with a man in his fifties. A Yorkshireman whose German father, it turned out, never became naturalised. This 'lost' man, who speaks no German and cannot understand why he is interned on the Isle of Man, teaches Henry how to make his own pipe tobacco by gathering certain leaves, mixing in a little saltpetre, and compressing it in a sardine tin under a leg of the bed.

'Peel was good,' Henry says. 'We were well treated and had plenty to eat. No shortages. We tried to make life reasonable. We sorted the mail, did lots of things that the army could not do, like roll call. We were allowed to go for walks, but only with soldiers carrying bayonets. So we sat down, refused, said "We're not going." These were older Jewish men, professors, academics, and they said "You must realise who we are? We should not be here!" One soldier said "They're not going to run away."' Eventually the men are permitted to go for walks, and sometimes even a swim in the bay, accompanied by a single unarmed soldier.

In Peveril, there are 'lectures galore' on philosophy, music and medicine. Henry sees men playing chess with their backs to the table, 'given ten seconds to call the next move'. The Austrian artist Hans Schwarz is also interned in Peveril, though Henry doesn't remember him, and while he is there he crafts a chess set out of scrap wood he finds, perhaps combed from Peel bay under the watchful eye of soldiers. To this day twelve roughly sculpted pieces survive, modelled, it is thought, on the faces of Schwarz's fellow internees and guards at Peveril.

It is an unspoken tradition that each man takes a piece of barbed wire from the camp as a memento. Henry cuts his from the high fence around Peveril and takes it home to Glasgow. Seventy years later, during the summer of 2009, he and Ingrid will be invited to return to the Isle of Man by the BBC. They will fly there, landing in the south of the island and then travelling west to Peel, where Henry will walk around the same Victorian house where he was interned. He will gaze out to sea and his memories will return with the tide. All around the island, traces of the camps remain. In the tablet-shaped markings on the tarmac where fence posts were once knocked into the middle of roads. In old railway lines impaled in cliffs where rolls of barbed wire were once attached to prevent internees climbing up and escaping. In a swastika, still faintly visible through layers of paint, carved on the wall of a house in Peel. In the gnarled lengths of barbed wire jutting from the posts of camp perimeters that now peek from wild foliage. On a whim, the young man who is showing Henry around will scramble up one of these posts and cut a rusty and misshapen piece of barbed wire for Henry. When he and Ingrid return home to Giffnock, Henry will frame the two sections of wire side by side, displaying this oxidised piece of his history on a shelf in his sitting room.

In Peveril there is culture. Some of the internees have instruments. No wireless, 'obviously', but newspapers are occasionally smuggled in. There is theatre, cabaret, and shows for the guards. On one occasion the men are taken to Douglas, the island capital, to see the Charlie Chaplin film *The Great Dictator*, Chaplin's first true talkie, in which he plays a Jewish barber and comically paranoid dictator called Adenoid Hynkel.

Henry, as usual, gravitates towards the kitchens. He starts baking 'in house', traditional German and Austrian jam-filled doughnuts called Krapfen that they sell to other camps. 'We had a little café,' he says. 'It became quite nice.' He is allowed to write a letter once a week on special 'shiny paper' that cannot be intercepted with invisible ink. Instead of writing to Mrs Hurwich in Glasgow he decides to send his regular letter to the *Manchester Guardian*, which 'unlike Lord Beaverbrook, the *Express* and the *Mail*, was for us'. He also writes to the MP Eleanor Rathbone, whose commitment to refugees is unparalleled and who is known to read out the letters of internees in the House of Commons. So perhaps Henry imagines his written words being spoken in Parliament by Rathbone, a Liverpudlian Quaker, suffragist social reformer and independent MP. This is 'the good side of British democracy', as Henry puts it, and 'in spite of being behind barbed wire' he continues to participate in it.

It was Rathbone who established the government's Parliamentary Committee on Refugees in the winter of 1938. And it is Rathbone who visits internment camps including Huyton, where Henry spent two nights, in the summer of 1940, reporting back to the House of Commons about it being 'almost entirely devoid of chairs, tables and beds, so that elderly people have to sleep on the floor on mattresses, or, as I have been told, on heaps of straw'. During this same extraordinary six-hour parliamentary debate on internment, which takes place on 10 July while Henry is still in Donaldson's, Rathbone speaks or intervenes no fewer than twenty times.

'Not merely are their services rejected,' she says of the 'avalanche' of interned enemy aliens, 'but they find themselves treated as dangerous people and interned, under present conditions, along with their lifelong enemies – Jews and political refugees with Nazis – and treated as so dangerous that they may not even receive newspapers or listen to the wireless and they live in conditions very similar to those of a convict prison. Is all that really necessary? Is there no better way?'

'These people entrusted themselves to us and came here at our invitation,' Rathbone says during another intervention. 'This is a question which affects our prestige as a nation, and we do not want to let it go out that our land is a land of oppression and not a land of the free.'

It is 27 October 1940. In London the bombs are falling nightly and will do so almost without interruption until the following May. Across the Atlantic, in Fargo, North Dakota, one of Henry's best childhood friends, Sigmund Mosbacher, who has emigrated to the US and now goes by the name of Stephen, writes to him: 'It is too bad that England does not seem to be in a position to make use of the wildest and most enthusiastic haters of Hitler and all that he stands for, but has to intern all of [sic] in the present moment'. He urges Henry to emigrate to the US. 'My dear friend, you know I was always very fond of you, and this feeling keeps for you for ever. I know you are very brave, honest, and just and these qualities are the best ones to become a real man.'

'Keep your courage and hope,' he continues, 'and you will get some day what you are deserving.' He closes with the hope that Henry isn't taking his present situation 'as a too tragic one.'

'Even if the present times may be disheartening, don't forget that you are part of a great fight, to rid the world of the very prototype of evil, Herr Hitler and his gang, and soon, with our aid, Great Britain will be able to beat them into surrender. Keep thinking of your future that awaits you when the war is over,' he closes. 'I am sure that it will be a bright one.'

Meanwhile, Henry is allocated to another room in house six of Peveril. He is sharing with a German officer, a metallurgist who works for the British Aluminium Company in Fort William and whose English is as perfect as his German.

'He was very nice, very kind to me,' says Henry. 'We spoke a bit and he got me drunk and pumped me for information a few times. Of course I had none!' After a couple of weeks, the man is suddenly taken away with appendicitis. It so happens that another man at the camp whom Henry knows is taken to the hospital wing too, and he reports back that the German metallurgist never turned up. During the rest of his time on the island Henry will hear rumours of this officer showing up in other camps. For the rest of his life he will harbour a deep suspicion that he was an MI5 agent planted to spy on him.

12 January 1941. Mosbacher writes another letter. 'I was sorry to have learned that you are in a camp,' he begins. 'We will do everything in our power to help the brave and courageous English people, who are holding off and will be beating into surrender the enemy of decency and civilisation.' He reports that his grandmother, who 'unfortunately, still is at Fürth', recently invited Henry's parents for coffee and cake, 'which she baked without any eggs or butter, which shows how bad things must be there and how effectively the British blockade is operating.'

Henry and Mosbacher continue to write to each other, always in English, during the war. In October 1941, Mosbacher will send a letter to house six, Peveril camp, writing that he hopes the 'change in your rating has been made and this letter won't reach you at this camp, but somewhere with your relatives or friends in Glasgow'. He will tell Henry he got the 'highest possible grades' in chemistry and is now back in Toledo, working in a factory manufacturing plastic goods, 'from thimbles to camera cases, toothpaste caps to automobile handles' while attending college classes at night. Mosbacher's letter, the last one Henry receives from him, will conclude: 'Good luck to you wherever you may be, and thumbs UP! So long, most sincerely, your friend, Sigmund.'

Two years later, in the summer of 1943, Mosbacher will

enlist in the US Army, where he will earn the nickname 'Moose' and become renowned for his cheerful attitude and insatiable appetite.

In the last days of the war, Sergeant Mosbacher's unit will cross into Germany.

He will be killed in action in the Ruhr valley.

Members of his family, including his grandmother in Fürth, will die in the Holocaust.

In the spring of 1941, the Isle of Man's camps continue to empty as a further 12,500 internees are released. On 25 March Henry attends another tribunal on the island where he is reclassified from a category-A prisoner to what the vast majority of Jewish refugees in Britain have been all along: category C.

A few weeks later, on 15 April, a stranger, Mrs L. Hahn-Warburg, writes a letter at her desk in Bloomsbury, London. She works for the Internees Welfare Department of the Refugee Children's Movement, the umbrella aid organisation that helped Kindertransport children come to Britain. She addresses the letter to the camp commandant of Peveril, to whom she has just spoken on the telephone. 'We have been advised that the above named boy – Heinz Martin Wuga – has been re-classified to "C" and would inform you that on his release he can proceed to 169 Queen's Drive, Glasgow, C/o Mrs Hurwich.'

Three days later.

18 April 1941.

Every prisoner interned in Peveril, including Henry, is transferred to Mooragh Camp, Ramsey, on the northeast coast of the Isle of Man. Here, between the park and sea, around thirty boarding houses and hotels have been requisitioned along a promenade. The reason for the sudden emptying of the camp at Peel is the imminent arrival of up to a thousand fascists. 'It is understood that this camp will very soon be the war-time home of 800-1000 of those individuals known as Fascists,' reports the *Isle of Man Times*, 'and one part of the camp will be for German Fascists and the other for "Wop" [a pejorative term for Italian] Fascists. The leader of the home-bred Fascists is Sir Oswald Mosley, but it is not known if he will be sent to Peel with the remainder of his dupes.'

On 26 April, Henry, now seventeen, is released from Mooragh.

The camp commandant tells him 'I cannot keep you a day longer'. Henry is given a pass and put on a boat. 'The journey home was frightening,' he says. 'All alone after being in a friendly community for ten long months.' At Preston he has to change trains for Glasgow. After all he has been through, it is the bustle of this Victorian railway station, with its high glass roof and slender cast-iron columns, that he finds terrifying. He has spent so long hemmed in on an island, imprisoned beneath giant skies, with all his meals provided, his every movement watched, and his freedom narrowed to a single sea view sliced neat in two by a dark band of horizon. He is not used to so many people, milling in every direction. He is not accustomed to freedom.

It is 2008, the year Barack Obama is elected the 44th President of the United States and the global financial crash begins with the collapse of Lehman Brothers. Henry is eighty-four years old. It will be another three years before we meet and I start telling his story. It will be ten years before he receives his file from the National Archives. At this moment Henry has never seen an official record of this extraordinary period of his life. The alien registration cards for all the men interned in the Isle of Man camps during the Second World War were destroyed in the 1970s. It is his memory that has carried these ten months through time like an egg balanced on a spoon. All he has had to go on is his own, forever retreating experience. Finally his curiosity, and specifically his suspicion that he was investigated by MI5 during this extraordinary time, compels him to write to the Home Office and the National Archives, and on 29 October he receives a letter containing copies of the original index cards issued by the Regional Advisory Committee. On the flip side of the cards the 'Reasons for Decision' are given, neatly typed out, stamped, and accompanied by handwritten signatures.

The back of the first index card, issued on 20 June 1940, the day of the High Court tribunal, states:

'Both parents are resident in Germany and he corresponds with them through the Red Cross and until recently through a relative in Brussels. He is above average intelligence having recently passed his Leaving Certificate in this country. He lived in what is now a protected area from September 1939 until recently. The Chief Constable, Perthshire, recommended internment and the alien failed to satisfy the Committee that he could with safety be left at liberty.'

The back of the second card is dated 25 March 1941. Nine months later. Henry's final tribunal on the Isle of Man. 'See how they refer to me now as a boy rather than an alien,' he laughs as he shows it to me. He has had both index cards blown up to A3 size and laminated so he can take them to schools and universities and share his history.

Together, in the endlessly disappearing time we call the present, Henry and I read out the words that procured his freedom.

'We see no reason why this boy should not go back to the care and friendly custody of Mrs. Hurwich and her son; Wuga has expressed willingness to do any kind of work in furtherance of the War Effort, and we think it should be represented to the Hurwichs that the boy should be put to some useful occupation within a reasonable time from now.

'Classified "C". No adverse Reports from Camp or MI5.'

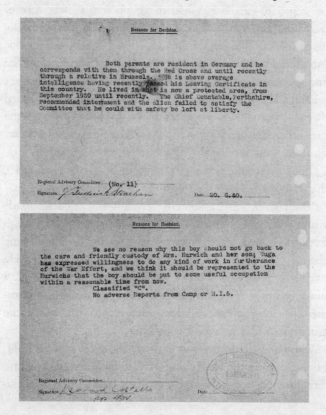

Reasons for Decision.

Both parents are resident in Germany and he corresponds with them through the Red Cross and until recently through a relative in Brussels. He is above average intelligence having recently passed his Leaving Certificate in this country. He lived in what is now a protected area, from September 1939 until recently. The Chief Constable, Perthshire, recommended internment and the alien failed to satisfy the Committee that he could with safety be left at liberty.

Regional Advisory Committee (No. 11)

Signature J. Frederick Strachan   Date 20. 6.40.

Reasons for Decision.

We see no reason why this boy should not go back to the care and friendly custody of Mrs. Hurwich and her son; Wuga has expressed willingness to do any kind of work in furtherance of the War Effort, and we think it should be represented to the Hurwichs that the boy should be put to some useful occupation within a reasonable time from now.
Classified "C".
No adverse Reports from Camp or M.I.5.

Regional Advisory Committee

Signature Leonard Costello
pro RAC   Date

'The law is a ass.'

When I am fourteen years old, our house in Richmond is repossessed. It is the early years of the Nineties, that weirdly inconspicuous decade of hedonism, cynicism, MiniDisc players and globalisation. Years which only in the future will come to be seen as ones in which the seeds of destruction were sown. Our semi-detached house is at the top of a hill and the end of a gravel drive. Unlike the other grand Victorian terraces on the street, in the bay windows of which twelve-foot-tall Christmas trees are placed each December, our house is brand new. We are the first people to live in it, and it smells like a freshly opened box when we move in. At one end of the street is the station, which itself is at the end of the line. At the other is the Victorian gothic church that gives the road heading for the hill its name, boasting a spire long and slender like a spear that can be seen for miles around. For somewhere so picturesque it is an exposed spot, where the wind whips around the church on the short days of winter. Once, when I am a child, I am briefly lifted clean off my feet here. I swear I take off, launched spire-wards for a terrifying second like a disgraced character in a Roald Dahl novel before my mother's hand yanks me back down to earth and, laughing our heads off, we carry on in the morning dark to school.

There are two houses on our plot: big, solid, square, and built out of smooth new terracotta brick. The other is owned by a man called Paul, a nebulous figure who, apart from his custom of barbecuing in his garden all summer and working 'in finance', I will not be able to summon in adulthood. At the back of the houses is a tall Lombardy poplar tree, my favourite spot in the garden, perhaps because here at last, like everything else around us, is something old. Next to it, a gate leads to an ancient passage that was once a bridleway leading to the church. Now it is a passage to the past proper, where the centuries-old London brick walls bulge like the bellies of stout Dickensian justices, bright green moss carpets the crevices, and the terraced cottages and their traditional gardens look as though they have been lifted wholesale from an English country village.

There is only one other modern building off this path: a care home right opposite the back of our house. This home, with its beautifully tended lawn and gleaming silver birches, frightens me. I have nightmares about it. Sometimes in bed at night I can hear screaming from behind the walls. It is a time when anything associated with mental illness, even disability, is spoken of in soft voices, interchangeable with 'craziness' and shame.

There is no build up to this memory. No before or after, just the isolated day projecting into the air like a church spire. On this day, our house has already been magically emptied of our belongings. The boxes are gone and the bailiff is on his way to change the locks. In my head he is something like the stout Mr Bumble from *Oliver Twist*, likely to turn up at the door with a hundred keys jangling at his belt, 'squeezing his hat emphatically in both hands', to pronounce that 'the law is a ass'. Who knows? Perhaps he does. The truth is, I am not there when he, or whoever it is carrying out the humiliating act of repossession, arrives. By this time I have been dispatched next door to Paul's house. My sister, presumably, is at school. Paul must be at work. So I am completely alone in this white man's house, which unfortunately is a carbon copy of our house, right down to the kitsch gold and glass chandeliers hanging from the ceilings. Except everything is back to front. In mirror image. Slightly off. And it is not our house any more.

Nor am I exactly alone. I must be revising for an end of year exam, probably my mock GCSEs, because I have a copy of *Romeo and Juliet* with me. I have just learned the word 'bawdy', referring to Juliet's nurse, who is unwittingly providing some much-needed comic relief in my tragedy as well as her own. Bawdy. A completely inapplicable word that will nonetheless be married to this moment from this day on. I have no idea how long I am here or what happens after my mother comes to collect me. The moment is elongated, pulled taut. I do not know, yet, that the Richmond house, as it will come to be known, will haunt me for the rest of my life. That I will never stop revisiting it, or the view from the nearby hilltop, in my dreams. That this moment will lead, like an old bridleway, to a flurry of life-changing moves and events. That when I walk these streets in the future, it will be at once an act of self-harm and the tenderest of homecomings. That the repossession will, in a few tumultuous years, land us in the council flat by the river that will come to be known as the happiest home of our lives. The centre of my world. How can I know that this moment will lead to a complete change of perspective? That some events rupture a life the way a church spire reorders the scape of a city. That this will be the making of me.

For now I am locked inside the moment, too young to throw open the door to the future. So I sit on Paul's sofa, in a house that looks exactly like the one that is no longer ours. I leaf through Shakespeare's great romantic tragedy, a play I will never be able to read again. I find my place, and start reading.

'The mustard is running over!'

I have never been to Nuremberg. In fact, for a spectrum of reasons ranging from my autistic son to the climate emergency I have not left Britain, nor been on a plane, for seven years. But I have visited 15 Fürther Strasse, Henry's childhood home, many times, courtesy of that most modern mode of transport, Google Street View. The routine is always the same, as if I were a resident treading a morning route to pick up a pint of milk. I click on the image and a satisfying rush towards the street takes place. I hold my index finger down on the touchpad and look this way and that, up and down the street, as if I am preparing to cross it. I examine the late nineteenth-century architecture of the building where the Wugas' flat was located on the ground floor, which appears now to be the offices of an insurance company. I picture Henry and his parents moving around the four large, traditionally furnished rooms separated by heavy double doors, with the warehouse and store for his father's stationery business towards the back. I imagine the thirteen-year-old boy with his brand new typewriter and desk. I imagine the room that, when 'things got difficult', is let to a German army lieutenant known for his friendliness towards Jewish people. A man who tries to protect the household, particularly Henry's mother, as much as he can from regular 'incursions', as Henry calls them, by the Sturmabteilung, the Nazi Party's paramilitary wing known as the SA.

My vision of all this is coloured, even contaminated, by a scene in *Austerlitz*. In Sebald's novel, which must be the most famous fictional treatment of a Kindertransportee, not that there are many, the titular character is a Jewish refugee sent on a train from Prague to London as a small boy. Jacques Austerlitz learns his history slowly, in fragments, just as we discover his life story through a disjointed series of encounters with an unnamed narrator across Europe. More than halfway through, Austerlitz describes learning how his father, Maximilian Aychenwald, who escaped Prague for Paris, was wary of the Nazi threat from the start. How, visiting Austria and Germany in the 1930s to 'gain a more accurate idea of general developments', he went to Nuremberg during one of the annual party rallies. There, he saw for himself 'the entire population . . . and indeed people from much further afield', standing 'shoulder to shoulder all agog with excitement along the predetermined route'. Maximilian watched a motorcade of limousines slowly gliding down an alley, parting 'the sea of radiant uplifted faces and the arms outstretched in yearning'. He stood in the square next to the towering medieval Lorenzkirche, a Nuremberg landmark a couple of miles from 15 Fürther Strasse, and saw the motorcade 'making its slow way through the swaying masses down to the Old Town' where the occupants of the old half-timbered houses with their crooked gables hung out of the windows 'like bunches of grapes'. When Henry tells me about Nuremberg in the 1930s, this is what I see.

Though for a few years he sees none of this. When hundreds of thousands of supporters gather in Nuremberg to watch the torchlight parades, Nazis marching with flags and swastikas, and Hitler's long hate-filled speeches, Lore and Karl send their son away to family in Heilbronn. But one year, for reasons children never know, Henry stays in Nuremberg. He looks out of the window of 15 Fürther Strasse and sees uniformed Nazis marching 'fifteen abreast' down the wide expanse of his street. 'We tried not to look,' says Henry. 'It was quite horrifying.' Alice, the maid, who will soon be forced to leave when the Nuremberg laws ban Jewish people from employing female German maids under the age of forty-five, opens the double windows to lean out over the marching crowds. 'The mustard is running over!' she screams, referring to the mass of brownshirts seething in the street. Karl pulls her back in and quickly shuts the windows. 'If they had heard they would have come and wrecked our flat there and then,' says Henry. 'How we weren't beaten up I don't know to this day.'

I direct the cursor along that same street, my hands long accustomed to doing the instinctive work of my feet. I swivel past two saplings to a café opposite Henry's building. People with pixellated faces sit at the pavement tables. The number plates of the parked cars are blurred out too, as are the buildings above the café and shop next door. But Henry's building has not been anonymised. I run the cursor up and down its stone walls. Vault over the top of 15 Fürther Strasse and the young boy's life playing out inside it almost a century ago.

Henry's building looks old. One has to keep in mind that when he and his parents moved in, it was new. Henry was six years old at the time. It was 1930, the year of the election in which the Nazis, having polled just 2.6 per cent of the vote two years earlier, gained more than six million votes and became the second-largest political party in the Reichstag. The year in which Henry's first memories also happen to register, soft and gauzy like dreams.

'Going to fetch milk from a local farm.'

'Sunday walks in the countryside with my parents.'

'My father lying down for a nap after lunch with his newspaper across his face.'

Henry emails me a photo of 15 Fürther Strasse. It was sent to him by his mother after the war, and arrives in my inbox upside down so I have to turn it once, twice, in order for my brain to grasp what I am seeing. A close-up, in black and white, of the doorway of the last place in Germany Henry called home. His address. Blackened. A history in ruins.

Today the Fürther Strasse building, like most of the old
walled town of Nuremberg, is as it stands an illusion.

On 2 January 1945, more than 500 Lancaster bombers
take to the air from bases across England and, in what will
be described by the RAF as 'a near perfect example of area
bombing', the historic heart of Nuremberg is flattened overnight. Afterwards, like so many of Europe and Asia's ruined
cities, the old town will be slowly reconstructed from the
ground up, exactly as it was. Like the quaint half-timbered
houses with their crooked gables, narrow cobbled streets,
walls, towers, fountains and bridges over the narrow river
Pegnitz, 15 Fürther Strasse will be rebuilt. A faithful reproduction in a faithless time. Another emblem of the effort
to move on. After the war, 1945 will sometimes be referred
to as Year Zero. A moment when time is literally suspended
by atrocity and the world responds by resetting the clock.
A speechless moment when a new word enters the lexicon
in an attempt to give language to the murder of six million
Jews by the Nazis. Genocide. A word I will grow up with,
as though it was there all along.

'My *special attitude*'

It is October of 1967 when a young man from Bangalore called A. S. Ramaswamy, known as Rama, arrives in London. He is a graduate in engineering, a Brahmin, a single man seeking adventure in the west before the arranging of his marriage, which will happen seven years from now, to my mother. He is my father, or at least he will be. Upon touching down in Heathrow on that freezing cold day, he becomes something else. An immigrant. His name both does and does not change accordingly. In the years to come everyone will still call him Rama, and the letters that drop on the mat will always be addressed to A. S. Ramaswamy. But what no one will understand is that his first name, the one his mother gave him, is actually Ramaswamy. My surname. I won't understand this either. It will take me three decades to first discover and then figure out the order and meaning of these letters, as if they are some indecipherable code and not the two initials and name of my father. It will take me longer still to keep knowing and not forget, as is my frustrating second-generation habit.

The A is for Arakalgud. A town 200 kilometres west of Bangalore, to which neither I nor my father have ever been. Arakalgud is the birthplace of his and therefore, I suppose, my ancestors. An initial designating the past as opposed to a present spoken name. No one calls him Arakalgud, neither here nor there. The S is for Subbaraya, the name of his father. Ramaswamy is his given name. In my thirties, shortly after this bombshell is dropped softly into the conversation, probably while we eat dinner in front of *EastEnders*, I learn that my mother, Shylaja, has her own invisible initials lurking at the front of her name. T. S., which make her sound, to me, like a scholar or twentieth-century poet. She dropped the 'T. S.' when she arrived in London in the spring of 1975, newly married to a man she had just met. Or perhaps it would be more fair to say the letters fell away like luggage lost in transit. The decision was not hers to make. She is called what she is called. The T is for Talya, the birthplace of her father's ancestors, the S for Subbarao, her father. On Wikipedia, the non-existent place where collective memory is stored, disambiguated and endlessly edited, I discover that Talya is a village near Chitradurga district known for its old Hanuman temple and large lake. The entry is a stub, and Wikipedia invites me to help by expanding it. This makes me laugh out loud, alone at home in Leith, with no one to share the joke with but the dog and the copy of *Austerlitz* lying open between us.

So my surname is my father's given name, at least in the western Christian sense. The only sense I know, though I am neither Christian nor a daughter of the west. Rama here and there, but for wildly different reasons. The rest is too complicated to explain. A name that in the UK appears to run back to front, prefaced by initials not intended to be spoken aloud? People wouldn't understand or care. It would bore them. Better to stick with the stub. Life is too short.

Which reminds me of something Henry once said to me about his own name changing when he came to Britain.

'So obviously you became Henry.'

In my family the discussion tends to close with a story, of which many immigrants will have a version, about a colleague. A man called, say, John, who says to my father not long after arriving in the UK, 'Rama is too hard to pronounce, shall I call you George?' To which my father politely replies, 'Of course, but only if I can call you Steve.' Or the one about my mother being praised for speaking really good English when she arrived, and replying, with a polite smile, 'Thanks, I learned it from ITV.' Politeness, good humour and dignity are the unspoken rule, handed down like an inheritance. Going high when they go low. All this is to be absorbed like a secret. And so we punctuate our stories, especially the sad ones, with a laugh. Move on with the fleet-footedness of families whose seeds are sown across the face of the earth.

When it comes to naming my children I find myself in difficult terrain. I want the Indian part of them to be named for at least the heartbeat of another generation. I want them to have my story, the contents of which I can barely speak myself, the remnants of which are so deeply concealed in my surname it took thirty years to break the code. I want them to carry a last name that in the last century, on a continent colonised by the one they call home, was a first name.

For their given names, I turn to maps of Scotland, where they took their first breaths and where I have passed more than half my life. Not because it is my home, but because it could be theirs. I travel north, via index finger, looking for somewhere to land. I hunt over slender lochs, moorland, forest and coast. I skim the tops of mountains identified by whorls of lines packed as tightly as thumbprints. I scan places small and aptly named. I swim rivers whose waters I have never seen furrow in thrall to unknown currents. I run across paths on which I have never set foot. I cross the body of a country to which I have no historical connection.

James Baldwin wrote with characteristically delicious irony about being 'a kind of bastard of the West'. When he followed the line drawn by the past, this particular native son wound up not in Europe but in Africa. Thus Shakespeare, Bach, Rembrandt, the stones of Paris and the Empire State Building could never be his creations. 'They did not contain my history,' he wrote, any more than the topography of Scotland, with its clear sense of itself and ancient rock pink and striated like human muscle, encloses mine. This bestowed upon Baldwin, and all us native sons and daughters of immigrants who have followed him, 'a special attitude'. And this is my perspective too, if I can acquire the ability to look out from behind my own eyes.

If I succeed, I find myself back on top of Richmond Hill. Where after school my best friend Suzanna and I run open-armed down the meadow dangling over the vale with the fearless commitment that only children can bring to a hill. Where we bunk off school, buy a can of Anchor cream each, and lie amongst the wildflowers and tickly grasses with our heads thrown back, squirting thick sweetened cream into our open mouths like a pair of rapacious Tudor kings. Where we take our red plastic sledges in the winter to race down thin skeins of London snow towards the river. Where we cycle at breakneck speed down Nightingale Lane, a one-way street hugging the meadow, named for the Wordsworthian birdsong that once resounded across the hill and renowned in my childhood for its crazy gradient. The purpose of everything we do, in this time, is risk. Our aim, always, is to disturb the peace. To test something boundless and as yet unnamed to us. To slap a streak of danger onto this canvas of pure English restraint.

At the most famous viewing point in the land I start to understand, however unconsciously, my unwritten place in this rarefied scheme. To feel complicit in something I never chose, simply by virtue of existing. Of being the only one. An irregularity in the landscape's calm composition. Or conversely this is where I begin to *not* understand, because it is where my education, which contains none of my history, begins. At a state school on top of the hill, moments from the nation's protected view of itself, part of which will be opened by Sir David Attenborough, known as our national treasure, the year after I enrol. Here, I learn the lessons of my era. To be bright, good-humoured, grateful, and to fit in. I learn how to be British without being English. I do not learn about my own perspective, which means it will be another twenty-five years before I realise I even have one. I do not learn that the selfsame view from Richmond Hill that I throw myself into every day after school once inspired an American planter, slave owner and colonialist called William Byrd to name another town, one he founded in Virginia overlooking a river with almost exactly the same bend, Richmond. How privileged this brown girl is, having this landscape painting come to life as her playground. How little she understands her place in it. That this scene, and all it stands for, is part of the history imposed upon her ancestors. That she must find a way for it to somehow belong to her too. Even if one day in the not too distant future the bailiff will come to the door and this view, along with everything else, will be seized from her. Not that it was ever really hers in the first place. Not that it can ever really be taken away because it will forever haunt her dreams.

The fact remains that when we go 'back' to India, for it is always framed as a return, we are interlopers in our own heritage. *The Britishers*, our aunts, uncles and cousins call us. Ours is the classic immigrant conundrum: too Indian in Britain, too British in India. Our true home lies in this *bewilderness*. In the incompetence we feel when we struggle to cross the choked roads. When my sister and I are told off at our cousin's wedding for not wearing saris and our mother, protective as a lioness, says 'How dare anyone say that about my girls!', and my sister and I cry and cry onto our ceremonial banana leaves covered with food, and none of us, in truth, know why the tears won't stop. When we cannot suppress the desire to raise our phones and take a picture of a cow held up in traffic. When we are instructed by our aunts to avoid street food because of our *delicate* constitutions. When we cannot help but be charmed by the sight of an Ambassador car cruising down the street like a boat on the tide of history, knowing full well that these shiny white automobiles are relics of the empire. When we pass the spanking white colonial architecture on the MG Road and feel humiliated by the spark of recognition, of aesthetic pleasure, lit in us. When we experience all of India's clichés not as the locals we appear to be but as the foreigners we are. When we cannot understand what our relatives are saying. When we cannot pronounce our own names.

In the future I will start to understand that belonging lies in the search. That disorientation is the true birthplace of millions of us. That ambivalence is my identity and concealment my natural habitat. That making myself at home in this bewilderness will be a life's work. And that I am not alone. I am like Austerlitz, who feels 'oppressed by the vague sense that he did not belong in this city either, or indeed anywhere else in the world'. I am like Henry cooking his way into Glasgow, into the Jewish community, into his own home. I am like Baldwin, born the same year as Henry. 'I would have to make them mine,' he wrote. 'I would have to accept my special attitude, my special place in this scheme – otherwise I would have no place in *any* scheme.'

In the end, I settle on glens. Those tremendously deep, often long, definitively Scottish absences in the land. Carved by ice, filled with water, shadow and restless northern light. Places identified as much by what surrounds them as what they are. Places to which I have always been drawn. I name my children after glens I have never visited. Places that are near me, that even border land I know and love, but upon which I have never actually set my little brown feet. And in the handful of years since, a period that everyone with children rightly says passes with the blink of an eye, I have not gone to those glens, in spite of their proximity and my half-hearted intentions.

After my children's births, there will follow a time when this is a source of shame. When I divulge the backstories of their names and then laugh politely, just as the world taught me. When I acquire a touch of imposter syndrome about my own children's names, which is almost as ridiculous written down as it is to experience.

But then more time will pass. And at some uncharted point, through the simple act of saying them over and over again, of watching my children become themselves, their names will bind to them like roots to the soil. They will come to signify their own specific and evolving persons more than any hollow in the land.

And in another moment, *this* one, it will occur to me. This deliberate forging of a connection, this stitching of a name to a particular place, is precisely the point. This is my special attitude. This is my special place in this scheme. This is how we belong to places. This is how we make them our own.

'I *went up to the gods.*'

The music programme is ochre, the colour of the past. A comforting size. Small, approachable like a book. Kept in a bundle of similar programmes and held together with a single perfectly centred elastic band. On top of the pile is an index card. The same kind used to document the internment of people during the war. People like Henry. The same kind used in my own youth to catalogue whatever it was I happened to be cataloguing. Books, which I developed a time-consuming habit of transcribing into notebooks, in the hope of making the words my own. Rubbers from WHSmith shaped like giant tablets. Small scented soaps printed with the crescent moons of my nail marks, and sometimes my teeth. Stones prised from the rough sandy paths of Richmond Park, which I took home and kept, like pets, in my father's used yellow Ship matchboxes. The stones, in particular, were a quiet source of disappointment, never as themselves as when they remained cupped by the paths unfurling across the royal park. Then again, it was the Eighties, and I had the misfortune of knowing someone with their own stone-polishing machine. It was not a time for appreciating things as they were.

Index cards are old now too, relegated to the past along with the music programme, those little boxes of Ship safety matches that populated my early domestic life, and, for that matter, stone-polishing machines. Yet I need only imagine a tall ship sailing across the canary yellow background of a little box, and there he is. A middle-aged man in a grey armchair, digging a match deep into his ear before retrieving it. Striking it with a single extravagant attempt. Lighting his cigarette and then shaking the match elegantly, one, two, three, to extinguish the flame. My father.

The words on the index card are printed in Henry's deft script, which I have come to recognise instantly, capitalised and hovering just above the line.

'THESE LIBRETTI AND TEXTS WERE COLLECTED BY ME FOR ANY OPERA OR PLAY THAT INTERESTED ME DURING 1937/8.'

In 1937 Henry is thirteen years old. An only child. The son of a German Jewish mother, Lore, from Heilbronn, and an Austrian stationer, Karl, from Graz. Henry's parents meet by chance on holiday before the First World War in the belle époque seaside town of Blankenberge on the Belgian coast. And after the war, during which the tall elegant Karl is held prisoner in a camp in the Italian Alps, something he will never talk about to his son, he and Lore are reunited. They get married. They settle in a suburb of Nuremberg.

Their teenage son is beginning to cultivate a lifelong love of food, the outdoors and music. This is the year Henry receives a desk and typewriter for his bar mitzvah, and from this moment on will never again be without a desk. He has a nursemaid, Alice, whom he calls A-la-la. Every month two women come to the flat to wash the tablecloths and bed linen. A seamstress comes every few weeks to repair their clothes. 'Look, that's how it was,' says Henry. 'We were lower middle-class but nevertheless we had a trousseau with an enormous amount of bed linen. We employed girls. You knew these people, ate breakfast with them, they were part of the family.'

The Wugas, and Alice, live at 15 Fürther Strasse. A straight wide artery penetrating the heart of what John Dos Passos will describe as the 'old city of toymakers and meistersingers' when he arrives here in less than a decade for the Nuremberg trials. Trials that will be held at 110 Fürther Strasse, the Palace of Justice further along the very same street. Nuremberg is the jewel in Bavaria's Germanic crown. A birthplace of European culture and science. It is in this old medieval town where it is first theorised that the world is round. It is the city of the world's first pocket watch and Europe's first railroad. A city, like London, Delhi, Paris or Tokyo, from which one is proud to hail. But for four years now Nuremberg has also been the most anti-semitic place on earth. In 1933 Hitler declared Nuremberg the 'City of Nazi Party Rallies' and work began on turning a 1,500 acre site on its southeastern edge into the location for mass National Socialist gatherings.

By 1937 the Nuremberg rallies have been running for more than a decade. The Zeppelinfeld arena has just been completed, and construction will begin over the summer on a vast stadium to seat more than 400,000 spectators. The anti-semitic Nuremberg laws have been in place for two years. *Der Stürmer*, the Nazi hate sheet, has been publishing for fourteen years, its first edition launching the year before Henry's birth. The November pogrom the Nazis will call Kristallnacht is one year away. The year after that, Henry will flee his home city for good.

'It was very nice,' Henry says of his childhood. 'Then of course the Nazis came. By that time I was ten years old. You knew what was going on. You sensed it from your parents. Times were difficult, particularly in Nuremberg.' The local Gauleiter, officials governing assigned districts under Nazi rule, is Julius Streicher, the founder and publisher of *Der Stürmer*. While Henry diligently collects his libretti and texts, Streicher's publishing company releases an anti-semitic book for children in which Jews are likened to poisonous toadstools.

'Nuremberg was always very, very anti-Semitic,' says Henry. 'The synagogue was burned long before the others. There were newspapers, horrible cartoons posted every-where with the big noses. I mean it was horrendous. At school I felt it. Possibly only one person would speak to you. The others were intimidated by their parents, by the regime. They were told to have nothing to do with Jews.'

There are three other Jewish boys in Henry's class at school. One day the four boys are segregated and made to sit at the back of the room. Nobody will speak to them from this moment on, neither the teachers nor the children.

'Songs were sung in the classroom while we were sitting there in tears,' says Henry. 'I don't forget this easily.'

Around this time Henry begins to quietly archive his own existence. To stack his music programmes at his new desk. He does this even as his life, which for now remains his to catalogue, becomes ever more restricted. A life now defined by a sole aspect of his identity, one he never much considered before. The red 'J' that in less than a year will be stamped on his Reisepass.

'You were a bit of a renegade, really,' says Gillian when Henry retrieves the stack of programmes from his archive. She turns to me.

'Did Daddy ever tell you about going to the opera?'

So Henry tells me about Hans Sachs, a German master-singer, shoemaker and poet from Nuremberg who wrote more than four thousand works in his life, which makes you wonder when on earth he found time to cobble. 'A real person,' says Henry with a starstruck expression, 'who lived four hundred years ago.' Hans Sachs is the historical figure on whom Richard Wagner based his mature opera *Die Meistersinger von Nürnberg*, the virtuosic prelude of which is amongst the most famous music he ever composed. Wagner worked on *Die Meistersinger* in various towns and cities during the 1850s and 1860s: Marienbad, Paris and Vienna. He completed the score in a stately manor on a hill overlooking Lake Lucerne that is eventually turned into a museum, with all the interactive displays and carefully worded interpretations we now associate with the more easeful digestion of history. *Die Meistersinger* debuted in Munich during the summer of 1868 with Franz Strauss, the father of Richard Strauss, playing the French horn at the premiere. It was an instant hit.

Set in mid sixteenth-century Renaissance Nuremberg, the opera is revered as a paean to the supremacy of German art. But by the time Henry hears it, it is also famous, more than any other music composed by Wagner, for its association with the Nazis. Hitler loved *Die Meistersinger* more than any other music by Wagner, and selected the opera to accompany the founding of the Third Reich in 1933. Leni Riefenstahl used the Act Three prelude to score a section of the 1935 propaganda film *Triumph of the Will*. During the war years it will become the only work performed at Wagner's own theatre in Bayreuth.

Still, when Henry learns that Wagner's opera about Hans Sachs is coming to Nuremberg, he decides to find a way to see it.

'I said "Well, this is an occasion,"' he tells me with a mischievous grin, rubbing his hands together. '"I would like to go."' Henry shakes his head at the chutzpah of his past self. 'I was thirteen! This was Nuremberg in 1937! My mother said "What do you mean? You are not allowed to go." How I got a ticket I do not know. My mother said I would be beaten to death. I said no one will know. A little boy? And they didn't.'

So much of the memory has vanished. Henry can neither recall how he got his hands on a ticket nor the walk home clutching his libretto, perhaps on air, perhaps already terrified at what had been risked. Gone is the moment of stepping into the exquisite art nouveau opera house on Richard-Wagner-Platz, home to the biggest stage in Germany. What's left behind is an opera of the senses. A young heart knocking against a chest in the freighted dark of a theatre. A hard seat against the fidgety legs of a small reactive body. The vertiginous draw of the height. The orchestra tuning in the pit. The heady thrill of getting away with it.

Were you frightened?

'No,' says Henry, and we laugh.

'He's too bloody-minded to be terrified,' says Gillian, and we laugh again.

I ask Henry to hold the libretto out in his hand, which is dappled with the universal hieroglyphs of age. Liver spots, veins, creases, errant hairs. There are only words on the libretto's cover, no pictures, and they are conveyed in a medieval romantic font. The kind that conjures up enchanting European fairy tales about princesses letting down their hair and empty turreted castles from a bygone era. The typeface of stories that never die out.

I bend over him, holding my phone as steady as my hand will permit. I let the automatic focus do its work then take a photo. Click. The crisp haptic reproduction of a camera lens blinking shut like an eye. The theatre curtain coming down at the end of a performance.

How did a Jewish boy come to love the same opera as Hitler?

'I know,' says Henry, making a fist with his hand. 'It was my fight against Hitler! It's unusual, but that's how it was.'

And that's how *Die Meistersinger* has been for a long time. A masterpiece not only stained with Nazi ideology and propaganda in the twentieth century but borne out of the nineteenth-century nexus of German nationalism, romanticism and anti-Semitism. Wagner's anti-Semitic twenty-five-page pamphlet *Jewishness in Music* was published in 1850, around the time he was beginning to think about *Die Meistersinger*. The character of Beckmesser, a hapless meistersinger and town clerk who is publicly humiliated on stage, is routinely acknowledged to embody anti-Semitic stereotypes. The finale, played during the section of the Nuremberg rallies when Hitler and his entourage arrived followed by a torchlit procession, closes with a triumphant call to German nationalism.

> Even if the Holy Roman Empire
> Should dissolve in mist,
> For us there would yet remain
> Holy German art!

In a moment snatched while my daughter trundles around the sitting room babbling to herself and my son watches YouTube videos of LNER trains on repeat in his bedroom, I listen to the famous prelude to Act One of *Die Meistersinger* for the first time. This unsettling concert for one falls in a tumultuous week, much like any other towards the close of the second decade of the twenty-first century. In America, the efforts to impeach the leader of the free world rumble on. In Germany, the far-right AfD has surged to second place in the east German state of Thuringia, led by an anti-Semitic politician who has been compared to Hitler. Closer to home, yet another Brexit extension is granted at the last minute and an end of year snap general election is called. The national mood is one of deep cynicism and despair. Meanwhile, Henry is travelling to Berlin to give a talk at the Jewish Museum. On the same day, the bodies of thirty-nine people are found in a lorry container on an industrial estate in Essex not far from the Tilbury port where the *Empire Windrush* docked. Nor far from Harwich, where Henry first set foot on British soil. Inside the Bulgarian-registered container the human cost of unsafe migration is portioned out in the deaths of thirty-eight adults and one teenager. Refugees, thirty-five of whom are thought to be from the farming communities of Vietnam's Nghe An province.

I go to Spotify, the digital music platform that has so seamlessly externalised our memories and cleared out our cupboards. I scroll down the list and choose a recording conducted by Daniel Barenboim, born in Buenos Aires to Jewish Russian immigrants, with the Bayreuth Festival Orchestra. I stand at the window of my flat, with its long systematic view down a peaceful residential street, the perspectival lines reaching like outstretched arms to the end of the road. So pleasing, so precise. This outlook is what made me fall in love with this place. I remember viewing it one freezing day in winter, standing upstairs at the window of my son's future bedroom with my four-month-old daughter strapped to my front, involuntarily bouncing up and down as mothers of babies do at that soft yet frenetic stage, watching a blizzard roll down the street. I saw the scene though my son's eyes. Occupied his five-year-old self, as mothers do so routinely and unthinkingly with their children even as they become ever more unknown to us. Deduced that my son's autistic brain, with its insatiable appetite for pattern-making, would love it too.

The prelude colonises my body. Rinses my senses. For

nine bombastic minutes and twenty-eight seconds I am transported to that vast Nuremberg theatre on Richard-Wagner-Platz. To a faraway seat in the gods, where the ghost of Henry still sits, alone in the last row, clutching his libretto. For a moment I am him. Then a magical switch takes place and in a breath I exit his body. I am no longer Henry, nor is he the ninety-five-year-old man whose story I am telling. I am the mother waiting at a window for her boy to come home. He is my teenage son. And though I know how the story pans out as surely as I can see the seconds of the music passing on my screen, I fear for him as if the past has not yet happened.

You will be beaten to death, she said.

I'm overwhelmed by the familiar tenderness and terror of parenting. The risk inseparable from love. The hammer of the heart that now beats in a whole other person. I wish Henry had not gone to the concert. I want the prelude, and the interminable hours of music that follow, to hurry up so he can come home to Fürther Strasse. I will the future to come quickly. I will it to never arrive.

John Berger wrote of how easy it is to lose sight of what is historically invisible, 'as if people lived only history and nothing else'. And so at the same time another train of thought is running on a parallel track. Its cargo is precious, light, almost undetectable. Pride in a bloody-minded German Jewish boy stripped of his citizenship. Awe at his dangerous love of the music inspired by his city, his people, his heritage. Respect for his capacity to give it to himself in the darkest and most ungenerous of times, because it belongs to him too. And love for the boy expressing, through the simple living of his one life, the words which will be written in exile by Bertolt Brecht and published two years after Henry goes to see Wagner's great German opera in Nazi-era Nuremberg.

In the dark times
Will there also be singing?
Yes, there will also be singing.
About the dark times.

'I'm still upright, aren't I!'

In the summer of 2011, I go to Giffnock for the first time. I am sent by my editor at the newspaper where I'm a staff writer on an assignment to interview an elderly Jewish couple in the run-up to Refugee Week. I spend the afternoon with the Wugas, who have just returned from giving a talk about their lives to a group of teachers in Ayr. My memory of this visit is in full colour, sharpened by the act of instantly turning it into copy when I returned to my desk the following morning. I will remember the finest textures of that day. The bottle of mineral water encased in a basket, wheeled in on a Sixties tea trolley that will become a running joke between the three of us. The bowl of Japanese rice crackers. The sensation of stepping over the threshold into a time hovering, according to the furniture, atmosphere, attire and sensibility of the inhabitants, somewhere around the mid-century.

Henry is impeccably dressed in a checked shirt, red tie and gleaming tie pin. Ingrid wears a pale pink twinset and pearls at her ears and throat. They are a rare combination of very proper and very warm. They are eighty-seven and eighty-six years old, and still skiing every year. They are long-term volunteer ski instructors with Blesma, the charity for limbless veterans, where Ingrid has gained a reputation for her ability to coax any number of traumatised ex-soldiers down the slopes. As well as skiing, they love music, food, culture and, after all it has dealt them, life. I am struck by

76

the generous atmosphere they create, even as we talk about some of the greatest atrocities known to humankind. I have never met anyone like them. Afterwards I ask the photographer to email me a photograph from their session together, something I have never done before. He sends me a picture of Henry and Ingrid on their sitting-room sofa, heads bent towards each other, grinning widely.

A few weeks later, the Wugas invite me back to Giffnock for lunch.

In the early days of our friendship, years before she is diagnosed with vascular dementia, Ingrid comes to collect me from the station. It seems impossible to me now, in the way it does when a person's illness begins to paper over their past selves, that she remained in the driver's seat well into her late eighties. This mischievous woman with a wit as dry as tinder. This quietly subversive character who the very first time I met her declared, with a defiant laugh, that 'One thing Hitler did for me is this: without emigrating I would never have met Henry.'

The car is parked outside Giffnock station. Ingrid reaches over to open the door, pats the leather passenger seat, and I am flooded with the warm sensation of being met at a train station by someone I love. I am young, free, a person at home with being on the move. I have bags that exist in a constant limbo between unpacking and packing in my hall. I talk about how tired I am, often, in the way that young people do, without a shred of self-awareness. I am an increasingly rare breed: a staff newspaper journalist in an industry already dying a long and naturally well-documented death. That can still afford, for now, to send one of its writers across the Central Belt, with a photographer in tow, to spend the afternoon with two Holocaust survivors in their home.

We head to the address printed on the lozenge-shaped gold labels the Wugas stick on the seals of envelopes, which I will soon begin to receive in the post. The genteel green and sandstone background of Giffnock parades past the window. The streets are wide, empty, the trees either very old or young. Then comes the procession of roundabouts alerting you to the fact that you have arrived in suburbia, a fact which, perhaps as much as the circling motion, always induces a slight queasiness in me. The sense of space, quiet and leafiness that tends to preside over affluent towns. Of people living out lives so different to mine behind closed doors. Ingrid's coiffured head is craned forwards, nose to the wheel. Her perfume fills the car. She points out the recently opened Whole Foods, which will close down in a few years, with a conspiratorial roll of the eyes. She looks at me as we talk, sometimes for long enough that I mentally beg her to redirect her gaze to the road. She cracks jokes. She asks after my parents. We pull up outside the block of flats, with its beautifully tended communal gardens, and immaculate entrance where the Wugas will overwinter their pots of geraniums in a few months. Inside, all is gleaming wood panelling and thick orange carpets. It is very quiet. I never see another soul. We take the lift a floor up. Henry is standing at the door to greet us.

Giffnock, home to Scotland's largest, longest established and dwindling Jewish community, is not my neighbourhood. I do not walk the wide tree-lined streets or shop in the supermarkets selling latkes and matzos. I know nothing of its Jewish restaurants, Jewish care home, Jewish community centre, kosher food bank, or synagogue, which is the largest in Scotland. I see Giffnock as we tend to see places meaningful to us solely because of the people who reside there. At speed, from a car window, on a single unchanging route. Through a pane of glass. Silently. As an outsider in every way. And Giffnock, equally, knows nothing of me. As I often do when I leave the metropolis for the high-vis suburbs or countryside, my self-awareness, by which I mean my sense of how I am seen, increases with every radius mile from the city. I disconnect from my surroundings and find myself bound, instead, to those who have beaten a path before me through places to which no one deems them to belong. To Baldwin's 'Stranger in the Village', which recounts his 1950s visit to the mountain village of Leukerbad in Switzerland. Its opening line plays like a jazz refrain when I walk through such places, which is to say most places I go.

'From all available evidence no black man had ever set foot in this tiny Swiss village before I came.'

And yet, within a few visits to the Wugas, the sight of Giffnock on the board at Glasgow Central, coming after the whimsical sounding Crossmyloof, Pollokshaws West and Thornliebank, will begin to induce a blood rush that can only be translated as belonging. I will stand there, already happy, on that vast concourse beneath the same great glass roof that once covered the head of a fifteen-year-old refugee called Heinz Martin Wuga. Just seeing that collection of letters on the list of stations forming the East Kilbride line will make me, a daughter of immigrants in a country I no longer understand, feel like I am, if not at home, at least on my way there.

Perhaps this is what it is like to visit grandparents. I never got to know my own. They all lived and died in South India, where my parents were born and raised, and which my sister and I visited rarely, and for twenty years not at all. No matter how many questions I ask, and for decades I asked none, these four people remain portraits. No voices to animate them. No gestures to make them shake off their poses, get up and walk out of the frame. Only a black and white photo of my mother's father, full-lipped, kind-faced, bespectacled, on our mantelpiece for years until, just like that, it was no longer there. Perhaps it was replaced by, possibly even hidden behind, the next generation: my sister's and my children. These photos are different, less precious partly because we inhabit the same time as them, partly because of their sheer number. High resolution, perfect, full-colour photos of mixed-race babies selected from hundreds stored on mobile phones and backed up in some faraway non-place. We print these photos out in Kodak Expresses that smell of the vinegar past and look like they are on their last legs. Or email a carefully mulled over selection to online print services that send them back in the post, restored to keepsakes from another time. Susan Sontag morbidly observed that the act of taking a photograph entails participating in another person (or thing's) 'mortality, vulnerability, mutability'. All photographs, she concluded, 'testify to time's relentless melt'. Every single one captures a moment forever lost.

I have a blurry recollection of one photo of my father's father. My grandfather, I should call him. The photo is on a wall in the flat of my father's brother, Shiva, in Bangalore. Blurry because it is old but also because it's glimpsed through a cascade of tears. I have only cried like that after the births of my children. It is the full-scale communal wailing of a family who never see each other, can't really understand each other, and bear so much that cannot be said that on the rare occasions when we do meet all that is left is tears. A tap that cannot be turned off. A kind of mourning for living things. The women of the family dabbing their eyes with the corners of their saris. The men smiling with shining eyes and shaking their heads, over and over again. Shiva flipping his right hand, palm up, then down, suggesting a kind of cavalier, 'what happens, happens' attitude. Same hand. Same gesture. Same philosophy. His brother, my father, right there.

This barely seen or remembered photo of a man from whom I am descended on a wall is it. I can see myself standing in front of it more than I can see what I saw. The fact is, these people, my people, are characters in my parents' life stories, not mine. The story I am living is elsewhere, closer to Glasgow Central, though when I stand on that concourse it eludes me again. When I get home from that trip, which will shake my life by the shoulders until it rearranges itself in a way I will never be able to articulate, I will try to tell my father, who was not with us in India, how things were. 'Ah, yes,' he will say, 'very emotional people, my family.' And his elegant right hand will flip this way and that.

Those early visits with the Wugas are about the slow evolution of friendship. The living of life, rather than the writing of it. There are no recordings. Mostly, it is about lunch, made long before I arrive by Henry, who despite being a retired chef and caterer I have never once caught in the act of cooking. Into the little dining room, wheeled in on the tea trolley I have come to anticipate like an old friend, comes bread in a basket lined with napkins. Salmon, poached to the palest pink. Cheeses and cold meats delicately draped on plates. Sliced boiled eggs smothered in a Marie Rose sauce, a signature Wuga dish borne out of catering kosher celebrations in the Seventies as an alternative to prawns. A tube of the most deliciously wobbly

81

Swiss mayonnaise. Once, homemade gazpacho that astonishingly tasted exactly like my mother's version. Another time, we ate Ingrid's homemade lebkuchen and she wrote down the recipe for me on a scrap of paper I have since, typically, lost.

At one of these early lunches, which over time have bled into one another so they now reside in my memory as one long delicious Marie Rose-tinted repast, our conversation turns to my life.

Am I married?

No.

Do I have a boyfriend?

No.

It is one of those casual, heart-hammering moments that afflicts all of us who must decide, right there and then, while the tea is being poured and the friendship struck up, whether or not to show ourselves.

I am not married.

I am bisexual.

My partner is a woman.

'Wonderful,' says Henry. 'Next time you must bring her.'

Eventually I start taping the visits to Giffnock. Around the same time the atmosphere in the town, and the world beyond it, is changing. The same week I first interview Henry for this book, the German chancellor Angela Merkel speaks about the country's 'spectres of the past'. About the need to be vigilant to the growing threat of far-right populism at home and abroad. 'Unfortunately there is to this day not a single synagogue, not a single day care centre for Jewish children, not a single school for Jewish children that does not need to be guarded by German policemen,' she says. A few days later Germany's ombudsman for anti-Semitism suggests that observant Jews would be wise not to wear a kippah in public.

And so it goes on. Anti-Semitism levels rise in the UK

and throughout Europe, and now and then security is stepped up at Giffnock's synagogue and Jewish school. During periods of increased risk, Jewish children are not allowed to line up in the playground. Though the number of hate crimes against Jews remains relatively low, this is a small community, numbering a few thousand, and there is an escalating and, for many, all too familiar unease.

'All of a sudden I begin to feel it again,' says Henry. 'One talks about it a lot. The police visit now and again, and there are certain meetings. But we have not been physically abused. There have been no attacks on synagogues. No swastikas, though it happens now and again at the cemetery. Physically it's been quite reasonable.'

At the same time, as pockets of Europe appear to renege on the promise to never forget, Ingrid's dementia advances.

'You mean I forget things,' she says.

'Well, it's more than forgetting things,' replies Henry. 'You can unfortunately not remember things at all. You will ask me the same thing five times. You wake up and say "What day is it? Where am I going today? What am I doing today?"' He turns to me. 'She wants to know, but she doesn't get distressed. She is quite happy.'

I turn to Ingrid. Are you happy?

'Yes,' says Ingrid. 'I'm here. Henry is here. My children are around. That's the main thing.'

Over lunch that day I learn that the Wugas received some unexpected visitors earlier in the week. The children of one of Ingrid's old classmates travelled all the way from New Jersey and came for lunch. It turns out their mother was at the Jewish school in Dortmund with Ingrid. This woman, who also has dementia, has always kept a photo of Ingrid on her bedside table, telling her five children that the picture is of her childhood best friend.

And so the family tracked Ingrid down on the internet, and following an eighty-year hiatus the two women talked on the phone. Despite their dementia, they recognised one another.

Ingrid listens intently to this story as we eat lunch. Every now and then she turns to me, grins and says, 'I'm still upright, aren't I!'

Before the woman's children left they gave Ingrid a message she wrote to their mother in a poesie album. I have no idea what a poesie album is until Henry produces it and I remember that this sweet youthful ritual accompanied my own schooldays in Eighties London, when we would get our classmates to sign each other's embossed and padded autograph books on the last day of term. It was a chance to practise our signatures but also, in retrospect, a rehearsal for life. For demonstrating the depth of our feelings to those we loved. For learning to say goodbye.

Ingrid's message is written in 1934. She is ten years old. Perhaps the future, as it tends to for ten-year-olds who have the fortune of growing up in loving, present families, seems certain, benevolent, uninteresting. Perhaps she has no idea the world around her is already changing beyond all imagination. The message is accompanied by a studio portrait in which Ingrid wears a dress with a rounded white collar and cuffs. It is the photo that sat, all those decades, on another Jewish woman's bedside table across the Atlantic. In it Ingrid smiles, the wide open-mouthed grin she is beaming at me right now across the table.

Her original message in German has been translated onto a Post-it note.

'Days go by fast. Whenever you get up in the morning ask yourself the question: what shall you do well today?'

'Now be the Heinz that left us.'

Henry first arrives in Glasgow on 5 May 1939. He is collected from platform one of Central Station, a glittering Victorian monument to the railway age, refracting the changeable skies of the city through 48,000 rectangular panes of glass. A station whose entire roof, in less than a year, will be painted black to protect it from the Luftwaffe. A change that will not be reversed until 1998. The year after I arrive in Glasgow.

Henry's second cousin, Grete Gummers, is waiting to meet him. She takes him south, across the Clyde, to 169 Queen's Drive in Govanhill. Henry's new home. He meets the owner of the handsome main-door flat. Mrs Etta Hurwich. A complete stranger. A woman in her sixties. His guarantor.

'An absolutely tremendous lady,' says Henry. 'Wonderful, welcoming, kind, a real intellectual. I was one of the lucky ones.' Mrs Hurwich is also a Jewish immigrant. She is from Libau, a Latvian port city on the Baltic Sea. She came to Glasgow in the 1890s with her husband, who started up a furniture upholstery business in Bridgeton. The couple had four children before her husband died, leaving her to raise them and run the family business alone. Which she did, says Henry with pride, 'from the very next day'. Now all but one of Mrs Hurwich's children, Simon, who helps her run the business, have left home.

Henry has nothing with him but a small leather case containing the clothes his mother packed for him a few days earlier. He is taken downstairs and given his own bedroom in the basement. 'A beautiful bed,' he recalls, 'everything lovely, fitted sheets, and blankets.' The sheets and tightly tucked blankets must be fought into with his bandy young legs, so different to the wadded continental 'downies' that sit, plumped up, on his bed back home in Nuremberg. It is an image that reminds me of the painter Max Ferber in Sebald's *The Emigrants*, in turn partially based on the Jewish refugee and painter Frank Auerbach. Fleeing Munich in May 1939, the same month Henry boards a Kindertransport in Nuremberg, Ferber passes his first night in Britain at 'a little émigré hotel in Bloomsbury'. There he finds himself unable to sleep, 'not so much because of my distress as because of the way one is pinned down, in English beds of that kind, by bedding which has been tucked under the mattress all the way round.'

It is through Grete, Lore's cousin, that Mrs Hurwich comes to hear about a Jewish boy in Nuremberg in desperate need of help. Henry will never be sure how it all played out. Perhaps Mrs Hurwich saw an ad in the *Jewish Chronicle*. Perhaps someone from the refugee committee in Glasgow already knew about an older Jewish woman with room for a child. This is how the majority of the children fleeing Nazi-occupied territories secured their place on the Kindertransport: via a stranger, or distant family connection, with the means to pay the upfront sum of £50 to guarantee any re-emigration costs after the war. Or perhaps it was the Gummerses who knew Mrs Hurwich. They had come to Glasgow when the government gave a few dozen German dentists permission to settle in Britain in the run-up to the war.

So through the joint efforts of Lore in Nuremberg, the Gummerses in Glasgow, and a Mrs Thelma Mann and Mrs Thora Wolffson on the city's refugee committee, Mrs Hurwich agrees to become Henry's guarantor. And he is, as he says, one of the lucky ones. The 'unguaranteed' children, those without sponsors, arrive in Britain with no one to collect them. They are dispersed to camps, sometimes for weeks, until foster homes can be found. They are the responsibility of the Movement for the Care of Children in Germany, later known as the Refugee Children's Movement, which is reliant on charitable donations. For it has been previously agreed with the home secretary, Sir Samuel Hoare, that no refugee child should become a burden on the state.

Two months after Henry arrives in Glasgow, another Kindertransport pulls into Liverpool Street, London, carrying a fifteen-year-old girl from Dortmund. Her name is Ingrid Wolff.

Her guarantors, the Dixons, live in Ashby-de-la-Zouch, a market town in north Leicestershire. They have no children. Their only son has recently died, though Ingrid will not find out about this until much later. Perhaps this is why the Dixons decide to sponsor a Kindertransportee in the first place. Perhaps this is why, when that child turns up, it is too much for Mrs Dixon to bear. 'Mrs Dixon told me she saw my picture and thought it was nice but they would rather have had a boy,' says Ingrid. 'I felt very unwanted. Certain things you forget, but I never forgot that.'

The Dixons go through the case Ingrid's mother packed for her. Inside, amongst the clothes, they find a copy of *Grimm's Fairy Tales*, and Ingrid's school uniform, in which they discover three German pfennigs.

'The Dixons unpacked the case for her, without her, and she didn't like that,' says Gillian. 'Her mum had packed it so lovingly. And the Dixons sort of . . . well . . . *accused* is a harsh word, but they suggested Mummy was going to sequester the money somewhere. Even though she couldn't use them here!'

'Where are the pfennigs?' Ingrid demands. Her eyes flit between Gillian, Henry and me.

'You got them back,' Gillian says. 'You kept them. Your grandson has one, framed on the wall. The others, I think, are in the Imperial War Museum.'

Once Ingrid's case is unpacked by the Dixons, they ask her what she would like to do while she is staying with them. She says she would like to go to school and eventually study nursing. But Mrs Dixon does not believe in girls over fourteen attending school. And so Ingrid's education is over. Instead she is sent to care for a local family's baby in a huge country house with a swimming pool in the garden. She becomes a live-in nanny. The family are kind, but the other staff will not mix with Ingrid because of her German accent. She speaks little English and meets no other refugees. On her half-days off every week Mr Dixon comes to collect her to take her home for a visit.

Then, just one week before the outbreak of war, Ingrid's parents, Erna and Ascher Wolff, manage to flee Germany. They get jobs as domestic servants for a family, the Watsons, in West Kilbride. Ingrid leaves Ashby-de-la-Zouch, abruptly and for good. She gets on a northbound train. On Scotland's west coast, in a tiny hamlet headed by an old pier striking out into the Firth of Clyde, the Wolffs are reunited on the eve of war.

'The Watsons had seventy factories,' says Henry. 'Really well established people. They made Scotch woollen hosiery. Their son would come running into the kitchen and say "Miss Wolff! Quickly put the radio on! They're playing classical music." People were very kind. This helps.'

Soon Ingrid gets a job nearby as a domestic servant in a cottage in Portencross, working for a bank manager, his wife and their son, who is a couple of years younger than her. She learns how to light a fire. She swims in the sea, which is just ten yards from the front door.

'"Let's go swimming," the lady of the house would say to her,' recalls Henry. 'Ingrid would answer "I haven't finished my ironing yet" and the lady would say "The sun is shining and the ironing can wait."'

'When was I in Portencross?' Ingrid demands. 'Why did I go there? Was it for a job?'

Meanwhile, in Glasgow, Henry is enrolled at the local school, Queen's Park, which he walks to every day. He is the only foreigner there but he is treated well. 'Mrs Hurwich introduced me to all her family,' says Henry. 'I was made welcome. I became part of the family. There were quite a few Jewish kids in the school. I was not abused for being German . . . well, war had not broken out yet.'

Still, adjustments must be made. At first, Henry is taken aback by the food at 169 Queen's Drive. He has never eaten tinned pineapple or chopped fried fish. He has never taken milk in his tea. His attire changes too. Henry is used to wearing shorts but is told this is not done, at his age, in Glasgow. He is taken to a tailor and kitted out in a suit. Mrs Hurwich takes him to the theatre, concerts and restaurants. He sees the Austrian Jewish actress Elisabeth Bergner in J. M. Barrie's play *The Boy David*, written especially for her. He misses his parents, desperately, but he has been away from home before on a nine-month apprenticeship in Baden-Baden, and now that time grounds him like an anchor. Keeps the homesickness at bay.

Then, less than four months after his arrival in Britain, war is declared.

Blackout curtains are hung across the windows, and air-raid sirens resound across Glasgow. The police start coming to the door to check on Henry. In Portencross and West Kilbride Ingrid and her parents, now deemed a security risk, are expelled from the coast. A policeman comes to the door of the cottage that opens onto the Firth of Clyde and says to Ingrid, 'You can't stay here any more. You're not allowed to live near the sea.' Erna and Ascher are advised to visit a local Jewish man, Mr Samuel, in West Kilbride who might help them. Mr Samuel offers them his house in the west end of Glasgow, rent-free. And so the Wolffs wind up in Scotland's biggest city. Erna and Ascher become housekeepers for a family in Pollokshields. 'The

Cuthbertsons,' says Henry. 'Piano makers. My mother-in-law was the cook. My father-in-law was the general factotum.' Ingrid, who at first has to stay in a hostel for women and girls, finds another job as a nanny.

All communication between Henry and his parents ceases. Until the middle of November when his uncle in Brussels, which for now remains neutral, starts acting as a conduit, passing the letters back and forth. Letters that in a matter of months will lead to Henry's reclassification as a dangerous enemy alien category A, and internment.

In these soon-to-be-incriminating letters Lore informs Henry that both she and his father have, coincidentally, broken their arms. Karl apparently fell, and then she had 'a run-in with a glass', cut through an artery, and was unconscious by the time she got to hospital. Lore mentions neither the war nor how dangerous the conditions in Nuremberg must by now be. Mostly she berates her son for not writing enough to her, nor his grandmother now alone in Heilbronn. Lore's laser focus, as always, is on Henry. She has no idea that he is in Perthshire. When she finds out she doesn't understand that he has been evacuated. She thinks her son is being disrespectful and ungracious to his guarantor. She is incensed.

'Dear Heinz,' she writes on 21 January 1940, 'we have done everything to bring you up as someone we could send to strangers with a clear conscience. Until now, you have brought us such pride. Now you are making us worry. You know that you and all the others on the outside give your parents hope as we are stuck here for the time being.'

Lore instructs Henry to return to Glasgow immediately. Her demand is definitive.

'Now be the Heinz that left us.'

By March, Lore has received two letters from Henry explaining his location at Rossie House, and letting her know that he has passed his exams. Her tone changes completely. Relief and love suffuse her sentences once more, and Lore gives Henry her and his father's blessing to pursue his love of cooking. 'If it brings you such pleasure and joy, the only right decision can be to once again choose that profession. So, my dear Heinz, my and indeed your father's view is this,' Lore concludes in the final long letter she will be able to write to her son on her beloved typewriter before the war's end, 'it is up to you, and a trade in hand finds gold in every land.'

One day, far into the future, I will visit the Wugas when my daughter is a baby. We will talk about this brief period in their histories when they were newly arrived in Britain. When life was so sharp, unfamiliar, tumultuous. After lunch my daughter will become fractious, and I will be dispatched to Henry and Ingrid's bedroom to breastfeed her. I have never been in their bedroom before. It feels like I am being summoned deeper into the family as I cross the threshold. And there, on top of the sheets, as I feed my daughter to sleep, I will rest my feet on a pair of thick eiderdowns. One for each of them, at the end of their bed.

'The other country.'

We are all born into vanishing time. But when a generation leaves or is forced out of the country of its ancestors, a branch is broken in our lineage. The family tree must now be dug up, lugged across the world, and replanted in foreign soil. There will be gains, and there will be losses. The roots now stretching across borders and thrusting under seabeds might become more difficult to trace. To hold on to. To naturalise. They might not take. And if they do you might end up going by another name.

I suspect this is why, no matter how many times my sister and I have been told the names of our grandparents, we forget them. Just like that, as though they are obscure character actors in old TV shows and not the same four people who birthed our parents. The work of forgetting is as powerful and unknown to us as that of recollection. 'For this is where day undoes what night had brought about,' wrote the critic and philosopher Walter Benjamin. 'Waking up each morning we hold in our hands, usually feebly and slackly, only frayed scraps of the tapestry of lived existence, as forgetting has woven it within us.' And by the end of the day, he continued, the 'ornamentation of forgetting' has been unpicked once again.

If memory is a tapestry woven from forgetting and recalling, what of the brief periods when I can summon my grandparents' names under my breath, shyly, with the self-consciousness of the non-native speaker? Roll them around in my mouth before they drop out again? Once or twice, I even write them down, these beautiful signifiers of the people who bore my parents, but always on pieces of paper that seem to slip through the cracks of everyday life, or a notebook seemingly bought for the purpose of misplacing after writing on the first few pages. It is my lifelong habit to store scraps of paper, banknotes, letters, postcards, photos, used train tickets, phone numbers, and anything else deemed important, between the pages of books. Immediately, I lose track of what holds what and drive myself mad shaking books into upside down fans in the hope that my grandparents' names might fall out. Or at least a tenner. Then again, once in a blue moon, I delight myself by picking up a random book and finding a piece of treasure. It can go either way. Years after I start doing this I will discover that the habit is borrowed like a library book from my maternal grandfather. A doctor known to slot cheques from his patients in his books. My uncle discovered dozens of them after his death. All uncashed, of course.

Perhaps it gets to the point where only writing a book will pin all this to the display case of my memory. An extreme solution, admittedly, to the second-generation afflic-tion of forgetting one's own story. If it is an affliction. Benjamin, a German Jewish refugee who fled his homeland in 1933 as the Nazis consolidated their powers, also wrote that it is not what the reminiscing author experiences that matters so much as how she weaves together her mem-ories. He called this process 'Penelope's labour of bearing things in mind. Or should one perhaps speak instead of Penelope's labour of forgetting?' For Benjamin, and so many European Jews, the weight of such labour was too great. On 26 September 1940, after a long, perilous journey across

Europe, Benjamin ended his life on the Franco-Spanish border while waiting for his visa to be granted.

I phone my parents. My mother answers first, a little exasperated by the reappearance of the question-asker – as I am known in my family – with the same old question. She spells the names of her parents in a hurry. No doubt a pot of saaru, that sour soupy hymn to lentils, tomatoes, tamarind and curry leaves, that is a staple of every South Indian home on the planet, is boiling vigorously on the hob. She never was one for simmering. Then it is my father's turn. He carefully spells out all four names, first his own parents', then my mother's again, using his own idiosyncratic version of the phonetic alphabet. His 'B', I notice, stands for British. His 'I' for 'Indian'.

I tap the names straight onto my computer.

It feels like an empty gesture.

It feels as though I am setting them in stone.

Parvathi
Talya Bhimarao Subbarao
Nanjamma
Arakalgud Subbaraya

Heinz Martin Wuga

I have never heard anyone address the man we call Henry by his German name. Heinz, his given name, the one attached to him by birth, however long after the cord fusing him to the body of his mother, Lore, who was in fact born Leonore Würzburger, was cut. A sturdy length of cable, body-made, bluish and braided like the trunks of certain trees if it was anything like the ones that tethered me to my babies.

Claire cuts this hidden part of me on a dazzling summer

morning in Edinburgh's Royal Infirmary. I don't feel a thing. Or rather, my feelings are elsewhere. Our daughter is here. We have made it. The memory blazes, like the hottest part of the flame, to the point of whiteout. Birth, like migration, is another kind of rupture. A hole punched through existence that once covered cannot be accessed again. Afterwards my daughter is thrown onto my chest like a wet flannel. There she lies, nameless, glistening, still. The butterfly wings of her upper back beat lightly. Her arms and legs are splayed like a spatchcocked chicken. She is as pink as a newborn piglet. Every metaphor derives from animals. There is nothing human about this, even though it is how each human begins. Her skin colour is a surprise against the dark brown skin of the body that carried her. That's what we will say: *remember how pink she was!* The image that sustains, forever developing in the darkroom of my memory, is the colour of her mixed-race skin, still mapped with vernix. And so the lifelong discussion over which she will have little control begins.

Next, snip with, of all things, a pair of scissors. The first break for freedom made. At some point a white identification tag is clipped around the delicate mini-bones of her ankle. Her first non-human contact in this world, late in our plastic age. On the tag are an official jumble of numbers, a date of birth, and a single handwritten word. Our surname. Ramaswamy.

'From what I was told by my mother,' Henry tells me of his own birth more than ninety years earlier, on 23 February 1924, 'she was not the youngest and they had to . . .'

He slaps his hands together to evoke the commanding of life into his just-born body. *Those hands.* I force myself to notice that they belong to the baby he is describing. It is an effort of will.

'They had to touch me a few times to get me breathing,' Henry continues. 'That's all I know.'

No one calls Henry Heinz. Not even Ingrid, though sometimes, during the early years of our friendship, she likes to address Henry loudly, impishly, often with a wink in my direction, as 'Wuga!' And I never hear them converse in German nor in the seamless mix of languages so familiar to me from listening to my parents. The sound of home, for me, is one I can only partially understand. My parents, nattering away in English and Kannada in the next room, vaulting continents and, it sometimes seems, characters as they argue the finer points of Sunday night's period drama or order one another to go and make the tea. An effortless two-step danced in so many immigrant homes between coloniser and old country, here and there, homeland and motherland. This migrants' move must be amongst the first sounds I hear in that gauzy pre-time before memory. Before the words ingested as easily as milk begin to fall away, one by one like opaline drops. Before I start to forget. Of course I will remember nothing of this loss. The early years of our lives are a time of sensation, action, not thought. A nameless experience. I will know only, in retrospect, that it happened. That at some indistinguishable point I no longer understood the mother tongue of my parents.

For Henry and Ingrid, language is not gradually lost over time but seized in a cascade of violent acts committed in their own country, by their own government. The words are stolen from their mouths when the land in which they are birthed and named rejects them categorically. When the police and courts will no longer protect them. When their books are burned. When their businesses and shops are boycotted. When they are excluded from military service and exams in medicine, dentistry, pharmacy and law. When they are not permitted to marry anyone who is not the same as them. When they are not allowed to vote. When they lose their citizenship. When they are banned from parks, restaurants and swimming pools. When they are forbidden bicycles, typewriters and vinyl records. When they are removed from schools. When they are banned from cinemas, theatres, concerts, exhibitions, beaches and holiday resorts. When they are forced to add the names *Sara* or *Israel* to their passports. When their passports are stamped with a red letter 'J'. When they are evicted from their homes. When they are not allowed out after curfew. When they are forced to wear a yellow Star of David if they are over six years of age. When they are forbidden from using public telephones. When they are forbidden from keeping pets. When they are forbidden from leaving the country. When they are forbidden from staying at home.

Years later, after the genocide of around two-thirds of Europe's Jewish population – what will not widely come to be known as the Holocaust until the 1960s – the loss will go on. Unrecorded but just as indelible. Henry and Ingrid will stop speaking German. They will never live in Germany again. The motherland will become the bosom to which they will never return. The mother tongue will twist into a language they will neither speak nor consciously pass on to their children. Though their German accents will never leave them, going back to Germany will become a form of trespass.

So, for wildly different reasons to my sister's and mine, Hilary and Gillian do not grow up actively speaking their mother tongue either. Some of us will acquire the language of our parents over the course of our lives through an enigmatic combination of osmosis and diligence. The picking up of scraps, turns of phrase, words for things that, like family recipes, crop up time and time again. Others, by which I mean myself, will retain only the arrested understanding of the child.

Snana	Bath
Magu	Child
Anna	Cooked rice

The one certainty, which is a condition of second-generation experience, is that each of the four of us will have a completely different, ironically inarticulable, and profoundly tender relationship with our parents' mother tongue. For my family the decision not to pass on the mother tongue is, as far as I see it anyway, an act of assimilation in Eighties Thatcherite Britain. A kind of insurance against not belonging. For the Wugas, it is wartime. German means the enemy. 'Refrain from speaking German in the streets and in public conveyances and in public places such as restaurants', advises a booklet issued to all wartime refugees in Britain by the Jewish Board of Deputies and the German Jewish Aid Committee. 'Talk halting English rather than fluent German – and *do not talk in a loud voice*.' Shadowing both decisions is the stigma that stalks immigrants and their children, wherever we go, in whatever era, for whatever reason. The value, which must be prized as high as one's own self-worth, of integration. The message filtered across the decades will be the same. Fit in, or go home.

'It wasn't a good thing to do,' Henry says of speaking German in the days, weeks, months, years, and eventually decades following his arrival in Britain. 'We said the odd thing, certain words, phrases, but we didn't *speak* German, certainly not in public.'

What happens when German no longer represents home, but danger, treachery, loss, the enemy? It becomes a boundary in the mouth, no more surpassable than a military checkpoint. In its place a new identity must be wrought. Quickly. And so Henry learns English at the dazzling speed dictated by necessity. The little German boy called Heinz who has been tossed from here to there in the hurricane of history emerges as both someone else and himself.

Henry.

Henry is not sure when this happened. He never changed his name officially, by deed poll. The National Archives file, dating from the mid to late 1940s, refers to him as Heinz Martin Wuga. Yet within a year and a half of arriving in Glasgow everyone, including Ingrid, was calling him Henry.

'It was quite straightforward,' Henry says with a shrug. 'Heinz was too German. It was wartime. So obviously you became Henry.'

The first and shortest section of Sebald's *The Emigrants* is about an Anglo-Lithuanian Jewish refugee called Dr Henry Selwyn. A man who spends most of his time in a hermitage in a remote corner of his garden in Hingham, Norfolk. Dr Selwyn left Lithuania in the late autumn of 1899 when he was seven. An exodus he has not remembered for years, but which starts coming back late in life. This is a returning theme in Sebald: the delay of memory, and the impact of Penelope's labour of forgetting. We find out very little about him but we do learn that at the end of school, when his confidence was 'at its peak, and in a kind of second confirmation' he changed his name. 'My first name Hersch into Henry, and my surname Seweryn to Selwyn.' The change is at once an act of becoming and concealment.

By the time I meet the Wugas, Ingrid has stopped speaking even the name of her birth country. She refers to Germany euphemistically, as if the land is a person who has betrayed her so badly their name will no longer be spoken under her roof.

We are at a Schubert recital in an austere converted church in Edinburgh. In the stalls of the Queen's Hall I am positioned in such a way that I can watch Henry and Ingrid as they watch the recital. They are perfectly still, perfectly straight-backed, perfectly turned out. A German soprano sings Schubert lieder, with solo piano accompaniment. I am not really paying attention to either singer or musician because I am transfixed by the noiseless drama unfolding off-stage. Ingrid's lips are moving with the music, forming words long ago stolen from her. Ingrid is mouthing German. How might the spectre of this language taste on an elderly woman's lips whose brain might already, for all we know, be beginning to strip the memories from its walls? Perhaps the words feel alien, bitter, treacherous. Perhaps they come easy like home. During the interval, we stand in small groups making light conversation and drinking water out of plastic cups. Ingrid tells me she knows all the words to Schubert's songs, but does not sing them out loud. It is too upsetting.

'It makes me think of the other country,' she whispers in my ear.

'Du bist ein cavalier'

The west end of Edinburgh's Princes Street lies in the shadow of a medieval castle, which in turn is perched on 350 million-year-old volcanic rock. History is striated like stone in the Athens of the North, the old town hovering in a higgledy-piggledy line above the new. Which is new by no one's standards but Edinburgh's. Princes Street, the main thoroughfare, is hemmed on one side by harmonious public gardens set in a valley that was once a loch. This deep depression, formed during the last Ice Age and turned into the city's most beautiful gardens in the 1820s, is known mostly to me, a couple of centuries on, for its excellent views of the trains coming in and out of Waverley Station. I have spent almost as long as an Ice Age here, standing with my son on a rickety wooden bridge over the tracks in all seasons. When the trains passed beneath us my son would leap and call out 'train, train, TRAIN', three times, with precisely the same inflection, like an incantation. Or a prayer. Often the train drivers waved at us, though my son never waved back, and when he did start to wave he did it backwards, as if to himself.

Today, I'm on the other side of the street, for the same reason as most visitors to Princes Street. To buy something. In Boots I head for the perfume section and scan the shelves for a bottle of cologne. 4711, Echt Kölnisch Wasser. The original eau de cologne. Though I had never heard of it until I met Henry, and have never smelt it, 4711 is more than two hundred years old. In fact, it is one of the world's oldest fragrances still in production.

The glass bottle perfectly expresses the heritage. Small and almost hexagonal in shape. History bottled, its beauty classic like a car. It bears a blue and gold label – though the blue, to me, is green – showing the address that gives the cologne its name: Glockengasse No. 4711 in, obviously, Cologne. This is where the eau de cologne has been produced since it was invented in the 1790s as a miracle health cure to be mixed with water or wine. Well, sort of. During the Second World War, the headquarters at No. 4711 were destroyed by bombing that left more than 90 per cent of the city in ruins, and the company had to move to a new address.

The scent itself, famously worn by Holly Golightly in Truman Capote's *Breakfast at Tiffany's*, is a closely guarded blend of bergamot, lemon, orange, lavender, rosemary and neroli. It also happens to be the signature scent of Henry's parents. Karl liked to dab a cotton ball soaked with 4711 on his hands after combing his hair. Lore wore 4711 all her life.

'It's the bottle as much as the smell,' says Hilary. 'It's so iconic. When I see it, I see Oma Lore.'

I take the box to the counter and ask the assistant whether they sell much of it these days. 'You'd be surprised,' she says. 'At least two a week.' And then she lowers her voice and her eyes dart around the shop floor. 'It's only ladies of a certain age who buy it, though.' She laughs, clearly tickled at the sight of a young(ish) Indian woman buying a bottle of old-world Europe's finest 4711. I laugh too.

Back on the street, in the shadow of the castle, I open the box and as people mill this way and that, filling a single street with a world of languages, I lift out the bottle. It is surprisingly heavy and fits perfectly in the hollow of my hand. I break the red seal and unscrew the gold cap. I lift the bottle to my nose, and take a deep draw.

It is 1975 in Glasgow, and the Wugas are living at their family home on Dalkeith Avenue in Dumbreck, a grand sandstone villa out of which they run their now legendary kosher catering business. Gillian has just won a prize at school, and her success has been published in the *Jewish Chronicle*. Soon afterwards Henry receives a letter from a Miss Rosa Schlesinger. A stranger whose sister is a patient in a psychiatric hospital in Epsom, Surrey: Horton Hospital, which during both world wars became a general military hospital for servicemen from all over the British Empire. On the same ward is a woman known to everyone, simply, as Wugie.

'Miss Wuga, either Annamaria or Mariele or possibly with another name in her passport or alien book, should I be lucky enough to get hold of them,' writes Miss Schlesinger on 3 March, 'was born July 12th 1894' though 'she looks fifteen years younger in my eyes'. Miss Schlesinger has tried to give Miss Wuga fruit, cake and chocolate but every time the patient hides her face, giggles and runs away. Almost nothing is known about her other than she was admitted in 1951, and then again in 1962, when she was found to be of 'no fixed abode'.

'I feel rather certain that Miss Wuga is related to you somehow,' Miss Schlesinger concludes. 'If this turns out to be the case, please do not make a special journey south. It would not be worthwhile.'

'She was my father's sister,' Henry explains. 'She was working in catering on the Isle of Wight. She had no proper address. I believe she was somewhat down at heel . . . an alcoholic. She had nobody to look after her, no papers, and so she ended up in hospital.'

'If it hadn't been for the name we would never have found her,' says Hilary. 'All because of the name Wuga.'

Refusing to heed Miss Schlesinger's advice, Henry goes directly to Epsom, travelling there and back in a day. He arrives to find Miss Wuga, who has not been forewarned of the visit in case she runs away, hiding beneath the covers of her bed. She will not show her face. 'We found the lady lying on her bed all covered up, counting aloud in German,' he writes afterwards to Miss Schlesinger. And so Henry introduces himself in German, the mother tongue he rarely speaks. To his astonishment, because he has been told 'Wugie' does not communicate with anyone, she replies. Annamaria speaks aloud his middle name. Martin. Then his mother's maiden name. Würzburger. Henry finds her lucid, with a fine sense of humour. He suspects no one knows she is bilingual. Before he leaves, Annamaria emerges from under the covers and looks directly at him.

'I had only seen my grandmother once,' Henry writes of a trip he made with his father to Graz, to visit his dying grandmother in a hospice. 'But I could see the resemblance.'

Miss Wuga is Henry's paternal aunt. She left Austria in

1936 to live with a family in Italy as a governess and no one heard from her again. The Home Office has no record of her. There appear to be no official documents relating to her existence in the country. But in 2020, while researching this book, I discover an internment card held by the National Archives issued at a wartime tribunal on 14 December 1939. It describes a German (Austrian) female enemy alien called Anna Maria Wuga, born 12.07.94 in Graz. It records that she is a domestic servant for a Mrs Grierson, living at 49 Broadfields Avenue, Edgware, in far north London. She is described on the card, which Henry has never seen before, as a 'non-refugee'. Exempt from internment, with no desire to be repatriated.

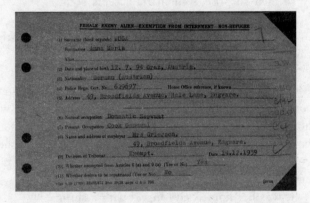

On 7 August 1975, Henry receives a letter from a consultant psychiatrist at Horton Hospital. Annamaria Wuga, Dr Mellett writes, suffers from 'chronic schizophrenia' and will have to remain in hospital for the rest of her life. Aside from her 'various eccentricities' she is settled at Horton. Of her past, about which he knows almost nothing because she does not communicate with staff, he surmises that if she ever did get to Italy 'she probably thought that the Fascist government of the time was unacceptable to her and came to England'.

Henry expresses a wish for Dr Mellett to list him as Annamaria's next of kin. He hopes that the visit has not disturbed his aunt. Dr Mellett writes that after Henry left Annamaria was 'unusually thoughtful', which he finds unsurprising. 'It must be remembered that while the thinking of a person suffering from schizophrenia is disordered and distorted,' he writes, 'the memory and a great deal of intellectual function remains intact.'

And so Henry continues to visit his aunt. The routine is the same. He always takes gifts, and she always refuses them.

Until one day, that is, when he and Ingrid take a bunch of carnations, and a bottle of 4711.

To their surprise, Annamaria accepts both.

'Du bist ein cavalier,' she says.

'You are a gentleman,' Henry translates for me with a cavalier's grin.

Over the next fifteen years Henry and Ingrid will visit Annamaria twice a year. When they go to London to attend concerts and recitals, they will stop by Epsom on their way home. Annamaria will become a part of their lives. At some point Henry will invite his aunt to come and live with them in Dalkeith Avenue but she will beg her nephew not to take her out of Horton.

'It was her home,' says Ingrid with a shrug.

In 1991, Henry and Ingrid are in London when they get a call from the hospital. Annamaria has died at the age of ninety-seven. Henry and Ingrid will take a train to Epsom to be present at her cremation. A decade later, Horton Hospital will be sold to a developer and most of the buildings demolished.

Henry and Ingrid will take his aunt's ashes home and scatter them, along with a bunch of carnations, in a place she never saw. The mouth of their home. The Firth of Clyde at Portencross. The place where Ingrid first lived when she arrived in Scotland. Where she was reunited with her parents a week before war was declared.

This leads me to ask Ingrid where her parents are buried.

'In Glasgow!' she replies, affronted by the thought they would be laid to rest anywhere else.

'In the Jewish cemetery, here on the south side,' says Henry.

'And am I right in saying one day . . . the same cemetery for you two?' asks Hilary tentatively.

'I suppose so,' says Henry.

'I'll let you worry about that,' says Ingrid with a chuckle.

On Princes Street I screw the cap back on the bottle and head to the bus stop. An idea is shaping itself. A biography of sorts about Henry. A collective memoir that will be alive to the changing historic moment. It will traffic between past, present and future. Between Henry's life, my life, our lives. An entire century will unfold at the same time. In the weeks to come, I will start writing. And when I sit down at my laptop in the early hours of the morning, before the children wake up and the working day is lost again, I will develop a little Wuga-inspired ritual of my own. I will unscrew the gold cap of my bottle of 4711, lift its open neck to my pulse points, upend it, and let my skin swig the scent of history.

'We tried to carry on as normally as we could.'

The Wugas walk east through the city in late winter to the Grand Synagogue of Nuremberg. The first stone was laid half a century ago, in 1870, the year Jews gained full civic equality in a united Germany. Here is a magnificent paean to integration, burnished with oriental detail, fronted by an immense rose window, and known, thanks to its great dome, as 'the pearl in the skyline and adornment of the town'. It is located on Hans-Sachs-Platz, named after the cobbler and meistersinger who will soon capture Henry's imagination so forcefully he will risk everything for a night at the opera.

This is where Henry has his bar mitzvah in February 1937.

He still has a photo of the Grand Synagogue of Nuremberg, probably taken on the day itself, seen through a screen of three trees, their spindly skeletons exposed by winter. The photo is small, monochrome, in perfect focus. It is taken looking up at the synagogue, so the building appears to rear up from the ground, its dome partially obscured by branches, its towers and smaller domes foreshortened. A child's view of the world.

Henry retrieves the photo, along with three others, from a careworn black leather-bound file. It has his initials, 'HW', embossed on its bottom right-hand corner in gold.

'It was a present for my bar mitzvah,' says Henry. He

rubs the initials with his forefinger, back and forth, back and forth. 'Stephen Mosbacher's parents gave it to me. I was so proud of it. Such a grown-up present – a leather folder for my desk with my own initials! I have kept it all these years.'

I take my phone out and snap away at each item as it emerges from the file. Henry pulls his hand back. I ask him to return it, to keep it there.

'When you think, I've kept it all,' he continues. 'My mother sent all this a week or so after I arrived. It was what was important to me . . . my favourite things. My Zeiss Ikon Baby Box camera, and these are pictures I took with it.' He leafs through them, one by one. 'This is a zeppelin taken in 1937; the hangar, perhaps taken from a train or a boat. These are two of my school friends: Stephen Mosbacher and Herbert Leiter. And this is the synagogue in Nuremberg.'

Inside the synagogue, Lore and Karl watch as their son is presented with a Kiddush cup made by the family silver-smith, Fassbender. A cup that against all odds will not only survive the war in Nuremberg but will be reunited with

Henry in Glasgow. Afterwards, Henry's friends and family arrive at 15 Fürther Strasse, and around a dozen people are seated for dinner. They are living in the early months of 1937, what they cannot yet know is a turning point in history. In seven months, Hitler will unleash his most blood-thirsty speech yet at the penultimate Nuremberg rally. This time next year what they are doing will be an even greater risk. The following year it will be impossible. For now, the Wugas can still walk home through their own city after celebrating their son's bar mitzvah. A collective calm still reigns over Germany's cities in particular. Emigration rates remain low and 10,000 Jews who fled to neighbouring countries two years ago have even come back. Jews still sit in pavement cafés reading Jewish newspapers. Henry and his parents still drive out to the country at weekends to eat in restaurants sheltered in ancient woodlands. Reason has not yet been entirely exchanged for madness.

'Remember,' Henry always says to me of this period, 'this was before Kristallnacht.'

And yet tomorrow already awaits him on the doorstep. Every time Henry and his parents leave or return to 15 Fürther Strasse they must pass the latest edition of *Der Stürmer*, displayed in a glass kiosk right outside their front door. Every time Henry steps over the threshold of his own home, this is what greets him.

'Look, it was horrendous,' says Henry, 'but we tried to carry on as normally as we could.'

The following summer *Der Stürmer* will publish an issue titled 'Synagogues are Robbers' Dens: The Shame of Nuremberg'. The city's Jewish community leaders will be assembled by the police and local administration led by Streicher, and told that the synagogue on Hans-Sachs-Platz will be destroyed because it is spoiling the look of the city. The Jews of Nuremberg will be permitted to hold one last Friday night service. On 10 August, three months before the Reichspogromnacht, the Grand Synagogue of Nuremberg and an adjacent Jewish community building will be demolished by the Nazis while Streicher addresses a large assembled crowd. And after the war, on 29 April 1946, the 116th day of the Nuremberg trials, when asked whether the destruction was carried out on his orders, Streicher will reply, 'Yes. Even before 1933 . . . I stated publicly during a meeting that it was a disgrace that there should be placed in the Old City such an oriental monstrosity of a building.'

Of his bar mitzvah, that milestone in a Jewish boy's life when he is deemed to become responsible for his actions, Henry will recall neither the fear underlying the celebrations nor the food served by his parents at home. Perhaps, by this point, concealment is second nature to him. Perhaps he simply accepts the situation in the unquestioning way of children. What will stay with him, 'to my shame', as Henry puts it, is fluffing his speech.

'Terrible really,' he says, 'just one of those things.'

'Good to see you and that lovely BOY.'

Near my old flat in Edinburgh, where I was living when my children were born, there is a small triangle of grass ringed first by pavement then cobblestones. The kind of scrappy urban patch where you instinctively know to watch your feet because there is bound to be dog shit. Every spring four small cherry trees blossom here with clusters of pink flowers so puffed up the branches disappear for a few uplifting weeks behind a homemade floral curtain. There are countless lovelier spots to view the annual spectacle of cherry blossom in Edinburgh, but this is the one that gets me. Other than that, John's Place, as it is appositely named considering its unwritten history as the workplace of Leith's prostitutes, is as unremarkable as the next street corner. A place for passing through, rather than stopping.

And yet this happens to be where a memory of mine is stored. More than a memory. A perfectly preserved section of my life spanning three years is buried like a time capsule beneath the setts. The years when I moved to Edinburgh from Glasgow. Got a mortgage. A dog. Discovered my mother had breast cancer. Became pregnant. Gave birth. Became a mother. Acquired, in other words, the midlife gift of responsibility. My foot alights on a section of the city no more than a square foot in diameter, and I am no longer here. I am there, and it is as if the past is located not in my self but below this uneven collection of cobblestones.

There, it is the summer of 2013. My baby is three days old and I have just left the house for the first time since returning from hospital. It is excessively bright, as though the path has been spotlit for the historic occasion of our first outing. Or perhaps it is just that I have been locked in the submarine of new motherhood. A dim and ethereal place where the rooms are quiet, the lights and voices soft, and the world outside passes by, slowly, brightly, hazardously.

I walk to John's Place, pushing the baby – my son! – in a cheerful yellow buggy to which a host of flies, wasps and bees will be drawn all summer. I am sporting a man's lilac shirt and black leggings and, beneath that, a slowly distending body that pulses and leaks milk, blood and fire. Possibly some cabbage leaves stuffed in my giant maternity bra. This is my body now. A body that belongs solely to me again though it does not, and will not for some time, feel like mine alone. A body that, no matter how unimaginable it is to me right now, will heal.

I have never pushed a baby, any baby, in a buggy for this length of time. Just as I had never held a newborn until I was handed mine a few days ago. At John's Place I push off the pavement and onto the cobbles. I am used to this precarious old terrain. Anyone who lives in Edinburgh knows the feeling of feet and wheels on cobbles. The sad anachronistic sight of setts hemmed in by a patchwork of poured black tar. How slippery they become in the rain. The unique pattern of bruises acquired from a cobble fall. When Claire drove us home from the hospital, we sang songs from *My Fair Lady* to try and stop the floppy woodland creature strapped into the brand new car seat with all its maddening buckles from emitting his owl-cry. I had just had a C-section and as we sang I wept for the pain brought on by bouncing over the cobbles. (First-time parenting in a nutshell: musical numbers and tears.) It was as if we were in an air cabin entering a patch of turbulence. It was tenderness in action.

In the months to come, the cobbles will become a tool in my maternal kit. Like many new Edinburgh mothers, I will learn to use the rhythmic jerk of the setts against the buggy wheels to help my son drift over to sleep. We will go on long buggy walks, all over the city. But for now I am stuck. The buggy rears up against the cobbles like a horse I cannot control. There is a moment of shame as the stitches of my C-section throb with the pathetic exertion and I imagine the scar opening like a mocking smile. I look around in terror in case anyone should witness my grand failure as a mother. But the baby doesn't wake. The buggy glides over the bumps and lands with a bounce on the tarmacked pavement. We have made it. Again.

Three days later we take him for his first visit. To meet the Wugas. Henry and Ingrid are stationed in the city as they are every August for the Edinburgh International Festival. This is where, during their first visit in 1949, they saw Kathleen Ferrier accompanied by Bruno Walter singing Mahler at the Usher Hall. Teju Cole wrote that all cities, to differing degrees, are 'places where traces remain of things that happened'. Often the traces are invisible to all but those who made them. Somewhere else in this city, and not necessarily where you might expect it, another memory is stored of a newly wed Jewish couple. Refugees holding hands in the dark. Listening to music banned in their homeland during the Nazi era.

Back in the submarine, we glide through the sea of Edinburgh in full festival flow. We sit in Gillian's lounge, where we never normally sit, and my son is passed around. He is wearing a terry-towelling blue and white striped babygro, which drapes off his long and slender newborn body. He sleeps the entire time, which makes me inordinately proud of him. I take photos of Henry and Ingrid holding him. Imagine a perfect future moment, as one is still able to sincerely do in the early days of the first child, when I will say 'Let me tell you about your first visit to meet the Wugas', and he will be blown away.

On the way home he cries and cries; the same heart stopping owl-cry that will desert him in a matter of weeks to be replaced by a more robust baby version. A cry I will miss like a person. Eventually, overwhelmed and exhausted, we pull over and I breastfeed him in the back seat, parked on a leafy street lined with grand Victorian villas. This is how life is now. Slow. Beyond our control. Glorious. When we get home there is an email waiting for me from Henry.

'Good to see you and that lovely BOY,' he writes, 'a long time since we held babies in our arms.'

Cobbles are as much a part of Edinburgh as the haar that rolls across the symmetry of the New Town. The depth of these setts surprised me the first time I saw them lifted from the street for a road repair, lying in a heap, waiting to be hammered back in again. I expected little grey tablets. Gravestones in miniature. These were more like blocks. I know now how to push a buggy over these embedded monuments without breaking a sweat. And I know that cobbles run deep, like the history they preserve.

'Wuga is a most unusual name.'

'**M**y full name at birth was Heinz Martin Wuga.'

In 2004 a man called Anthony Grenville travels from London to Giffnock to do a long interview with Henry. This is the statement that opens it. Henry and I will not meet for another eight years and it will be longer still before Henry sends me a transcript of the interview, which runs to more than 24,000 words. Perhaps this statement, like the opening line of a Dickens novel, is the first – certainly the most memorable – time I see Henry's given name in print. It disarms me. Briefly turns the man whose life I am beginning to know more intimately than those of my own parents into a stranger.

The interview is carried out by the Association of Jewish Refugees, formed during the Second World War, and is one of 235 filmed Holocaust testimonies given by Jewish survivors and refugees from Nazi Europe who rebuilt their lives in Britain. The testimonies are archived online, alongside photos and a brief biography. One of the photos I have never seen before. I cannot stop returning to it, as if it is a painting beckoning me to stand in front of it in a gallery. As if the static figures might have something new to reveal to me each time I come back, which they do. In the words of the chief archivist at the Jewish Museum in Berlin, where the original is held with the rest of Henry's records, it is an 'iconic' photo and is often on display in their core exhibition.

It is a studio portrait of Henry seated between his parents, taken a few months before he left Nuremberg. Henry's mother, Lore, leans back against her son, her head ever so slightly tilted towards him. She wears her hair in rolls, a white bow at her throat, the ribbon falling straight as an arrow down her dark dress. She has a natural smile for such a forced occasion. Henry looks older than his fourteen years. His hair is sharply parted to the left. He wears spectacles, a suit jacket and, of course, a bow tie. His father Karl, on his other side, is also wearing a bow tie. Of the three of them, he looks most directly at the camera, an inscrutable half-smile playing on his thin lips.

Here they are, the Wugas, shoulder to shoulder. A trio of people dangling over the maw of history looking totally at ease. I imagine the person, likely a man, behind the camera positioning them, concertina-ing his hands together in the way photographers through the ages do. Moving them closer.

People in old photographs are frozen in time, unable to see the future that awaits them. The future in which we too find ourselves trapped, looking back at them, unable to do a thing to alter the fixed course of history. In the last interview Sebald did, in his office at the University of East Anglia, he showed the interviewer a sepia photograph of a boy from his mother's Bavarian side of the family. A boy who would later return traumatised from the First World War. Just as Karl, Henry's father, did. 'This was before he knew,' Sebald observed. 'I find that frightful – the incapacity to know what's round the corner.'

This interview took place just twelve weeks before Sebald was killed in a car crash in Norwich.

When I read the interview between Henry and Anthony, I am blown away by the level of detail. Anthony, a consultant editor of the Association of Jewish Refugees, is now retired but I track him down and ask if I can quote from the transcript, and what he can remember about meeting Henry. He emails me back with a generous response and an apology. He doesn't have any detailed memories of the interview. He has done dozens of them, had to pack them in while he was in Glasgow, and soon enough the conversations begin to blur, an uncomfortable truth that I understand perfectly as a journalist. The knowledge falls away. Someone else's story moves in to replace it.

There is a formality, but also an ease to Henry and Anthony's conversation so different to our interviews. Ours are characterised by pauses for lunch, explanations of Jewish or German rituals and phrases that pass me by, the search for a particular document or photo, the clamour of family members talking over one another, often in contradiction. And sometimes, when I can't organise childcare, the increasingly sophisticated chatter, cries and demands of my daughter as our recordings unintentionally track her development from baby to toddler. Anthony, the son of Jewish refugees from Vienna, and Henry speak once, at great length.

They are men who share culture, religion, heritage, language, understanding. What we term 'background', that poor approximation of the rich topography of a life. Henry and I share something else entirely.

Early on, the two men get talking about what Henry describes as 'this strange name Wuga', and how little he has been able to find out about it. He says his father, Karl, was a 'very smart man, very nice man, very vain, if I may say. I mean, the business of combing his hair with the mirror in the back till everything was absolutely perfect and rubbing his hands with a little cotton wool with 4711 on it. Very pukka gentleman, yes.'

To me, Henry says, 'He was Austrian. In our family book, under religion, my father put "dissenter". Now for a Catholic son in Austria in 1910 to say "I'm a dissenter" is unusual. But he just washed his hands of it. He didn't go to synagogue or chapel. Religion meant nothing to him.'

'He was a good person,' says Ingrid. 'Never mind religion.'

Henry describes his father to me as 'a very dapper gent', which is also how I might describe Henry. And, for that matter, my father. Another man of the world who always likes to examine up close any new item of clothing or shoes, and who in my earliest memories is to be found on the floor, cross-legged, the thin, frayed sarong he changes into when he gets home from work stretched taut across his knees. He has laid down neat squares of newspaper, probably from the *Sunday Times*. He has a hand in one shoe. The other holds a rag, formed from an old pair of pants, smeared with black Kiwi polish, which he buffs back and forth, rhythmically, across the leather upper. It is a kind of magic to watch the transformation from dull to glossy. From suited man of the city to my father in a panche.

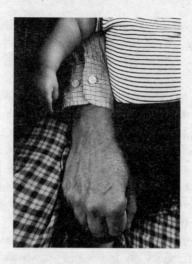

'He had very little to do with his family,' Henry tells me of his father. 'His mother lived in Austria. His father had passed away. His brothers and sisters lived in Austria but there was very little connection with the family and that was fine.' Only once, in 1937, does Henry meet his father's side of the family, when Karl's mother is terminally ill. He decides to take Henry to Graz to meet his grandmother for the first and last time. 'Wow,' says Henry. 'We travelled by train from Nuremberg through the Alps. It was very exciting for me. I remember the journey well.'

It is because of the lack of contact between Karl and his family, which Henry stresses to Anthony had nothing to do with the fact that he married a Jewish woman, that he has no idea of the origins of the name Wuga. 'We tried to do some research, very difficult,' says Henry. 'I believe his father came from Maribor, Marburg, in what is now Slovenia, and I believe his father, or grandfather, changed the spelling of the name.'

'There are no Wugas,' Henry continues. 'I am the last of the Mohicans, so to speak, and I have no sons.'

Fifteen years later, Henry and I also find ourselves talking about his surname. 'I looked everywhere,' he says. 'In New York, phone books, everywhere for the name Wuga. Eventually we found somebody in Graz and I corresponded with him. He must have been a cousin of my father. We sent pictures of our families back and forth. I've kept it all.'

What happened?

Henry shrugs.

'When they heard we were Jewish the correspondence stopped,' he says. 'These people might have known more but they simply didn't want to know. It's unbelievable, but that's how some people are.'

'Wuga,' concludes Ingrid, 'is a most unusual name.'

'We *wanted you to have* everything.'

In the summer of 2018, as I am beginning work on this book without quite realising it, I am commissioned alongside five other writers to pen a love letter to Europe. The letters will be projected onto buildings across Edinburgh during January of the following year, as the first of a cascade of parliamentary votes on the Brexit withdrawal agreement takes place. I decide to write my letter to Henry and Ingrid. I can precisely locate the tone it will take – elegiac, grateful, apologetic – but when I sit down to write it, something unexpected happens. My fingers alight on the keyboard, and a single word issues from the cursor.

Then.

And with it a different time is ushered onto the page. Our family holidays in Spain on the Costa del Sol in the Eighties, before our house was repossessed and we never holidayed as a foursome again. I find myself writing about the 'Spanish couscous' (I eventually realised it was Moroccan) that we ate in the same restaurant every year, which my mother faithfully recreated, as in completely Indianised, when we returned home. I write about the pristine white villas we stayed in with their glassy private pools though neither of my parents, who are from land-locked Bangalore, could swim. I write about how my sister and I continued to holiday together in Spain into adulthood. How we were sometimes seen as locals there, a case of mistaken identity we embraced because it never once befell us back home. I write about how touching I find this vintage snapshot of a brown-skinned immigrant family trying to do the right thing. Holidaying just like the English do.

My letter is projected onto the side of the oldest custom house in the land, presiding over Leith's seaport, which for centuries was Europe's trading gateway to Scotland. A song and video are made to accompany the text, in which I am filmed making the Spanish-Moroccan-Indian couscous from scratch; self-consciously watching coriander and cumin seeds sizzling in a pot, chopping turnip, carrot, onion and garlic, and making the accompanying hot sauce from soaked dry red chillies that would cause sweat to stream down my father's shiny head during those boiling summer fortnights. In order to do all this, I have to phone my mother to get the recipe. Her breast cancer is now incurable and she has recently returned from hospital after being rushed to A&E with hypoglycaemia. Time is pressing down on us, fastening each moment to the railroad of our lives. There is a terrible fixity to the present when you know someone you love is going to die. Nothing can be changed. In that way, it is like living in the past. Not for the first time, I wonder if writing in the midst of all this is becoming an act of preservation. The tending of a memorial I will be able to revisit when she is no longer here.

Memoir is a finicky trade. So before the letter is projected onto the worn stone of the Georgian house where every evening it will play on a loop, hovering over its upside down reflection in the river's mouth, I send it to my family. My mother always says I can write whatever I want, especially if it's in the service of comedy. But this time she wants to talk to me. She has been thinking about my image of the immigrant family holidaying like the English do. She doesn't want me to change a word, but this is not how it was for her. 'Your dad and I discussed it,' she says, 'and it was never about doing what the English do. It was never about *trying to do the right thing*.'

My words in her mouth. Picked so lovingly, so carefully. They make me cringe.

'So why did we always rent villas with swimming pools when you couldn't swim?' I ask, which releases something and makes us laugh like a pair of drains.

Then my mother gets serious.

'It was because we wanted you to have everything.'

'I saw a piano fly out of a first-floor window.'

On the night of 9 November 1938, Henry is in Nuremberg with his parents. He is just home. Only yesterday he returned from Baden-Baden, abruptly cutting short a hard-won chef's apprenticeship. Perhaps he is still disorientated from the travel, his mind somersaulting between two bedrooms, not quite sure in which one he is going to wake. Except tonight he cannot get to sleep. He can hear the high sharp sound of glass smashing outside on the wide street. He goes to the window and sees a Jewish man being chased out of his home next door. He sees the pavement lined with SA men. He watches them beat up his neighbour.

'My father was not Jewish,' Henry says, 'so they did not come to us.'

A few weeks earlier, while Henry is cooking in the kosher kitchens of the Hotel Tannhäuser in Baden-Baden, more than 12,000 Polish-born Jews living legally in Germany are expelled from the country on Hitler's orders. They are forced from their homes by the Gestapo to the nearest railway station where they are put on trains to the Polish border. Thousands are refused entry to Poland and end up waiting in villages along the frontier to be taken in by someone, anyone. Two of these traumatised people are a couple who have lived in Hanover for more than twenty-seven years. The parents of a boy three years older than Henry, Herschel Grynszpan, who is studying in Paris. When Grynszpan hears of what is transpiring on the border, what his parents are being forced to endure, he buys a pistol, loads it with bullets, and on 6 November takes a metro to the German embassy. He tells the doorman he has a document to deliver to the ambassador. He is directed to the room of a German diplomat called Ernst vom Rath. He fires five shots, one of which gravely wounds vom Rath, who is rushed to hospital.

'You are a filthy Boche,' Grynszpan reportedly shouts as he takes aim, 'and here, in the name of 12,000 persecuted Jews, is your document.'

Two days later, as Henry is travelling back to Nuremberg, all Jewish newspapers and magazines are ordered to cease publication. All Jewish cultural activities are suspended. No Jewish child is permitted to attend 'Aryan' state elementary schools, although Henry has long ago been moved to and then taken out of the Jewish school in Fürth by his parents. That night, Henry's first back in his own bed, riots break out across Germany. Synagogues are burned. The windows of Jewish shops and businesses are smashed. Jews are driven from their homes and beaten. In Buchenwald around seventy Jewish men who have been incarcerated for months are executed.

The next day news reaches Berlin that vom Rath has died. On the evening of 9 November Hitler is in Munich celebrating the anniversary of the Beer Hall Putsch of 1923, when he tried to seize power in the Bavarian capital. Goebbels, who is with him, records Hitler's response to vom Rath's death in his diary: 'He decides: demonstrations should be allowed to continue. The police should be withdrawn. For once the Jews should get the feel of popular anger.' Goebbels gives the police the order, and addresses a speech to the party leaders. 'Stormy applause,' he writes. 'All are instantly at their phones. Now the people will act.'

Over the next twenty-four hours, the orchestrated orgy of destruction the Nazis will call Kristallnacht is carried out by brownshirts, the blackshirted SS, and civilians. Ninety-one Jews are killed. More than a thousand synagogues are set on fire. Tens of thousands of Jewish shops and businesses are destroyed. Jews are attacked in every city, town and village in the Reich. In Baden-Baden, every Jewish man is rounded up and forced to march through the streets to the synagogue. Inside, the men are beaten and forced to read out passages from *Mein Kampf*. Less than an hour later the synagogue is set alight, and the men are deported to concentration camps. Across the country, more than 30,000 Jewish men – a quarter of all those left in Germany – are arrested and taken to camps where they are tortured for months. More than a thousand die.

In Dortmund, Ascher Wolff, Ingrid's father, is one of those arrested men.

The Wolffs are still recovering from their last run-in with the SA. When Germany's Jews were forced to register their addresses with the police, Erna and Ascher added the name of a local Jewish girl of Polish descent. A girl whose parents were frightened of escalating anti-Semitism and wanted their daughter to attend a Jewish school, Ingrid's school, and needed a local address to get her a place. Erna and Ascher offered to help.

But when Hitler gives his order to expel every single Jew of Polish descent from the country, there comes a knock at the door. Brownshirts force their way into the Wolffs' flat, search the rooms, and find a little girl fast asleep in her bed. They order her to get up, which she does. They prepare to drag her away.

The little girl is Ingrid.

Ascher explains the mix-up to the police. This girl is not Polish. She is his daughter. Incredibly, the men let Ingrid go.

On the night of the November pogrom, she is not taken. The following morning the family wakes up unaware of what has happened, and Ingrid goes to her Jewish school as usual. At first she is confused. Dortmund's Great Synagogue has already been forcibly sold to the Nazis and destroyed, and she doesn't see the city's other synagogue in flames. So she walks past the smashed shop fronts, feels the crunch of glass beneath her shoes, and thinks there has been a burglary.

'Then I realised it was all Jewish shops,' says Ingrid. 'And I found out at school that some of the fathers had been taken away. [That day] somebody came to the door and said "If you don't go to the police you will be taken to a concentration camp." So [my father] went to the police.'

'Can I interrupt?' asks Henry. He turns to me. 'That's how frightened we were. They didn't come for you, so you went to them and said "I'm here." Think of that.'

'Some men just went into the woods,' Ingrid continues. 'But if you did that you might be shot.'

When Ascher, who owns a textiles agency, goes to the police he is arrested and taken to Sachsenhausen. Six weeks later he returns home. He will never speak about what happened to him there.

'I have a feeling he was beaten,' says Ingrid. 'Well, at least he survived.'

Before I leave, I ask Henry and Ingrid how hard they find it to keep retelling their stories.

'We've done it so often,' says Henry, 'but Ingrid still feels it. Tonight, she won't be quite happy.'

'I'll have a big drink before I go to bed,' she says with a wink.

In Nuremberg, on the morning of 10 November, Henry and his parents will venture out to check on some friends and Henry will see certain things. Images that brand his memory and turn him into an eyewitness of history.

'I saw a piano fly out of a first-floor window,' Henry says. 'A baby grand. It crashed on the pavement.'

'There were feathers everywhere because they had ripped open the downies.'

The Reichspogromnacht is covered in newspapers all over the world. It will become a turning point in twentieth-century history, and yet another pivot in Henry's life. In the following days he will learn that many of his friends' fathers have been taken away to Dachau. What has long been suspected will now be clear. Life in Germany is impossible.

'Suddenly everyone wanted to emigrate,' he says. 'That was the thought in everyone's minds, all the time. "How can we get out?" And nobody wanted anything to do with us, neither Britain nor America. Our mothers, of course, continued to try. That's how it was, and nothing has changed. That is still the question. And just like then, who wants refugees now? No one.'

Yet, after the Reichspogromnacht, British public opinion shifts. The prime minister Neville Chamberlain writes to his sister telling her he is 'horrified by the German behaviour to the Jews', though at a Cabinet committee meeting on Palestine the following April, he will also say that it is 'of immense importance' that Britain should 'have the Muslim world with us', concluding that 'if we must offend one side, let us offend the Jews rather than the Arabs'. Five days after the Reichspogromnacht, the prime minister receives a deputation of eminent British Jews calling on him to permit the temporary admission of children and teenagers from the Reich and pledging to pay their guarantees.

The following day the Cabinet meets. The committee decides to accept an unspecified number of unaccompanied refugee children under the age of seventeen years. Though no quota is specified, after the British Colonial Office turns down a request to allow the admission of 10,000 children into British-controlled Palestine, 10,000 becomes the unofficial adopted figure.

21 November. The Home Secretary Sir Samuel Hoare meets a delegation of Jewish, Quaker and Christian organisations working for refugees. They, and other aid organisations, have come together to form an emergency non-denominational body called the Movement for the Care of Children from Germany. It is agreed that group lists instead of individual travel documents will be issued to speed up the process of temporary emigration. It is agreed that every child must have a £50 guarantee, paid for by their individual sponsors. It is agreed that the Jewish community will provide the funds. It is agreed that the children will not become a burden on the state.

At 9.35 p.m., at the end of a long day debating the plight of the Jewish refugees, Sir Samuel Hoare takes the parliamentary stand. 'There is no page in our lifetime which is so tragic as that of the sufferings of the refugees in the last twenty years,' the Home Secretary begins. He presents a policy to temporarily accept an undisclosed number of unaccompanied refugee children as a moral responsibility of the British Empire, 'from the fact that we possess a great part of the surface of the world and that, owing to our wealth and other resources, we can play an important part in any attempt to deal with this tragic problem'. He presents it as a great humanitarian gesture. He refers to his earlier meeting with the Movement for the Care of Children from Germany and how 'they told me that they would be prepared to bring over here all the children whose maintenance could be guaranteed, either by their funds or by generous individuals, and that all that will probably be necessary will be for the Home Office to give the necessary visas and to facilitate their entry into this country.'

'Here is a chance,' he concludes, 'of taking the young generation of a great people, here is a chance of mitigating to some extent the terrible sufferings of their parents and their friends.'

The motion is passed.

The Movement for the Care of Children from Germany, which will soon become the Refugee Children's Movement (RCM), sends representations to Germany and Austria to set up systems for selecting and transporting the children. On 25 November, the first broadcast appeal for foster carers airs on the BBC Home Service. More than five hundred people respond. On 8 December, seven days after the first Kindertransport departs from Berlin carrying around two hundred children from a Jewish orphanage destroyed during the Reichspogromnacht, ex-Conservative prime minister Stanley Baldwin gives a speech on the wireless to raise funds for Jewish refugees. More than £500,000 in donations pours in from a million British people. Out of these funds a Georgian hotel on Gower Street in the heart of London's west end is purchased by the RCM and turned into Bloomsbury House. Here, in the headquarters of this hastily assembled group of organisations, more than seventy volunteers process several hundred applications per week.

By now the Wolffs have left Dortmund for Hamburg, a bigger city where they hope it will be easier to get visas. Ingrid goes first, staying with an aunt until her parents can follow. She briefly continues to attend a Jewish school while taking domestic science classes in preparation for emigration, and caring for children in a Jewish orphanage.

Meanwhile, in Nuremberg, all of the Wugas' energy is focused on getting out of the country. Karl takes Henry to the American consulate in Munich to try and get the three of them visas. He takes him again, and then again. It will never be known at what point Lore and Karl abandon the hope of the family leaving together and start considering the heart-wrenching alternative. Getting their son out by himself. Lore writes to everyone, everywhere. 'I had distant relatives in America who would accept me and stand surety but it never happened,' says Henry. 'I never got there, though my mother tried hard.'

Henry's days are quiet and formless, slowly accumulating into weeks and then months. 'I spent the next three months with nothing to do,' he says, 'just trying to stay at home. These were very difficult times. The pressure was terrible. We simply withdrew. We had no more contact with people who were not Jewish except a very few who stuck with us. You couldn't go to a theatre, concert, cinema. You no longer took part in public life. You lost your identity. You were no longer a citizen. You were a nobody.'

One day he goes with his mother to the town hall with all their silver cutlery. 'We were not allowed to possess any silver,' he says. 'I remember we got a piece of paper for it. People were trying to hide what they could. I remember rings being sent away in a tin of Nivea cream, that sort of thing.' Now and then he ventures out with his best friends Sigmund Mosbacher and Herbert Leiter. 'We could go to the local park as long as we kept ourselves to ourselves,' says Henry. 'Once or twice we were chased but it didn't happen often. It must have been . . . it *was* difficult, especially for my parents. But they still managed to take me to the countryside at the weekends, for a walk and a meal at a restaurant in the woods. After the horror of Kristallnacht we made it as normal as we could. My father was great for that. He loved his weekend walks.'

Sometime during the early months of 1939, Lore makes it happen. 'She went to the committee in Glasgow, through her cousin, and found someone to sponsor me,' says Henry. 'I suppose I got priority because there was somewhere for me to go.'

And now she breaks the news to her only child. The news that is at once a miracle and a tragedy. Mother and son know the drill. They have gone through this before. It was only last year that Lore was sitting Henry down to tell him he would be leaving school to go and work in a Jewish hotel in Baden-Baden. Now, behind the closed main door of 15 Fürther Strasse, she tells him again.

She has found a way.

Henry can leave the country.

He is going on a train to a place called Glasgow.

'Was it anything to do with us both being German?'

It is September of 1944 and Henry is cooking a wedding banquet for more than a hundred guests in the former home of Sir Walter Scott. One of the most famous houses in the land. Abbotsford lies on the banks of the River Tweed, a country estate dreamed up by Scotland's myth-maker himself, and built on the proceeds of his success. On the accumulation of words. Words that by the time Scott is living at Abbotsford have accumulated into a completely new literary form. The historical novel. So Henry finds himself staying in a house built on the strength of stories about the past.

Scott buys his 'mountain farm' in 1811 and is planting trees on the land by the time he moves in. Over the years, he keeps adding to Abbotsford like a chef perfecting a signature dish. The estate becomes his prize possession, and the original icon of Scots baronial architecture. It is at once a home and a romance penned in stone. He describes the increasingly whimsical baronial mansion as the Delilah of his imagination, his 'Conundrum Castle', and a 'flibbertigibbet of a house'. And on 21 September 1832, Scott takes his last breath in the dining room of this grand house, the same room where Henry's food will be digested by his descendants in the next century. Scott dies in a bed made up for him at the window so he can look out at his gardens and the river. 'It was so quiet a day,' his son-in-law noted, 'that the sound he best loved, the gentle ripple of the Tweed over its pebbles, was distinctly audible as we knelt around his bed.'

Precisely one hundred and twelve years later, on another autumn day in September, Henry arrives to cook for the wedding of Scott's great-great-great-granddaughter. He is twenty years old. He is grieving the death of his father, which he only learned about three months ago in a Red Cross letter from his mother in Nuremberg. He is a young man in love, engaged to a girl called Ingrid.

It has been three years since Henry's release from the Isle of Man. He was invited to go into business with Mrs Hurwich at her upholstery factory but he declined. As he and his parents have always known, he is a cook. And now he is a sous chef in a busy Glasgow restaurant, the Corn Exchange, on Gordon Street. The restaurant serves hale and hearty food to Glasgow's suited and booted businessmen. On Wednesdays, market day, a farmer might bring in a whole sheep's head, which Henry watches being cooked 'jaw in, and everything', accompanied with brain sauce as the main dish on the menu, which never costs more than five shillings. As soon as they run out of meat and fish each day, the restaurant has to close. 'That was rationing,' Henry says, 'but we got a fair amount of meat, and we managed.' The Corn Exchange is owned by the Grosvenor, where Henry also works; a sumptuous Alexander 'Greek' Thomson building along the same stretch of Gordon Street that in twenty-five years will be partially destroyed by a fire. For now, this is the Grosvenor's heyday and the building is home to a heady mix of dining and tea rooms, smoking lounges, a cocktail bar and one of the grandest function rooms in the city, reached by a sweeping marble staircase.

Both the Grosvenor, recently refurbished into six floors of grade-A office space, and the Corn Exchange, now a Betfred betting shop, are located opposite the main entrance to Central Station. So this row of buildings housing Henry's induction into the catering trade will be the first thing I see when I arrive in Glasgow during the autumn of 1997.

When I will get in a black cab with my minimal luggage, spark up a Marlboro Light and fail to understand a word the garrulous taxi driver says. When we will speed west through the grid of a city I have never visited, that feels akin to a small northern Manhattan, past the university where I will be studying for the next four years. When I will mistake this blackened neo-gothic landmark for the city cathedral because not only have I never been to Glasgow, I appear to have not even seen the prospectus.

At the Corn Exchange, Henry's boss is a German called Hausdorfer, who came to the city for the Empire Exhibition in 1938 and never left. The two men become friends, speaking to one another, always, in English. 'He looked after me,' says Henry. 'He advanced me in my profession. It was nothing to do with me being Jewish. I mean, he didn't know . . . but I don't think it would have mattered to him.'

Did they talk about the war?

'No, not at all,' says Henry immediately. 'That was never mentioned.'

It is Hausdorfer who recommends Henry to cater the wedding of Major General Sir Walter Maxwell-Scott's daughter. 'He was responsible for sending me to Abbotsford,' Henry says. 'I don't want to be self-aggrandising but he must have had confidence in me. Was it anything to do with us both being German? I don't know. I've often thought about that.'

Henry takes a train to Galashiels station on 6 September and is taken to Abbotsford House. He is given a room in the tower and instructions on what he will be cooking over the next three days. The main baker in Selkirk, Robert Douglas, whose bakery is famous for a tea bread known as a bannock, arranges all the supplies and provides three kitchen maids to assist him.

'Dear Mr Wugga [sic],' begins Douglas in a letter written on thick headed paper and sent to Henry on 28 August. 'I was very glad to learn that you would be able to come to Abbotsford – the home of Major General Sir Walter Maxwell-Scott and prepare one or two meals.' On Thursday, Henry will be in charge of preparing a 'simple lunch for seven people at 1pm'. That evening he will cook dinner for sixteen: consommé, lobster, grouse or partridges with 'vegetables, etc, as you desire', chocolate soufflés and grapes for dessert.

'The dinner party included the archbishop of Scotland, as well as all the Scotts and their descendants,' Henry recalls. 'I did smoked salmon with grouse and bread sauce. The gamekeeper's wife, who happened to be French, helped me.'

The following day is Friday. The day of the wedding. Henry makes lunch for 120 guests: a buffet served in Scott's famous library, the likes of 'which can be eaten,' Douglas advises in the letter, 'standing about without knives or forks'. The provisions – a generous list in the midst of wartime rationing – include sliced bread, finger rolls, tongue, ham, grouse, partridges, rabbits, fresh lobsters, anchovies, cheese, eggs, butter and tomatoes. 'I thought to offer you six dozen small meat turnovers,' Douglas adds, 'carefully made with good pastry', which Henry may or may not accept. 'As you will notice the dinner is simpler than might be expected,' he concludes, 'but that is the menu.'

And so, while the battle on the eastern front continues between Nazi Germany and the Soviet Union, and Lore remains alone and grieving in Nuremberg, Henry watches Scotland's aristocracy hobnobbing in one of the most famous literary houses in the world. Perhaps he thinks, with a jolt of pain, of how much he would love to tell his father, the man who introduced him to the power of bow ties, good stationery, and manners, about this elegant spectacle playing out before his eyes.

He watches the guests drink champagne and eat food made by a Jewish refugee taught to cook in a German kosher hotel on the brink of war. He hears the sound of the pipes drifting in from the gardens, and the babble of the Tweed. The light conversation between pebble and water that so pleased the house's original owner. It is the most 'splendid afternoon' at the most catastrophic of times, and Henry will never forget it.

A few months later, on 27 December, Henry will marry Ingrid. The wedding will take place in Pollokshields synagogue. Afterwards the newly married couple will go by car back to Ingrid's parents' flat on Maxwell Road where, with a handful of guests, they will dine on noodle soup, turkey and pomme croquettes, cooked by one of the chefs at the Corn Exchange. For dessert Henry will serve ice cream bombes, which he made himself earlier that morning, using a local Italian shopkeeper's machine, then filling his bath with ice and sea salt so he could freeze the bombes in their moulds.

During the day a wedding cake, silver in colour because it is coated in inedible papier mache cake boards, will arrive on the doorstep. A gift from Robert Douglas himself. 'A two-tier wedding cake – mind you, no icing.' Henry explains. 'We still had rationing. We were delighted. Such a kind gesture. And do you know he offered me a job in his bakery in Selkirk, too.'

'We didn't want to live in Selkirk,' Ingrid protests.

'No,' agrees Henry. 'We were quite happy in Glasgow.'

'I was a sun child.'

In the early 1930s Henry is sent across Germany and Switzerland to a series of Jewish children's camps known as Kinderheim. He is a sickly child and his mother decides the experience will be good for building him up. The first camp is in the saltwater spa town of Bad Dürrheim east of the Black Forest. 'I'll never forget as we walked in,' says Henry, 'the matron stands there and looks at us. Left, right, and you were either a sun child or not a sun child and were allowed to stay outside or not.'

Which was he?

'I was a sun child,' says Henry with a smile.

Henry attends these camps until 1937. At a Hakhshara, one of a number of pre-war agricultural camps in which Jewish youth are taught preparatory skills for emigration to Palestine, he learns to make sourdough, which in another century will become the most hipster-signifying of breads. 'Starter Sour Dough, well kneaded,' writes Henry in a short essay about the Kinderheim. 'The oven was filled with wood. When it had burned it was raked out. The loaves were put in, oven sealed. After eight hours baked on diminishing heat it was ready. Delicious wholemeal bread.' The Hakhshara is located in a large farmhouse near Salem in southern Germany, the town where the renowned German Jewish educator Kurt Hahn founded Schule Schloss Salem, one of Europe's most elite schools. The year before Henry learns to make sourdough in the Hakhshara, Hahn is forced to flee Nazi persecution and move his school to Gordonstoun on Scotland's Moray coast.

The same stretch of northeastern coastline where I happen to start writing this book.

Those first words, so difficult to summon from a place that feels like nowhere, will be tapped out in the early hours in a holiday cottage deep in a valley lodged between the mountains and the sea. I will write every morning, against the clock, until my children burst in and put a stop to it. In the afternoons we will go to the beach, explore the old fishing villages, buy seafood from sparse fish shops at the end of coastal roads. We will walk from the cottage to the old Bridge of Alvah, which arches high over a gorge and river and has terrifyingly low walls. The men fishing for salmon down below on the river bank are so far away they look like figures in an old romantic painting. I will not be able to enjoy this pastoral scene. My stage of life will not permit it. All I will see is the impending lurch towards disaster. In the nights, I will fall asleep to the repeating vision of my four-year-old son or the dog careering towards the low stone walls of the bridge. A vision that will make me gasp out loud, emitting the same involuntary yelp the dog makes when I accidentally stand on her tail. But I do this to myself. This is what my mind can make. In the mornings, sane and fearless once more, I will open my laptop and the search for the story will begin again.

'It all goes back to the house on the hill.'

The house on the hill is at 358 Sauchiehall Street. It is simple in style, a child's drawing come to life, with a pitched roof, five large windows and a portico held aloft by slender columns. It stands back from the street, perched in another era at the top of the steep slope that gives it its nickname. Enclosed in its own landscaped garden. Hemmed in by younger tenement cousins. It is arrived at by a long flight of stairs that ascend at a slant from one of the most famous thoroughfares in Glasgow. Here, for now, is the place where Henry and Ingrid meet during the wartime summer of 1941.

The river of history is running fast. Though the building, originally part of a terrace of Georgian villas called Albany Place, has been here a century, it is already a throwback to a vanished time. A time when Sauchiehall Street was the residential address of wealthy merchants, many of whom made and inherited their fortune through the transatlantic slave trade. A time when the street meandered like a river and was named after a water meadow of willows. Now Sauchiehall Street has been straightened and widened. And almost all of Albany Place has been submerged by the incoming tide.

Entire houses are interred in the street as a bombastic style of architecture sweeps through the second city of the empire. The tenement. At street level, department stores, cinemas, ballrooms, hotels, restaurants, galleries, commercial businesses and tearooms open. The trams come. The Glasgow School of Art, one of the finest art nouveau buildings in the world, opens its doors. By the time Henry arrives back in blackened, bombed, poverty-stricken, economically depressed and irrepressible Glasgow following his release from the Isle of Man, there is only one incongruous Georgian villa left on the street. And it's being used as a refugee centre. There are around two thousand people who have fled Nazi-occupied Europe in Scotland now, and most of them have wound up in Glasgow. As war rages on in their homelands dozens of these German, Austrian and Czech refugees, many of them returning from internment, find their way to 358 Sauchiehall Street. The young men and women climb the stone steps. They open the heavy front door flanked by columns. They enter a shabby old merchant's villa filled with the strong scent of continental coffee, revolution, and home.

'It was a very powerful youth club,' says Henry. 'Its members, I think there were around sixty of us, were from Austria, Czechoslovakia and Germany, though not all Jewish. The people there were a few years older than we were. We learned a lot from them. It was our first contact with music and art. One of the chaps was a chorus master, and we sang Mozart. It was a most interesting way to find out what being young is all about.'

'Henry!' Ingrid protests. 'It wasn't my first contact with music. I've *always* loved music.'

'Yes,' says Henry, 'but it all goes back to the house on the hill. Music, politics, art, painting. It was a hotbed of culture. We sang for Mrs Churchill's aid to Russia fund to raise money for a second front. We made our own costumes and performed Czech and Austrian songs in the Usher Hall in Edinburgh, St Andrews, all over Scotland. We went on rambles together. We took the number four tramcar to Clarkston and Croftfoot and walked up into the hills.'

He turns to his wife. 'You tell the story, Ingrid . . . about the sandwiches.'

'The sandwiches were put in the middle,' says Ingrid, looking intently at Henry.

'Why?' Henry prompts her.

'Because we wanted everyone to have the same.'

'You weren't allowed to eat your own,' Henry explains. 'You put them in the middle and it was a lucky dip.'

They were Marxist sandwiches!

'That's right,' Henry laughs. 'That's how it was.'

At the refugee centre there is a library, theatre group, meeting rooms, and a canteen famous for its proper coffee and cheap meals cooked by Austrian chefs. Soup, rye bread, liver sausage. The continental cuisine becomes locally renowned and students begin to drift over from the art school for a bowl of soup. When Henry enters the house on the hill he steps inside a world that to the rest of the city is foreign, but to him is home. A home, moreover, that does not reject, persecute and seek to obliterate him. A home that no longer exists for him in Germany, and never will again, but is somehow here, in a shabby Georgian mansion. And here, for once, assimilation is not the ultimate aim of every interaction. Here, Henry can be free. Amongst his own. He can speak German. Sing German songs. Talk about his internment. Eat the food of his childhood. Stay up late discussing what might become of Europe. Share news of the war. Listen to young men and women talk about returning to rebuild their countries after it's all over. Make friends for life. Fall in love.

Henry and Ingrid meet at the house on the hill a few months after his return from the Isle of Man. Perhaps they first smile at each other in the canteen over the rim of a coffee cup, or get chatting on one of the centre's organised weekend rambles in Cathkin Braes, throwing those first bashful pleasantries into the wind that whips across the highest point in the city. Maybe they find themselves sitting next to each other on the pitched roof of the house on the hill, beneath threatening night skies, as the refugees take turns fire-watching; sitting out all night with buckets and stirrup pumps in case German air forces drop incendiary bombs. In any case it happens quickly; the blossoming of love sped up like a time-lapse film by the inexorable machinery of war. At a New Year's Eve party at 358 Sauchiehall Street, marking the entrance into another year of the war, Henry and Ingrid become a couple.

The house on the hill is the centre of their world. Chess, music, philosophy, medicine, literature, politics, war, anti-Semitism, home: everything is up for discussion under the probably leaking roof of 358 Sauchiehall Street. It is here that Henry is politicised. He writes left-wing pamphlets with the future academic and humanitarian Henry Prais, attends lectures on Marxism, sings anti-fascist songs in the choir and marches alongside the trade unions on May Day. An old German song, 'Die Gedanken sind frei' – a famous anti-fascist paean to freedom of thought – is sung so often that seventy years later, when so much else has vanished from Ingrid's memory, the lyrics will remain, the notes imprinted on the bar lines of her past. She will sing 'Die Gedanken sind frei', in German, all her life.

The house on the hill's activities are funded by the Labour Party, trade unions and the Co-op. The address is shared with left-wing groups including Free German League of Culture and Free German Youth, of which Henry for a time becomes leader. After the war the building will be taken over by the left-wing Unity Theatre – itself composed of members from the Glasgow Jewish Institute Players.

It is this proud history of activism that will threaten Henry and Ingrid's application for naturalisation in the near future. A history that for the refugees is a matter of moral and political obligation both to homeland and host country during the war.

This place they call home, where they meet, fall in love and together become themselves, will in a few short years be viewed as a cause for suspicion. A sinister place. A potential risk to their British citizenship. 'Do not join any Political organisation or take part in any political activities,' advises the booklet issued by the Jewish Board of Deputies and the German Jewish Aid Committee. This is what it is to be a refugee in wartime Britain. This is how fraught with danger belonging can be.

'Daddy did say I shouldn't go there,' says Ingrid.

'Your father didn't like it,' Henry agrees. 'He said "You're too political, you march on May Day, you're too left-wing." It could get you into trouble. Well, he was right, we now see. It just shows you that whatever you do somebody is watching you.'

16 June 2018. I'm in Giffnock to talk to Henry and Ingrid about the house on the hill. A conversation that will stoke the embers of Ingrid's memory and glow in mine afterwards because it will be the last time I am able to officially interview her. It also happens to be the morning after history is made on the very same site where Henry and Ingrid met. The previous night, at 11.15 p.m., a fire ripped through the Glasgow School of Art. The roof and upper floors were completely destroyed. Debris and embers the size of fists rained down through the night, and the heat from the blaze could be felt several streets away. Only four years earlier a much smaller fire devastated parts of Charles Rennie Mackintosh's masterpiece, including the world-famous library, and its restoration, including a new fire suppression system, had almost been completed. After

this engulfing second blaze the damage will be deemed irreparable, a public inquiry into both fires will be repeatedly called for, and the debate over whether stone-by-stone reconstruction or twenty-first-century homage is preferable will begin. Meanwhile, the chasm ripped open by the fire will continue to look as disturbing as a set of front teeth knocked out of a mouth. On the day I visit the Wugas to talk about how they met, a renowned architect who trained at the art school visits the scene and compares the smoking ruins to Second World War bomb damage.

'It's very upsetting,' says Henry. 'Our little house on the hill was just below the Mackintosh building so we were very aware of it. It was through the club that we got to know the work of Charles Rennie Mackintosh. Once we were taken up to see it. It was his masterpiece. It was part of Glasgow.'

'That was . . .' Ingrid pauses, thinking hard . . . 'Renfrew Street.'

By 1946 the war is over and the refugee centre is dissolving. The last Georgian villa on Sauchiehall Street will not be here for much longer. In a couple of decades the house on the hill will be demolished to make way for an extension to Glasgow's dental hospital. By the time I arrive in the city, you would never have known it was there.

During my student years, when I am the same age as Henry was at the house on the hill, I will also spend most of my recreational life on Sauchiehall Street. The party street of Scotland's party capital, as it has now become. This is where I will go drinking at the weekends, filling my belly with greasy noodles before the long stagger home in the dark, picking my way past the piles of vomit and abandoned polystyrene trays lining the street. This is where I will go clubbing, see bands, art exhibitions, and watch films in a newly refurbished gallery a few doors down from the dental hospital. This is one of the places where I will fall in love with a woman for the first, and only, time in my life. The woman with whom I will go on to have children, and share this precious life. For a few charmed years this gallery will be a beacon for people like me. The place where my new love and I will sit, cloaked in the dark of a tiny cinema nestled in the building, watching a double bill of films, Richard Linklater's *Before Sunrise* and *Before Sunset*, that in another fifteen years will influence the words I am writing now. This bold reset of Alexander 'Greek' Thomson's Grecian Chambers, all millennially spirited steel and glass, light and exposed sandstone, will be my very own house on the hill.

At the time, I am oblivious to my surroundings. This is what it is to be young, carefree, not yet rebuilt by the passing of time. Living out your life inside its most present part, in the spacious rooms of youth, guarantees that you cannot appreciate it. Nor do I know this. That when the refurbishment of the gallery begins and decades of plaster-work and false ceilings are removed, layer by layer, day after day, a ghost from another time emerges. A lost Georgian villa of Sauchiehall Street, towering fifteen feet high on iron stilts in the midst of the Grecian Chambers. Part of the same terrace as the house on the hill. Entombed in the street for more than 140 years.

'There was more to Austerlitz than he could ever know.'

In the spring of 2008, I am sent to London by my editor to interview the Scottish rock band Biffy Clyro. The quartet are making a music video for their upcoming single, 'Mountains', and I have been invited to watch them shoot it and, if it works out, appear in it. (It doesn't, thankfully.) The video is to be made in a Masonic temple hidden inside the revamped Great Eastern Hotel, right next to Liverpool Street Station.

Back in 1884, the Great Eastern opens its doors for the first time, a decade after the construction of the station. Here is one of London's great railway hotels. A monument, erected in rich red stone, to the industrial age, British imperialism and the expanding network of tracks streaking the body of the country like veins. Hotel and station are coupled up from the beginning. The Great Eastern boasts its very own private track running into the building, delivering provisions including fresh sea water for the guests' salt baths every day. Soon it also contains a clandestine Masonic lodge, formed deep within the hotel as an afterthought by the Great Eastern's chief architect Charles Barry Jr. The son of the designer of the Houses of Parliament.

More than eighty years later the temple is said to be rediscovered when engineers are working on a restoration of the hotel, which by now is just another shabby Victorian behemoth in London that requires dragging into the twenty-first century by Terence Conran or razing to the ground. A false wall on the first floor is removed, and behind it a mahogany-panelled antechamber is found, as perfectly preserved as a pearl within an oyster. The construction workers go into the antechamber and find a pair of heavy studded doors anointed with brass lion knockers. They open them and step into a vast windowless room. It is wrapped from floor to ceiling in twelve types of Italian marble. Decorated with a host of arcane symbols and insignia, lined with cream-and-red veined marble pillars and bookended by two giant mahogany thrones. Above is a domed ceiling bearing a five-pointed star and ringed by the signs of the zodiac. Underfoot is a sunken black and white chequered marble floor. Here in the bowels of one of London's original railway hotels is a jewel in the crown of inveterate male privilege. The most magnificent Freemasons' lodge in the land.

When I arrive at the entrance of the Great Eastern hotel I know none of this. The forty pages of 'cuts' in my rucksack, interviews gathered by the newspaper librarian – these are still, just about, the glory days when such a role exists – are about the formation of Biffy Clyro in mid-Nineties Kilmarnock, not the Masonic temple discovered around the same time off a hidden antechamber of the Great Eastern. And the lodge has not been opened to the public either. It will be another two years before Lady Gaga does a shoot in the lodge for Italian *Vogue*, titled 'Masonic Glamour', in which the superstar appears seated on one of the thrones, clad in a dress made of Hello Kitty toys. Before the temple undergoes its typically twenty-first-century reincarnation into fashion location, exclusive party venue and scene of the occasional 'secret' screening of a cult horror film by candlelight, with a cocktail included in the ticket price.

I'm taken up to the first floor of the hotel by a member of staff. A nondescript door, the kind that lines old carpeted hotel corridors in every major city in the country, is opened to the wood-panelled antechamber. It smells like the inside of a military medal display case. It smells of a particularly masculine, upper-class, British strain of authority.

My hands grip the cold brass lion knockers. I pull open the doors. I am standing at the top of a flight of marble stairs, looking down into another era of time. Well, aside from the producers running back and forth issuing commands into their headsets, and the paraphernalia of cameras, screens, lighting equipment and cables snaking across the chequered floor, which looks like a supersized chess board. The room is cold and artificially lit. The enormous gold star bursting from the dome of the vaulted ceiling blazes above us. The lead singer of Biffy Clyro is seated on one of the thrones, dressed all in white, singing the same lines over and over again.

I have never been in a room like this.

Has anyone like me?

Three years later I meet the Wugas, and read *Austerlitz* for the first time. I've never read Sebald before. Somehow, I had received the message that it was not for me. That it might be beyond me. Instead, I become obsessed with this strange and beautiful novel about a Kindertransportee, published just weeks before Sebald's untimely death.

Opening in the summer of 1967, which happens to be the same year my father arrived in Britain, *Austerlitz* may have a beginning and an end like any other book but the prose somehow continues to flow invisibly on either side of it. You read it convinced the story goes on beyond its 415 pages. That it started long before you cracked the spine. That you are only wading into a small section of the river's inevitable course. *Austerlitz* is William Faulkner's observation that 'the past is never dead. It's not even past' in unending action.

No matter how many times I read the book, it always feels like going into the same proverbial river that you can never enter twice. I know neither what's coming next, nor where I've just been. And when I close *Austerlitz*, I arise from the text as if from a dream. Austerlitz, an obsessive photographer, speaks of the moment in the darkroom when the image emerges from the exposed paper, 'as memories do in the middle of the night, darkening again if you try to cling to them, just like a photographic print left in the developing bath too long'. Similarly when I close the book I instantly forget my place in it, despite the ritual folding down of the page corner or replacing of a bookmark. A bookmark that happens to be a note written by my mother containing her email address (hotmail, that most antiquated of domains) and password. An uninteresting scrap of paper until my mother's breast cancer returns, incurable this time. Each time I open *Austerlitz* the note tucked deep in the spine begins to mean a little more to me, its worth increasing with the diminishing of my mother's life.

Over the years, as I get to know Henry, I keep reading *Austerlitz*.

And at some point, as sometimes happens with great art, *Austerlitz* begins to read me.

Sebald's masterpiece is published two months after the Twin Towers come down. It is a twentieth-century novel published as the curtains are thrown open to a new millennium. Perhaps the first great novel of the troubled new century. Its effect is displacement, as well as a kind of cultural confusion. Here is a novel about the Second World War with a McDonald's in it.

Many of the meetings between the two lonely white men at its centre happen near or around stations. In fact

Austerlitz is bookended by major European railway stations, opening in the Centraal Station in Antwerp, and closing at the station with which the protagonist shares a name: Paris's Gare d'Austerlitz. And, of course, Sebald's stations are more than places of transition. They are weird and murky terminuses of history. They share a quality of light and atmosphere with photographic darkrooms.

The Great Eastern is in *Austerlitz*, too. It is in the saloon bar of this old hotel that Austerlitz begins to break the silence permeating the novel's heart. This is where he runs into the narrator, who is killing time in the bar while waiting for his train home, quite by chance. The two men, who have not crossed paths for twenty years, immediately pick up where they left off. Austerlitz begins by telling him how he spent the afternoon in the hotel, 'which was soon to be thoroughly renovated'. The Portuguese business manager – it is often immigrants who lead Austerlitz where he needs to go – agreed to show him around and took him 'up a broad staircase to the first floor', where he 'produced a large key and unlocked the portal of the temple'. Austerlitz found himself standing in the Grecian Masonic temple. He describes the hall 'with walls panelled in sand-coloured marble and red Moroccan onyx', the black and white floor, and the vaulted ceiling with a star at its centre 'emitting its rays into the dark clouds all around it'. It was in that secret room, says Austerlitz, that he realised he had to find someone to whom he could relate the story of his life. The story kept from Austerlitz until his fifteenth year, which he will now begin to tell. A secret history that is somehow handed back to him, in fragments, in that long-buried Masonic temple.

Novels are like buildings. They can be home to any number of hidden histories. And there is one antechamber so deeply buried in *Austerlitz* it is never laid bare. Sebald partially based Jacques Austerlitz on a real-life Kinder-transportee. A woman whom it is said he discovered through a 1991 BBC documentary called *Whatever Happened To Susi?* It is now on YouTube, split into three grainy and unintentionally Sebaldian parts. The film tells the story of a German Jewish girl, Susi Bechhofer, who came to Britain on a Kindertransport in May 1939, two weeks after Henry. She travelled from Munich with her twin sister Lotte. The girls arrived into Liverpool Street Station the day after their third birthday. 18 May. The same day on which Sebald would be born five years later.

The girls were adopted by a Welsh Baptist minister and his wife, Fred and Audrey Legge, who immediately changed the children's names, a fate which befell many Kindertransportees. Lotte became Eunice Legge. Susi became Grace Legge. And with the changing of their names, their true histories were erased. Until more than a decade later, in 1954, when Susi was being seated for an O-level exam according to her position in the alphabet and she was told out of the blue by the school mistress that 'Today, Grace, you're going to be with the B's.'

Like Austerlitz, decades passed before she discovered more about her past. But it is Bechhofer, not Austerlitz, who is struck by a final act of renaming. Her past is fictionalised by Sebald. Turned into someone else's story. A great story. A man's story. Austerlitz's story. This is what writers do, but what did Bechhofer make of it? After all she had been through, did it feel like due recognition or yet another act of erasure? At some point in the years that followed, Bechhofer started to go by her real name. She apparently corresponded with Sebald shortly before he died. And when she died in 2018 the obituaries remem-bered her not as Grace Stocken, but as Susi Bechhofer. Her birth name. Her Jewish name. The one that inspired a novel called *Austerlitz*.

The title of Sebald's novel is itself a play on names. A name that is at once a place, a Parisian train station and a historical battle. It must be a common misconception, certainly one I made, to assume Austerlitz refers to a place, not a person. And there is another alias ghosting Austerlitz. What the critic James Wood terms Sebald's most beautiful act of withholding. The name which never appears in the novel. 'The name that begins and ends with the same letters,' writes Wood, 'the name which we sometimes misread Austerlitz as.'

Auschwitz.

'Ingrid lost uncles, aunts, and cousins,' says Henry. 'So many died.' On her father's side, two of Ascher's brothers, Julius and Willi, died in Auschwitz. It was Willi who, when his brother Ascher pleaded with him to apply for domestic work in Britain, replied that he would not have his wife working as a servant in another country. He, his wife Thekla and three of their seven children were murdered in Auschwitz.

'Some survived,' Henry continues. 'Emil. He was a tough guy.'

'Emil?' asks Ingrid. 'What happened to him?'

'He did whatever he could to survive,' says Henry. 'He came out of Auschwitz, came back to Germany . . .'

'He was my cousin,' says Ingrid. 'His father was my father's brother.'

'He and his wife, who was also in Auschwitz, both refused to get the numbers tattooed on their arms removed,' says Hilary. 'He was a real toughie.'

'And Ingrid's aunt came out of a camp and died a week later,' says Henry. He believes her husband, separated from his wife and child, was murdered in Riga.

Ingrid stays silent.

This is the moment when Henry and I start talking about *Austerlitz* for the first time.

'Wow!' he says, shaking his head. He has just finished reading the novel, having bought it on my recommendation. 'He describes everything! A girl's artery pumping, a lizard on a sunny rock with its tongue out. I said to myself, this is going to be different. It goes on and on: "said Austerlitz . . ." over and over again. Then about halfway through I suddenly got the hang of it.'

In that stretched moment, I am carried by the wings of memory south, back to London a decade ago. To the gleaming windowless room in the depths of the Victorian hotel beside Liverpool Street Station. There I am. Standing on the checkerboard floor. Beneath the blazing gold star. Inside a cube of hidden history.

'Got the hang of what?' asks Ingrid.

Henry pauses for a long time. He takes off his glasses and rubs his eyes. Finally, he looks up. His face appears naked and calm.

'How he felt there was more to Austerlitz than he could ever know.'

'Hello, Cheetah!'

My first day of school falls in the autumn of 1983. The days, months, even years around it are mired in a vapour of forgetting. But the actual moment of arrival at the school gate is fossilised in my mind at least partly because it is my first recorded experience of the mispronunciation of my name. And one of my earliest memories. The recollection is short, taking up no more than five minutes of my entire life. It is complete, suspiciously so, as if I have already written it down though I swear I never have until now. Unlike so many of my other childhood memories in which I remain outside myself, guiding my progress through life like an omniscient narrator, the memory already parsed into story, in this one I am in my own body. Looking out through my own eyes.

Lavender bushes flank a short path, bowing fragrant spears to the flagstones. The drunken din of bees tickles my ears. I am close to the ground, the plants running alongside the path at head height. My mother's big square hand is snapped shut over mine, encasing my small hand like a brooch in a box. Her sari swishes against me. A place, warm, cave-like, where I like to hide, running my hands up and down the concertina folds. A place so connected with my mother, practically an extension of her body, that once, in India, as we are standing around somewhere hot on a roadside, next to a car, I caress a passing

162

woman's sari by mistake. When the stranger inside it turns to me and smiles, I am flooded with humiliation.

This is southwest London in the Eighties. A rarefied world of big white houses stacked on a hill, Garbage Pail Kids cards traded in the school playground and *The Jewel in the Crown* on the telly. Or, when my sister and I get our way, *Top of the Pops*, a place where men wear make-up and Madonna writhes on the floor in a wedding dress, which we watch with stainless-steel plates of rice and saaru burning our laps. We have not yet made the wholesale switch to Western crockery, which means that when we do, stainless steel will somehow retain the composition of my childhood. The sensation of a cool rim of a steel cup pressed to my lips, sometimes held by my mother, and the accompanying tinny taste of London water, which everyone loves to say, usually while watching you drink it, that it passed through eight other people before it got to you.

In this era everyone apart from the four of us and the owner of the newsagent at the top of the hill, whom everyone assumes must be my father, is white. On the television in our sitting room they are white. In the books on my shelves they are white. The world, as I know it, is white. I am an anomaly here. So is the thick black hair on my head that springs vertical at every opportunity and requires the kind of quick violent plaiting that brings tears to my eyes to contain it. The hair of a witch, I am told. So thick and luscious, I am told. Impossible to manage, according to the hairdresser. Other things seem impossible too, like my perennially dry charcoal knees and elbows, the pressure cooker producing endless vessels of rice on our stove, my mother in her sari at the school gate, and the lime pickle in my sandwiches. This may be my life, the proof of which I inhabit every single day, but it appears to exist nowhere else on earth.

So here we stand in the playground. My mother and I.

Holding hands. Around us, other parents and children mill and talk and exercise their beautiful belonging. A teacher, nameless and faceless, eventually comes over to introduce herself. The drone of adult conversation plays out in the faraway land above my head.

She turns to me, this kind and well-meaning stranger with the *Blue Peter* voice.

'Hello, Cheetah!' she says brightly.

It is the first of countless such mundane instances, which over decades will accumulate into a kind of songbook of alienation. Many of these mispronunciations will be well-meaning. Many I won't mind in the slightest. Some I will even cherish. Others, few in number but powerful enough to infect the many, will be wounds.

This time, like virtually every other one stretching into the future, each for now retaining its potential like a star in reverse, I say nothing.

The conversation goes on.

We stand in the playground, frozen in our poses.

The memory ends. There is nothing on either side of it but the steep fall away into the oblivion of forgetting.

I will forget my mother leaving.

I will forget walking into the school.

I will forget the rest of the day.

I will forget my mother coming to collect me.

I will forget going home.

But I will never forget this.

'It was the first time I went in the sea.'

Rocks at Carrick is a small oil painting by the artist David Sassoon. It's held in the Stewartry Museum in Kirkcudbright, and depicts, in simple colour and form, the view from nearby Carrick Bay on the Solway Firth, painted by Sassoon in 1935. The light over the bay must have been bright that day, because the sea is whitened to a single alabaster note and the grey of the granite rock formations in the foreground is mellow rather than menacing. 'Rocks at Carrick' is a calming painting, radiating a stillness, flatness, and softness of light that anyone who has been to this particular stretch of Scotland's southwestern coastline will immediately recognise. Here, the shallow waters of the Solway Firth form the most opaque of borders between England and Scotland, creating a kind of ongoing debate between the nations drafted by the fast-flowing movement of the tides and, beneath the water, the endless shifting of the sands. On a very low tide day, if you really know what you're doing, it is said to be possible to criss-cross the Solway on foot, from Scotland to England and back again, following one of the ancient 'waths' – a Norse word for fords – used for centuries to traverse the border.

The Solway Firth is mostly famed for its vast tidal range, one of the largest in the world. Twice a day, every day, the sand flats and salt marshes along the coastline are uncovered. The islands out to sea become temporarily accessible on foot. The strong currents alter the location of the channels, rearranging the sand banks like furniture in a room. This is at once a precise and endlessly changing world. There are fish in these shallows that smell exactly of cucumbers. Tadpole shrimps thought to be amongst the oldest living creatures on the planet have been found here. And it's territory difficult to navigate. A place where the eye is easily deceived by boundaries that appear to evaporate between land, sea and sky.

This is where Henry washes up for one unforgettable summer before the advent of war. He is fifteen years old, and has been in school for a few weeks before the summer holidays kick in and he is invited via Mrs Thelma Mann, on the refugee committee in Glasgow, to stay with the Sassoon family in Kirkcudbright. It is only the second time Henry has seen the sea. And the first time was just weeks ago when he arrived at the Hook of Holland on a Kindertransport and boarded a ferry across the moonlit channel. Now Henry finds himself staying with descendants of one of the greatest Jewish dynasties in the world. The 'Rothschilds of the east' who made their fortune during the previous century in the British-ruled country of my descendants. India.

'David's cousin was Siegfried Sassoon,' Henry explains. 'What a family! More British than the British, you know? They had a beautiful house in Kirkcudbright. That's where painters lived in those days.'

Kirkcudbright is known as the artists' town, where the pastel houses and unexpectedly wide streets cluster around an old fishing port. The town is bathed in the soft and ever-changing light particular to the coastal region, which has drawn artists like moths here from as early as the 1830s. A century on, in 1926, David Sassoon moves to Kirkcudbright from Chelsea, London. He ends up painting mostly for enjoyment, becoming known locally as a quiet and self-effacing character who harbours a tendency to give paintings away for free. For the next twenty-five years David, his wife Vera Rosenberg and their two sons will live in a beautiful Georgian townhouse at 3 and 5 High Street, still known as Sassoon House. It happens to be on the market as I am writing about it, permitting Henry and I an online snoop around.

'Persian carpets, and beautiful silver,' sighs Henry. 'This is why my mother kept complaining that I did not write often enough. There was too much going on!' For most of the summer the Sassoons and the refugee boy in their charge will stay at their black-washed summer hut at Carrick Bay. This is where David likes to paint in his studio overlooking the bay fringed with grasses and gorse spiked with the scent of coconut. Beyond the rocky outcrops lies the shallow sea and the low slope of Ardwall Isle, which can be walked to on foot at low tide. This is the view, or at least a section of it, shown in the oil painting David makes four years before Henry arrives to see it for himself.

'There was no running water, no electricity, it was very primitive,' says Henry. 'We had a Primus stove and got water from a well at low tide. It was the first time I had ever been in the sea. I learned to swim. I was stung by a jellyfish. There were rabbits everywhere, millions of them. I met lots of other young people. Oh, it was fantastic. I felt so lucky.'

Every day he swims in the bay with the Sassoon boys, one of whom, Joey, will become the first Jewish coxswain in Britain, and Henry's friend for life. Henry is mesmerised by the tides, which go out for three miles and come in 'like an express train'. The boys take a little boat, which they leave far out in the bay at low tide, to Ardwall Isle. Henry wakes to the laughter of wheeling gulls and goes to sleep in a hut beneath a night sky embellished with stars. He knows nothing of the tumultuous future that awaits him. Neither the war that will be declared in a matter of weeks, nor the months of internment across Britain that will follow. He cannot know that a view out to sea will soon become commonplace for him. That when he is held behind barbed wire on the Isle of Man, it will become a metaphor not for freedom, but confinement.

It will be almost eighty years before Henry receives the documents regarding his naturalisation from the National Archives. Before he finds, on page twenty, a report written by the procurator fiscal of Kirkcudbright on 3 August 1948, and sent to Edinburgh's Crown Office.

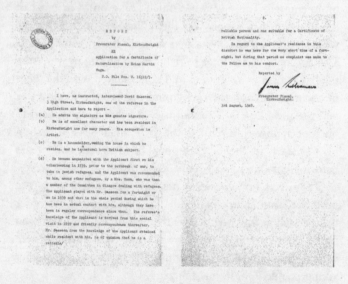

'I have, as instructed, interviewed David Sassoon, 3 High Street, Kirkcudbright,' the letter opens. The procurator fiscal confirms that Mr Sassoon is 'of excellent character', has been resident in Kirkcudbright 'for many years' and that his occupation is 'Artist'. 'He became acquainted with the applicant first on his volunteering in 1939, prior to the outbreak of war, to take in Jewish refugees, and the applicant was recommended to him by a Mrs Mann, who was then a member of the Committee in Glasgow dealing with refugees.' The procurator fiscal writes that 'the applicant' – Henry is not once referred to by name – stayed with Mr Sassoon 'for a fortnight or so in 1939', and they have been in regular correspondence since. Mr Sassoon, he concludes, 'is of opinion that he is a reliable person and one suitable for a Certificate of British Nationality'.

As for his short stay in Kirkcudbright during the summer of 1939, which Henry will remember for the rest of his life as his glorious introduction to the sea, 'during that period no complaint was made to the Police as to his conduct.'

'What will happen to Europe?'

The UK's exit from the European Union looms on the horizon for months on end. Suddenly, after three years of debate it mutates from a fog creeping over the earth's curve to the mountain propping up leaden skies behind it. Immovable after all that. Henry and Ingrid are heartbroken by the prospect of the breaking of an agreement which was born out of the wreckage of the Second World War. Of their lives. The EU began, after all, as the European Coal and Steel Community. At the point of its enactment in 1952 it was a pledge, however flawed and unrealistic, for hope and co-operation in a ruined world.

'Ingrid gets very upset about Brexit,' says Henry when I visit Giffnock on one of the strange suspended days after the 2016 vote. Brittle days. Braced days. Days characterised by a sense that we are living inside something enormous, old and fragile as it is breaking. Mostly the impact is closer to exposure than shock. To a kind of facing up to where we are. And how we got here.

Ingrid shakes her head over and over again.

'She does not accept it,' says Henry.

'No, no, no!' replies Ingrid, punctuating each rebuttal with a little whack of her chair arm. 'We should all be able to live together. If there is going to be a war again, I don't want it.'

For Henry, Brexit is 'horrible', 'a disaster', 'very upsetting'.

He has walked the streets strewn with broken glass the morning after the Reichspogromnacht. He has seen how swiftly the world can change. Now he feels he is the eyewitness of another seismic shift, so creeping and normalised at first, so difficult to cease in the end.

Meanwhile the Wugas' daughters, grandsons and thousands of other British Jews find themselves in the previously unthinkable situation of applying for German citizenship. Gathering documents and supporting evidence, filling out the right forms, and then waiting for the identity stolen from their parents and grandparents to be returned to them by the German government. The baton passed down through history, signifying if not identity exactly, then birthright. Whether they consider themselves German is another matter entirely.

'They're entitled to it,' says Gillian of her two sons. She pauses. '*I'm* entitled to it. It feels a bit wrong taking on German citizenship after everything that's happened. But then again, we were stripped of it. *You* don't get to decide. *We* decide.'

On Brexit Day, a countdown clock is projected onto Downing Street. Union flags are flown around Parliament Square. 'Britain's Brexit Shrug: Just "Get On With It"' runs a headline in the *New York Times*, which doesn't necessarily capture the local spirit but says something about how this fractured island on Europe's northern edge might come to be viewed from the other side of the Atlantic, through the binoculars of history.

They just got on with it.

Meanwhile, as a million commemorative coins flood Britain printed with the doublethink of 'peace, prosperity and friendship with all nations', Greece reveals plans to build a sea barrier off Lesbos to deter migrants. Lesbos, where nearly a million refugees fetched up in Europe during the mass exodus from the Syrian war. Where 'migrant clashes', as they are termed in the press, are increasing between the 25,000 people trapped in overcrowded camps on the island and local riot police. The government solution to this situation, described by a regional governor as a 'powder keg ready to explode', is a floating wall almost three kilometres long, bolstered by pylons fifty metres above the water, and strung with flashing lights. A seaborne lighthouse, designed not to guide lost people to safety but to make them turn back.

The seventy-fifth anniversary of the liberation of Auschwitz happens to fall during the same week as Brexit Day. To me, immersed in Henry's life, the two events are fused in time, strung like lights across a century of history. The observance of the liberation of Auschwitz is deemed especially significant this year. Anti-Semitism and hate crimes against Jews are on the rise globally and in the UK a record number of anti-Semitic incidents has been recorded for the fourth year in a row. Globally, in a world whose order was constructed, however shakily, in the shadow of Auschwitz, Holocaust denial is increasing, particular in younger generations. One newspaper report on rising levels of anti-Semitism, published a few months before the seventy-fifth anniversary, opens with a chilling statement.

'The future of Jewish life in Europe is being called into question.'

The seventy-fifth anniversary is also the last major date to be marked during the lifetime of first-hand survivors. The last generation, as this amorphous and international group are increasingly called. Many, like Henry and Ingrid, are in their tenth decade. The time to remember is more urgent than ever, as though history itself is located in the bodies of this ever decreasing group of people and with the passage of time is becoming thinner, frailer, more endangered.

On the day itself, fewer than two hundred survivors of Auschwitz gather at Birkenau to testify one last time. Some speak against a backdrop of the gates of hell, ghoulishly lit for the purposes of television as if what happened there is not illumination enough.

'Where was everybody?' one survivor asks. 'Where was the world, who could see everything and yet did nothing to save all those thousands?'

Another makes reference to Auschwitz survivor Elie Wiesel's darkly prescient observation that 'the opposite of love is not hate, it's indifference'.

'I'm absolutely devastated with the political situation,' says Henry. 'The whole drift to the right in Germany, here in Britain, Poland, Hungary, the anti-Semitism, the anti-immigrant rhetoric . . . it feels like the 1930s all over again. It's frightening. What will happen to Europe?'

'You can't always push people away,' says Ingrid.

'You just can't,' Henry agrees.

'If they pushed us away,' says Ingrid, 'where would we be?'

'I *am* the last one left.'

We meet outside the main gate of Glasgow University, an archway as grandiose as one would hope for in the fourth-oldest university in the UK. Henry is giving a talk to a group of students from the Jewish Society and has invited me along. The location, high on a hill with a bell tower that can be seen from all over Glasgow, is meaningful to us both. I was a student at Glasgow University in the Nineties, as was Gillian, a couple of decades before me. This is the X marking the spot of my move to Scotland at the age of eighteen, when north, to me, meant north of the River Thames.

The nostalgia hits me long before I set foot in the city. An anticipation for what has already been starts on the train, which is a particularly effective mode of transport for journeying into one's own past. It is also true that whenever I look out of a train window, no matter where on earth it happens to be headed, I feel like my father. When I see my face reflected in the blacklight of a window as the train whizzes through a tunnel my expression belongs to him. And until I alight there it remains, in the turn of my mouth, the beadiness of my eyes, and my outlook on the world. Just as when I open a pat of unsalted butter, upend it into a milk pan, switch the hob on and stand over it like a sentry, I turn into my mother. Long before the butter has clarified into thuppa, boiling itself into something

174

umber and fudgey and destined to cause type 2 diabetes, the transformation has taken place. I am not just doing what she taught me. I am her.

I'm travelling west from Edinburgh after a week of unusually violent storms. The wettest February on record, again. The fields are flooded with reflections of lagging blue skies. There is a clarity to the light, the shining northern kind that follows a spell of strong weather. It is also a brightness emanating from my own head. The night before, while I was getting the children ready for bed, I experienced two migraine auras in succession. A migraine, for me, is an event. A warning written in kaleidoscopic lights. I have had less than a dozen of these visions in my life and this is the first (and I sincerely hope last) time I have ever been assaulted by two in a row. After the lights comes the pain, and the sun striking the train through the trees hits my eyes like strobes. At Falkirk High the gentle hills of Stirlingshire and Perthshire in the far distance look like a rolling bank of cloud. Fleeting. Untrustworthy. I'm not quite sure where what I am seeing begins and ends. I write a few notes. Google anti-Semitism on UK campuses, which has increased exponentially over recent years and is conveyed via the usual channels of hate: swastikas, fascist stickers, Holocaust denial leaflets. I look out of the window and feel like my father.

There he is. My adopted Jewish grandfather, leaning on his stick outside the main gate of my old university. A gentleman, the kind one still comes across now and then in all the major cities of the world. Standing on a pavement, carrying nothing it seems but the clothes on his back. Often wearing a hat. The kind of man one struggles to imagine dressed in anything other than a suit. The kind who seems to have walked here directly from the past. Who, chameleon-like, blends into whatever landscape he happens to be crossing while remaining irrefutably himself. The kind who is in complete command of the story of his life. The kind often described as *a real character*. Henry. A man whose life I have been writing about in one form or another for almost a decade.

My heart soars at the sight of him. He is wearing a flat cap and beige mackintosh, shaded glasses, and a burst of colour at his throat from what appears to be an exceptionally bright bow tie. He is surrounded by students milling this way and that. The future on its way, just as I was twenty years ago. I watch Henry for a while, perched on a stone bench on the brow of a hill, where I might once have sat eating a floppy panini and missing a lecture, blissfully oblivious to the liberty contained in such choices. Then I walk down to greet him. We embrace, and it is unclear which of us enjoys the spectacle of a middle-aged Indian woman cuddling a white nonagenarian gentleman beneath the gothic arch of a fifteenth-century university more. I ask Henry if I can take his photo. He instantly stands back and assumes his photographer's grin, a constant in the images of him traversing a century. I sense as I take this picture, as we sometimes do upon freezing an instant in time, that I will treasure it.

We are taken to a lecture theatre by a Jewish pharmacology student from London. As we negotiate lifts and stone-flagged corridors, she tells me she is concerned about ongoing campus protests which, although they aren't directly anti-Semitic, often trigger anti-Semitism. Does she mean pro-Palestine marches? 'Yes,' she whispers quietly. We reach a room with the number 466 printed on it. Like many such rooms housed in historic buildings to which they bear no relation, it is all low-panelled ceilings, strip lighting, institutional blue carpets and laminated pine. Thirty students have turned up. I join them, and Henry stands in front of us, at a table on which he quietly sets out his history. He has done more than a hundred of these talks, mostly in schools around Scotland alongside Ingrid, and divulges his past like a professional. It is a pleasure to watch him. I feel like a proud parent.

First, Henry gets out his and Ingrid's Third Reich passports stamped with a red J, the name changed on his from Heinz Martin Wuga to Heinz 'Israel' Wuga, and on hers from Ingrid Wolff to Ingrid 'Sara' Wolff. Next, one of the letters that shuttled between Henry in Glasgow, his uncle in Brussels and his parents in Nuremberg. Now the 'white card' he had to show when he landed at Harwich in May 1939, stating he would not be able to work but not, of course, that being a Kindertransportee would become a kind of job for life. And a copy of his class photo from 1937/8, by which time the Nazi regime had moved Henry to a Jewish school.

'And this of course is the horror.'

He holds up the cloth yellow star his mother was forced to sew onto her clothing from 1941 until the war's end. 'Horrendous to have all these things, nevertheless . . .' Henry stalls. 'We must face facts and deal with things as they happen.' This is the sentiment that opens and closes his talk, just as it parenthesises his life. 'We have to tell the truth because the truth is there,' he begins. 'We are duty bound to do it.'

One of the stories Henry tells is a piece of his history I am struggling to write. It is about the period in which he was moved to a Jewish school in Fürth, which he neatly explains to the students is to Nuremberg as Paisley is to Glasgow. It is about how, a few months later, he was moved again by his mother to go to Baden-Baden and take up a chef's apprenticeship in a kosher hotel. It is a story about the ever tightening stranglehold of the Nuremberg laws, the Wugas' forced withdrawal from German society, the complex formation of Henry's Jewish identity, and the fortitude and canniness of his mother. It is a story about carrying on as normal in the most abnormal of times. And in the times in which we are living in room 466 and beyond, the past seems at once too perilously close and far away for me to write about it.

Only after I spend this day with Henry in Glasgow will the words start to come.

The setting is springtime in Nuremberg, 1938, when in one of the large traditional rooms separated by double doors at 15 Fürther Strasse, perhaps the one Henry describes as tending 'a bit towards Biedermeier', his mother takes him aside. 'We can no longer stay in this country,' she says. 'We have to leave. And you would be best to learn a trade.' Whenever Henry tells me this story, which is like a pivot around which his past and future revolve, his mother's words are slightly different, becoming over time like musical variations of a famous theme.

Sometimes Lore breaks it to him gently: 'I am sorry. The way things are going we have to get out of here soon. You better learn something.' Sometimes Henry relays her speech with the cool efficiency of a reporter: 'Then my mother decided to take me away from school. "To learn something," she said.' Sometimes there is more context. 'I liked school and I hated having to leave. But my mother was very wise, yes? She had foresight.' Sometimes there is hindsight provided by the son turned great-grandfather, looking down the kaleidoscope of history for patterns. 'Everyone knew the dangers that lay ahead. My friend Herbert's parents had business interests in Birmingham, so he was sent to Britain. That was no problem in the early days. My mother looked at it differently. She said you have to learn a trade.'

Over the years, the variations of this story will become part of their character. Like Edmund De Waal listening to the tales of his great-uncle Iggie in *The Hare with Amber Eyes*, I find their repetition wears them smooth like a river stone. So it is with Henry, though to me his stories become not the stone but the river itself. Swift, unfathomable, difficult to grasp, even if all the tributaries run into the same sea. Even if the destination remains inescapable.

Henry has to leave school.

Henry has to leave home.

Henry has to learn a trade.

How do these words land upon the shoulders of this fourteen-year-old boy with his devotion to bow ties, Wagner, and truth? A boy whose life has already been squeezed so systematically, so swiftly as I see it from my own shifting standpoint atop history, that the recent past must feel like an absurd dream. Children, after all, live in the present. It is their skill, however transitory, and is part of what makes this brief and magnetic period of our lives

179

so alluring once it passes. So perhaps these words fall not like knives but as softly as the cherry blossom in the parks they can no longer enter. The parks where, as recently as five years ago, Henry would go with his parents on warm summer evenings, bringing their own schnitzel and salad to listen to music.

'I asked "Why?"' says Henry.

His mother's reply never follows. Perhaps this is because shock has a habit of digging holes in our memory and Henry does not know what came afterwards. Perhaps it is because there is no sane answer to the question.

Henry is to go to Baden-Baden, the centuries-old spa town on the edge of the Black Forest where everyone from Napoleon to Marlene Dietrich took the waters. He will be working in the kitchens of an orthodox Jewish hotel owned by a family called Kohler-Stern. It is thanks to the Wugas' connections in catering that the apprenticeship, which must have been extraordinarily difficult to organise, is secured. Lore's father, whom Henry never knew, owned a brewery and restaurant in Heilbronn in southwest Germany where his mother ran service during the First World War. This was while her brother, one of the 100,000 German Jews who flocked to serve their country, was in the army.

Catering, as it is often said of professions handed down through generations like heirlooms, is in the blood. When Henry was growing up he spent his summer holidays in Heilbronn with his cousins, aunts and uncles, and grand-mother. Sometimes he would be sent there alone, put on the train at Nuremberg station by his mother. A boy of six with a label tied round his neck like Paddington Bear so fellow travellers could help him change trains.

'Nobody was afraid then,' says Henry.

In Heilbronn, Henry spent all day in the kitchens with the chefs. These will become some of his happiest childhood memories. Unremarkable, largely forgotten time spent with family in an old Jewish town between the wars. Now this natural interest and heritage is to be expedited into a skill. Perhaps even a future in some unknown land.

By this point all Jewish children have been expelled from German state schools. Henry was moved to a Jewish school by his parents last year, a pattern replicated throughout Nazi Germany. So now, instead of walking to the school where he was forced to sit separately at the back of the class, taunted by teachers and classmates daily, Henry takes a tram to Fürth, on the way passing the Palace of Justice where the Nuremberg trials will be held in less than a decade.

'It was a straight line and it took twenty minutes,' says Henry. 'In the tramcar boys and girls were not to sit in the same coach. It was a very orthodox town.'

Fürth's history of Judaism dates back five hundred years. Long known as the Franconian Jerusalem, at one point its Jewish community was the most flourishing in Germany, with the country's first Jewish hospital and one of its oldest cemeteries, which will be desecrated and destroyed by the Nazis both before and during the war. Henry's school, the Israelitische Realschule, opened in 1862. By 1937, its numbers have swelled. There are fifty-two children in his class alone.

'It was a good school,' he says. 'We had good teachers. Though one of them had to be "Aryan", there were no tensions. There was religious input, a rabbi, and we learned to read Hebrew.'

Henry Kissinger, a future ex-US secretary of state who will soon flee to America with his parents, is in the year above Henry. Another boy, Herbert, the one who manages to get out because his father has business interests in Britain, will become a friend for life. In his brief time spent at the

Jewish school Henry's life is peaceful, sociable, safe.

It is also religious. The children coming from assimilated Nuremberg families suddenly find themselves immersed in Jewish orthodoxy. The Wugas are not observant. The family belong to the main liberal congregation in Nuremberg. Though Henry's mother is Jewish, and Jewish descent is traced through the maternal line, his father is Austrian and has no interest in religion. So although Henry has his bar mitzvah, shabbat, and often goes to his family in Heilbronn for festivals, until he starts taking that tram to Fürth he is German first, Jewish second. Now he finds himself wearing a kippah most days. As a direct consequence of living under Nazi rule, Henry becomes Jewish.

The previous summer. We are sitting side by side at Henry's desk in Giffnock as he shows me, for the first time, a photo of his class of 1937. The former schoolboy runs a trembling finger over each small blurred face, trying to summon names. 'Otto I remember,' he mutters. 'Some of these boys went to Israel . . . This girl I remember, this girl, this girl.'

There are so many pupils in the photo that the arms and shoulders of those on its outer edges have been cut out of the frame. They are split into two rows, with their Jewish teacher, Dr Heinemann, standing in the middle at the back, with black-rimmed spectacles and a bald pate. In the front row, the children sit in various positions, giving the overall image a pleasing lack of uniformity. Two boys in the back row have their hands on their hips, assuming the universal pose of bravado, all the more touching for its affectation. A few are smiling broadly, while others, as is the way of some children when presented with a camera lens, are scowling. Each one looks perfectly like him or herself. Styles forming. Gestures being laid down. Chapters in the midst of being written.

At first I cannot make out Henry. An absurd panic comes over me. My eyes flit from face to face as though the last seconds of an exam I am failing are counting down.

Then, hiding in plain sight right in the front row, I see him.

My boy.

He is almost sprawling. One of his legs is straightened out to the side. The opposite hand bears the weight of his neatly attired body. Nobody else in the photograph is sitting like this. How on earth did I miss him? There is the side parting, the direct gaze, the deep certitude. That ease in himself that will survive with him. That he will take wherever he goes. The position is pure insouciance. So *Henry*.

Looking at him makes us both burst into laughter.

'I know, I know,' says Henry.

Does he know what happened to Dr Heinemann?

'He didn't survive,' he replies. The words come fast, like the smooth lip of water rushing over a weir before it meets the cascade. Then he moves on. 'One girl went to Israel and I corresponded with her for many years. I mean, it's amazing how we kept in touch.'

Does he know how many children survived?

'I'm not sure,' he eventually says.

Those who do survive end up scattered across the world. Most flee to the United States. Many change their names. One former pupil in Henry's class, a boy called Franz Hess, becomes an American soldier and emigrant called Frank Harris. He settles in New York, and in the 1970s begins to arrange Nuremberg-Fürth reunions in the Catskills. This is where the class of 1937 first come together, immersed in the pristine swathe of mountains, forest-ringed lakes and vacation resorts of upstate New York. Jewish New Yorkers started holidaying in the Catskills in the 1890s, and by its wartime heyday this vast expanse ranging into the Appalachian Mountains was known as the Borscht Belt. The first Nuremberg-Fürth reunion takes place in the summer of 1978 at Grossinger's, the legendary kosher hotel founded by Austrian immigrants which ushered in the era of giant self-contained Jewish resorts in the 1920s. At its height Grossinger's boasted its own post office, landing strip, and had the honour of being the first ski resort in the world to use artificial snow. It will also, in my own so-called teenage heyday, become the inspiration for the fictional Kellerman's in *Dirty Dancing*, which I will rewatch, sometimes twice in a single day, through the early 1990s. At Grossinger's, it is said, vacationers could get anything from gas for their car to a gown for an evening dance. It was like a kingdom, and in 1954 was described as 'to resort hotels as Bergdorf Goodman is to department stores, Cadillac to cars, mink to furs, and Tiffany to jewellers'.

Grossinger's closes in 1986. And in 2018, as I start writing this book, it is demolished.

Henry is tired by the time he finishes his talk. He has been standing for almost an hour and politely asks permission from the students to sit down while they ask him questions. These come thick and fast. What is his relationship with Germany like now? Has he noticed an upsurge in anti-Semitism? Does he see similarities between the Nazi concentration camps and the US camps on the border where refugee children are held and separated from their parents? Did he ever consider moving to Israel? What are his views on Scottish nationalism and independence? What direction does he feel Holocaust education should take? Does humour have a role to play? And what is his view of the divide in Glasgow between reform Jews and the orthodox community? Henry answers each question patiently, generously, sensitively. Meanwhile I feel increasingly protective of him.

Afterwards Henry accepts a card and a bunch of yellow tulips, which he says he will take home for his wife. He poses for photos. He watches as the students crowd around the table, looking through the belongings he has brought with him.

Finally we return to the main gate, the two of us alone again, to wait for a taxi to take Henry home. This turns out to be the usual farce involving cabs failing to turn up and irate drivers failing to appreciate the heroics involved in getting in and out of a cab when you are ninety-six and have just spoken about the Holocaust for an hour. 'I'll have what he's having,' a local passer-by says, just like a character in a Nora Ephron anecdote, as the two of us marvel at Henry shuffling along the street with his stick towards yet another black cab.

Before we part Henry gives me a little blue canvas bag with a handle. It is printed with an image of the bronze memorial sculpture located in the forecourt of Liverpool Street Station, where Henry, Ingrid and all the other Kindertransport children arrived into the country. The sculpture is by Frank Meisler, himself a Kindertransportee, who came to London three months after Henry. His parents were arrested three days after his evacuation from Danzig, held in the Warsaw ghetto, and murdered in Auschwitz.

The words on the bag read 'Celebrating 70 years of Kindertransport, 23 November 2008, London'.

'You can have this,' says Henry. 'I think it will interest you.'

Inside are all the Nuremberg-Fürth reunion newsletters. Tributes to Frank Harris, who died in 2017. A photocopy of the class photo of 1937, accompanied by the handwritten names of all the children the survivors were able to identify. I see, for the first time, a small original photo of Henry's classroom and the children at their desks on what must have been a warm day. The windows are wide open, casting a soft bleaching light into the room. The boys' caps hang on pegs along the back wall, the sort of incidental detail that tugs the heart as much as the children themselves.

The first reunion is attended by more than two hundred Holocaust survivors from all over the world. In the years that follow, they will become some of the largest gatherings of survivors in the world. On the cover of a few of the DIY newsletters Henry has kept, which are packed with long attendance breakdowns by state, country and generation, events, invitations to talks and pledges to never forget, is a photocopied image of the Grand Synagogue of Nuremberg on Hans-Sachs-Platz where Henry and many of the First Generationers, as the newsletters refer to them, had their bar mitzvahs under Nazi rule. Henry and Ingrid will attend many of these legendary reunions in the Catskill Mountains. Eventually, in 1992, Henry will put up a notice asking for people from the class of 1937 to come forward. He will write a brief handwritten request, which of course is also in the bag on a scrap of A4, asking for classmates born in 1924, the year of his birth, to meet in the hotel lounge after dinner. And beside every single name, one of which is 'Henry Wuga', a little red tick is drawn signifying attendance. Everyone comes. Four photos of the class will be taken in the years between 1992 and 2008, the quality of the photos improving over time as the pupils' numbers dwindle. In each one Henry will appear grinning, just as he does in the photo I take of him outside Glasgow University.

'At that first meeting there were eighteen of us,' says Henry. 'Then fourteen, then twelve, then eight at the last one. That was ten years ago.'

And now?

'I am the last one left,' he says with a rueful smile.

'You are prepared for whatever will happen.'

There is a hole in this story. It is mother-shaped, and I do not know how to fill it. Motherlands and mother-tongues. These are the landmarks engraved on the maps of our lives, so elemental they are impossible to track. The histories so comprehensively silenced we forget that those invisible lives are, in fact, our own. The images cut out of the photos so that only their outlines remain. Mothers are not just central to our histories, their bodies are the literal sources of them. And yet every day when I open my laptop in the early hours of the morning, which ever since I acquired children and lost the gift of time is when the best words come, history, the kind recorded in books, repeats itself. The sentences laid down are invariably about men. Men in wars, men in power, men going places. Boys heading off to school on trams. Fathers alighting aeroplanes on foreign soil. What fissure might appear where I can insert Lore's wartime letters? Where is my own mother in this story?

Then life intervenes, and blasts the narrative open for me.

A few days after meeting Henry at Glasgow University, my mother nearly dies.

It is the beginning of March 2020, when the promise of spring is finally fulfilled and a respiratory virus buds into a global pandemic. In Edinburgh the crocuses bordering the paths of my local park are in full bloom. Each time we see them my daughter points at the rumpled borders of yellow, white, and lilac and bellows 'They're growing bigger!', although crocuses tend more to droopiness than ascension.

I am in two minds about their flowering. There is a familiar lightness; that hoist of the heart that accompanies the lengthening of days, even and perhaps especially when one is in crisis. But there is also the downward pull of a sadness I already know is a rehearsal for the full-length opera of grief. A show for which my family has been warming up for eight years ever since my mother was diagnosed with breast cancer. Three years ago the uninvited visitor, whom we had begged never to darken our door again, came back. This time the cancer was incurable. It had metastasised, a word I still struggle to spell or say out loud so overloaded is it with consonants and hopelessness.

After I meet Henry at Glasgow University, I go for a solitary lunch at a nearby Vietnamese canteen. I have just acquired a job as a newspaper restaurant critic and am here to do a review. The canteen, which is rammed mostly with students, happens to be a shortish walk from Maryhill Barracks, where Henry was briefly interned with twenty-five German sailors during the dizzying summer of 1940. So as I turn the laminated, slightly sticky pages of the menu, I briefly entertain a fantasy of wandering up there after lunch and taking some photos. The reality? I'm in a rush to get home to pick up my children. Bound to the tyranny of the clock. A mother first, always. And, as it turns out, a daughter. I stir aromatics into a bowl of pho. I take photos of the lampshades fashioned out of traditional Vietnamese conical hats hanging from the ceiling. It is an arrested moment; time itself paused by appreciation. I am lucky. I'm ravenous, and lunch has just arrived. I get to review one of my great passions – food – for a living. I have just seen Henry, whose mere presence always injects a massive dose of joy into me. I'm writing a book about

189

him. We have just booked tickets to visit my parents in London for my forty-first birthday in a few days. I am rushing with the sweetness of life.

Then a text arrives from my father. My mother is in A&E again with severe breathlessness.

Everything that follows the breaking of this charmed moment seems to play out at terrifying speed.

My mother loves flowers, from the brief romantic encounter of magnolia to the tenacity of a bunch of reduced alstroemeria from the supermarket. In recent years, as she has been able to go out less and less, the latter has become the more garden variety experience in her life. My mother now only leaves the house for hospital appointments. This fact, which I have been coming to terms with for a while, will keep hitting me like a truck throughout spring. It is a bit of a problem when nature itself becomes a prompt. When every flowering cherry tree induces a shower of grief. When resurrection, which Teju Cole acutely observed is 'far too close to death', becomes a motif of loss. A particularly strong, even perfumed, childhood memory of mine is of walking the streets of southwest London and having to stop repeatedly to witness this small, round, apple-cheeked Indian woman hitch up her sari to grab a cutting from some random posh garden. My mother, the guerrilla gardener. She once took a young monkey puzzle tree from outside a derelict house, had a nightmare about it, and dug it up and returned it the next morning. In more recent years, she commandeered the concrete back court behind their block of council flats and got planting in a space that anywhere outside of London would have been a car park. It all began when a single slab cracked, then buckled. My mother prised it out, 'chucked some seeds down' to use her turn of phrase, and turned it into her own miniature patch. The last garden of her life. It grew and grew, became beautiful and then impossible to manage, and finally died a routine devastating death.

I wanted to go home for my birthday, to the flat overlooking the garden long since removed by the council. This is where my parents and I endured my raging teens. The place on earth I will always call home, though none of us own it, and I left when I was eighteen. I predicted it would be my last chance to spend a day in the company of the sole person who birthed me. And my mother wanted to see her grandchildren. One last time, one or perhaps both of us said. We had got to the point where we could say such things. Chuck them into a conversation like seeds into a square of soil without shedding a tear. Me in my little garden in Leith, talking as I witnessed the daily progress of our plants in pots, and my mother at home on the sofa four hundred miles away, BBC News or BBC Parliament invariably rolling in the background, as was the torturous national habit in those months encircling Brexit. It was a lovely, sweet, unmemorable conversation that I have since racked my brain to remember because it was the last one like it. I recall shifting into the warm square of sun that hits our bench in the early afternoon. I had just been to the dentist for a filling and my face was numb. The abnormality of the numbness has preserved the memory, and I am grateful for it.

You poor sweetheart, my mother said.

A few days after taking the call from my father in the Vietnamese canteen, all four of us travel to London by train. It is a triumphant journey, the first time we have used disability assistance for our son. I take a photo of him on the platform at Waverley, leaning against a poster of the new fleet of Azuma trains – Japanese-designed, British-built, a train to travel on in strident and globalised times – and with which our son is obsessed. He watches trains incessantly on his tablet, so the sight of a real live LNER Azuma has taken on a visceral power for all of us. Every train I see now is through the saucer eyes of a six-year-old autistic boy. Onboard it is a little quieter than usual but people are still going about their business, however warily and with however much more handwashing. By this point less than a hundred coronavirus cases have been confirmed in the UK. No one is wearing a face covering. A person can still travel the length of the country to be with her dying mother on her birthday without thinking twice. Life has not yet changed beyond all recognition.

The following morning, as the first known death from coronavirus in the UK is reported, I take another train to the hospital where my mother is on an acute assessment unit. Like a train in an overly signposted novel, it literally passes through the stations of my early life. Richmond, where we lived until our house was repossessed. Twickenham, my first home. Strawberry Hill, which at some undesignated point in my childhood merged with both the Beatles song 'Strawberry Fields' and Box Hill, the famous picnic spot and bracing scene of Emma's bad behaviour in Jane Austen's novel. Finally Kingston, where I spent hungover Saturdays as a teenager, killing time in the brutal town centre. Waiting, as one does for a train, for the future to arrive.

My destination is the hospital where my mother worked until she retired as a cytology screener. Where she studied cervical smears for eight hours a day, walked in Richmond Park on her lunch break, and made some of the best friends of her later life. She was not always a cytology screener. In Bangalore, my mother trained in medicine and was the first female pathologist in the entire state of Karnataka. This is what relatives have told me in any case, which according to my mother is 'utter nonsense'. In the 1970s, when she came to London following her arranged marriage to my father, she worked as a house officer in what was then the National Hospital for Nervous Diseases in Queen Square. There was talk of her becoming a registrar and six weeks after giving birth to my sister she did indeed return to work, and her mother came all the way from Bangalore to help with my sister. The only time she ever came. All I know about this period before I was born is that my father took his mother-in-law to the Chelsea Flower Show that spring of 1976. It tickles me like pampas grass, the thought of this dapper Indian man and his visiting mother-in-law walking amongst the technicolour displays and handlebar moustaches of mid-Seventies west London. Drifting in and out of heavily scented marquees. Bending dark heads to the year's best roses in a sea of white.

Three years later my mother had me and decided not to go back to work. Long before having it all became a perky catchphrase and then an albatross to hang around twenty-first-century women's necks, she gave up a pioneering career as a doctor to be a full-time mother. As the story goes, or perhaps as how she carefully told it to us, her second-generation daughters, she never once regretted it.

Here she is. This same woman, five years older than the National Health Service to which she has devoted her professional life, in her old workplace. She is lying diagonally in the first bed of the bay, head off the pillow. She looks tiny, doll-like. She looks both like herself, the guerrilla gardener stealing forty winks post-raid, and like anybody on the brink of death. There is a packet of Fisherman's Friend lozenges on the table, which I have never seen a single soul on earth but my mother eat, and which is an anchor hurled from the past. Never, ever will I forget how my mother looks in this hospital bed. *This is it*, I think, and adrenaline sounds through my body like a siren. A call to action. There is something perverse about the fact that witnessing someone you love close to death can make you feel outrageously, necessarily alive.

My mother is confused and having seizures. She is refusing her meds, water, food, a drip – everything required to sustain human life. She keeps saying the word 'eejit', which I have never once heard her say and pronounced just like that in the Scots form. This is a good joke and for an insane heartbeat I think I must tell it to my mother. She seems to recognise me and calls me 'my darling'. I rise to the occasion like a lioness, becoming a version of myself I have seen only twice elsewhere in my life, at the births of my children.

In my bag is an old sweet-smelling copy of *Carry On, Jeeves* by P. G. Wodehouse, one of my parents' favourite authors. Like many Indian immigrants of their generation, born if not like Salman Rushdie's fictional *Midnight's Children* on the stroke of independence then within its peripheral timeframe, they are as British as they are Indian. Possessors of what Rushdie calls the 'partial and plural perspective of the migrant', an outlook written on the spines of their often vertically arranged bookshelves. Agatha Christie, Georgette Heyer, Miss Read, Dickens, the *Bhagavad Gita*, Somerset Maugham, Ruth Rendell, D. H. Lawrence, Arundhati Roy, the Upanishads, a book of reflections on love by Sister Wendy Beckett, and many, many more written in Kannada, my parents' mother tongue, which I can neither read nor speak. I grabbed the Wodehouse off one of their shelves before I left that morning, perhaps in some strange premonition but also because books are companions in hard times. And it is difficult to think of a more cheerful consort than Wodehouse.

And so I read to my mother from the start of *Carry On, Jeeves*. 'Now, touching this business of old Jeeves – my man, you know – how do we stand?' I begin chirpily, pulling out all the stops, feeling like the musician tuning her instrument on the *Titanic* while two nurses insert a cannula in the crook of my mother's miniature arm and hook her up to an IV drip. She lets them. I use every distraction technique under the sun, skills honed from six years of parenting an autistic child. I feel like everything I have ever done, been, known and seen was training for this precise moment in time. The marathon of death. I monologue about the East Coast Main Line from Edinburgh to London King's Cross, describing each station in the purplest of prose, then comes a breakdown of a programme, *Britain's Lost*

Masterpieces, I watched in my mother's overstuffed TV planner the previous night. My mother is transfixed. She starts waxing lyrical about the scientific advances required to remove centuries-old grime from Renaissance paintings. It is the first and last time we will ever discuss what it takes to restore a Raphael. 'You're so good at this,' the nurse's assistant says to me, and it is one of the proudest moments of my life.

The word 'thingummy' comes up a few pages into *Carry On, Jeeves*. My mother turns to me with a mischievous smile and we share a laugh at the trusty deliciousness of language. Each word is a life raft. And once on board, a fragment of memory rises to the surface.

A girl with plaits twisted tightly enough to make her parting ache a little is walking down the street, the long twisty one that goes from the town to the doctor's, holding her mother's hand. She sees a house covered in scaffolding and asks her mother what this is. Her mother, who knows the words for things and pronounces them in her particular rich, low, singsong voice, tells her. '*Scaffolding*,' the girl repeats. 'That's my new favourite word.' A feeling passes between them, transmitted by hand. The mother strokes the girl's hair. They carry on walking.

I pause to turn a page and my mother, who in her confusion is acquiring the powers of a sage, tries to predict the word that will follow. A word I have tragically forgotten, which she speaks aloud, with great urgency. In that moment I am convinced she is right. As I turn the page the drama heightens to hammy proportions as all four of us – me, my mother, the nurse and her assistant – hold our breaths for the big reveal.

The word is not the word.

My mother is wrong.

It is my madness that is right.

I thought it was one of the worst days of my life until

196

I understood that it might be our last together, and then it became one of the best. My mother rambles on and on about wombs, babies, flowers, the Ice Age, India, her childhood, her parents, the prime minister, whom she loathes and insists is hiding 'in a bunker', and the physicist Brian Cox, whom she adores. I remember my father saying to me that the night before she was rushed into hospital my mother watched a Brian Cox programme about the universe and 'seemed to enter another realm'. In this dimension time runs not like a train on its regular route but like a plane hovering over past, present and future, surveying all of life at once. Except the view from on high is obscured by mist. I understand now. At the end of one's own life on earth, time unhooks from chronology. 'It makes one's head heavy and giddy,' writes Sebald in *The Emigrants*, 'as if one were not looking back down the receding perspectives of time but rather down on the earth from a great height, from one of those towers whose tops are lost to view in the clouds.'

In real time, it is the eve of my birthday. And so it occurs to me, as I feed my mother a few forks of rice and hold her hand, that precisely forty-one years earlier she was in labour with me. Enduring those early electric pangs as my little black-haired head bore down on her pelvis. Here at the other end of life, death is as much of a process to be borne. My mother speaks in a visionary torrent of Kannada and English. She sings lullabies, her voice sweet and high, and I remember my sister once saying 'have you noticed how much more Indian she seems when she is ill?'. Another woman in the bay, a white woman, yells at her to shut up, and I fear the abuse, however coded or overt but always anticipated in every single possible scenario that might follow. 'You're not the only ill person in here,' she shouts. 'Just shut your mouth.' I come out from behind the blue curtain and say, in my most cut-glass Richmond accent and with a calm summoned from the depths of a place I did not know existed, 'That woman is my mother. She is a lovely person, and she can't help it.' The woman never says another word.

A consultant arrives, a mixed-race woman with glasses and a Zadie Smith head wrap. 'She has a little kidney failure,' she says to me. She speaks gently, as if the breakdown of a major organ is as everyday as a sniffle. Probably, for her, it is. I lose all control and burst into tears. My mother looks at me, momentarily shocked out of her confusion, and starts crying too.

'I'm sorry for everything I've put you through,' she says.

It is like being branded.

We hold hands.

We cry in communion.

The consultant averts her gaze.

Later, a junior doctor comes to attend to my mother. A British Indian like me, though a generation younger. In the parallel universe immigrants and their offspring drop into from time to time, to affect, spook and on occasion torture ourselves, I might have been her. A more conventional kind of dutiful daughter. A doctor. A speaker of mother tongues. Edward Said calls this capacity to inhabit two spaces at once 'the contrapuntal awareness' of the exile, a kind of double vision shared by refugees, immigrants, and their children. Back to Dickens and the *Bhagavad Gita*, side by side in my parents' sitting room. And there is no knowing when we might pay a surprise visit to the motherland or how long we will stay there. 'Every immigrant has a second, spectral autobiography,' writes Eva Hoffman, the daughter of Holocaust survivors. In this autobiography written in invisible ink and read by no one but ourselves we tell the story of the spectral life in the motherland we never left. Where I was born in the same country as my parents. Where I speak their language. Where I know how they want to die.

I tell the junior doctor that my mother is from Bangalore.

'She grew up in the Indian Institute of Science,' I say proudly. 'She trained as a pathologist in the 1960s.' The junior doctor whistles through her teeth. It means something to her too. Then just like that she turns and starts talking to my mother in Kannada. I watch my mother magically transform into her first self on what could be the last day of her life. Her Indian self. No longer the foreigner, the immigrant, the doctor forever mistaken for the nurse, the lone mother in the sari at the school gate, but the matriarch, the cherished eldest child, the physician's daughter from Rajajinagar, the Brahmin, the pathologist, the commander of respect. She seems not only to be dying but going home. And in every possible way I cannot follow her. I can only watch, bowled over, from what suddenly feels like the other country. It is like being behind a pane of glass. I watch the two of them, dark and silver heads bent conspiratorially towards one another, nattering away. I cannot make out a word they are saying.

My mother is in intensive care for almost a week, machine-run, talking like a prophet through parched lips. In the quiet room to which one never wishes to be led, and in which I begin to feel curiously at home in those long suspenseful days fuelled by packet sandwiches and the adrenaline rush of grief, we are advised to stop her active medications. To start her on end of life care. To let her go.

One morning she is unresponsive for an entire hour. We rush to hospital in a taxi and, like characters in a Richard Curtis film – if ever such characters looked like us – get stuck in Richmond Park behind a cavalcade of cyclists decked out in all the trappings of health, wealth and Lycra. I hate them. I resent their lithe neon-clad bodies. Their freedom. The fact that not one of them is spending the morning in a race against time to see their mother before she dies. We weep and swear and rally in the back seat. We understand that we are inhabitants of another world. We overtake them.

I do the things we do to ease the passage of those we love into the country of which we will all, one day, become resident. I say goodbye, and mean it, every time I leave. I hold my mother's hand, paint the red dot on her forehead with the lipstick from her handbag, play her favourite songs, stand like a fool in the corridor calling for a doctor, small-talk with the nurses, weep openly in the street, and moronically answer the taxi driver who, after a long day at my mother's bedside, turns to me as soon as I get in the car with my father sitting in the back, and asks 'Where are you from?'

I should have answered: my mother.

I wash my hands until my knuckles start bleeding whenever I clench them. I drift down the aisles of the Sainsbury's Local beside the station as if I am a ghost haunting my own life, buying treats for the children in an attempt to stem the flow of grief. I catch the train home, travelling in the other direction this time, back to my present, as I scroll through the increasingly staggering news and try not to sit near anyone, touch anything, or breathe too deeply. The coronavirus has been declared a global pandemic. There have been more deaths. School closures are being discussed. The efficacy of masks. A national lockdown seems likely. Never before has the planet seemed so aligned with the unravelling of my own life. I walk home in mellow sunshine, floored by the magnolia trees in full bloom. By the merciless fact of renewal in nature, but not our lives. I arrive home to the flat I lived in as a teenager, rearranging my face at the door as I used to do to look sober in front of my mother, so that when it opens and my children spill out I can greet them, hand out chocolate bunnies, hear their woes and pull them onto my lap with a wonky smile.

One night I wake up and, feeling sick and dizzy, knock an entire glass of water onto my laptop. A disaster so small in the scheme of things yet so appallingly personal I actually laugh in the dark, to myself and the bright green parakeets beginning to screech their tuneless chorus in the plane trees outside. I get up, go to my parents' sitting room, with its vertical book towers and photos of the grandchildren on the mantelpiece, and email this manuscript and the transcript of all my interviews with Henry, which at this point run to more than thirty thousand words, to a separate account. Living in this darkness brings astonishing clarity. My whole life is spotlit. I can see what really matters, and the list is small, whittled down like poetry. It consists of a few people, my dog, some memories, a couple of places, writers, songs, flowers, plants and trees. It contains these words, which I have saved, and which might save me. Then I go back to bed.

The next day I email Henry, Ingrid, and their daughters. 'I feel as if we are family now, the Ramaswamys and the Wugas, and this book about us brings us closer every day,' I write, high as a kite on grief. I tell them my mother is dying. Henry and Ingrid have only met my parents once, years ago, during the interval of a morning recital at the Queen's Hall in Edinburgh. The same venue where I saw Ingrid mouthing along to Schubert.

'We remember well meeting your parents at the EIF many years ago,' Henry emails back. 'Just a short hello but so good to meet this lovely Indian couple, we were impressed.' He goes on to praise my mother's career in medicine, and acknowledge the essential and too often unacknowledged part played by immigrants in the NHS.

Finally, Henry tells me to be brave.

'You are prepared for whatever will happen,' he says. 'Be strong.'

He signs off 'your adopted grandparents, Henry & Ingrid'.

A fortnight later I feel like a storm-damaged tree. I am back in Edinburgh and to everyone's astonishment my mother has returned home. She remains confused and the delirium, like Ingrid's dementia, runs deep now, permanently fused to the motherboard of her self. She is being looked after by my father and a small band of NHS carers, all of them black women, who by day and night travel the length of unpeopled London on public transport, some for more than two hours. There is to be no more cancer treatment. The do-not-resuscitate order has been signed. There is a lot of euphemistic talk about making my mother comfortable. It is likely that I will not see her again or be able to attend her funeral.

This is because, in the meantime, we have all become inhabitants of a terrifying new world. One ruled, it seems, by an invisible airborne virus. A virus that might have originated in a wet market in China and might now be hanging in droplets on the air outside our homes, or smeared on the cardboard packaging of the deliveries left at our front doors by men in gloves who are gone by the time we get there. In this new world we paste rainbows on our windows, and our children draw in pastel chalk on the streets. We dream more and sleep less. Lockdown, social distancing, self-isolation and 'the new normal' are the lingua franca of the pandemic and overnight we become fluent. Every day the deaths of hundreds of people are announced in the UK alone. Every Thursday night we clap for the NHS on our front doorsteps, or, as the weeks go on, refuse to clap because what people risking their lives really need is more PPE, ventilators, a government willing to fund a public health system long ago cut to the bone, and fewer avoidable deaths.

Long-existing inequalities are torn wider open. People of colour die in disproportionate numbers. Refugees and migrants are abandoned as the US suspends its asylum system, Italy closes its ports and the UK refuses to take unaccompanied children from Greek island camps threatened by the virus. It becomes a cliché to say that we are not in the same boat. Climate scientists say that we have done it to ourselves. That we created the Anthropocene age, mined the seabeds and poisoned the skies, and now

202

the natural world we tried to domesticate for 12,000 years is biting back. Some predict the world will be different, better, slower, kinder, after the virus. Others fear greater unbridled nationalism. 'I don't think history repeats itself, but nor does it learn,' says the barrister and writer Philippe Sands in a newspaper interview. 'You get variations on a theme. When the coronavirus crisis is over, nationalism could be rampant. Or we could remember the lessons of the 30s; that the only way out of recession is via global solidarity and trade. Either way, we need to pay attention.'

Time seems to bend in accordance with the narrowing of our horizons. The present fans out so that the recent past, whether catching a train to hold the hand of your dying mother in hospital or going to watch your adopted Jewish grandfather give a talk at your old university, takes on the hue of a sepia photo from a lost world. Blurry and thin like the membrane of early memories. It seems preposterous that we lived like that for so long. What were we thinking? The future becomes as evocative, risk laden and best avoided as the past. There is only this; the continually unravelling present of our collective days.

Hilary has temporarily moved from London to Giffnock to take care of her parents. We talk on Skype and begin, as one does in a pandemic, with practicalities. I update them about my mother and ask after Henry and Ingrid's great-grandchildren: twin babies born three months earlier to Hilary's son and his wife. They are well, oblivious to all but the sweetness of milk, sleep and their parents. In Giffnock, Hilary is making sure that when the shopping arrives from the supermarket it is left out on their small balcony for a few hours before they bring it in. The Association of Jewish Refugees, the organisation that carried out the lengthy interview with Henry sixteen years earlier, has offered to send food parcels. The orthodox Lubavitcher rabbis sent two soups, at which point Hilary repeats 'Two soups!' in a tribute to the classic Victoria Wood sketch and the two of us share a lip-twitch in the midst of a crisis. The daily paper – *The Times*, 'Though we used to take the *Guardian*,' Henry reassures me – has been cancelled. Henry is reading the news on his computer, which he hates. The fear is that if the virus crosses the threshold of the building it will be, as Hilary puts it, a 'care-home scenario'.

'These are unprecedented times for everybody,' says Henry, seated at his computer in customary shirt and tie. 'It's so different to wartime. Wartime was wartime. We were afraid of losing the war, being in a camp, getting taken by Hitler. This is a completely different kettle of fish.' Ingrid sits beside him, not only following our conversation but contributing a little. This is unusual. In recent months during our interviews Ingrid has either sat dozing in her chair or been absent altogether at a local Jewish daycare centre where she spent two days a week. Lockdown has unexpectedly improved Ingrid's dementia. It is as though the shrinking of her immediate world has somehow cocooned her memory, just as the simplification of life that lockdown necessitates seems to benefit my son. While he is adapting to going out once a day to scoot a triple circuit of our local park with Claire, Ingrid is taking a short stroll to the end of the road with Henry, using her walker which has a seat so she can rest when she needs to. I picture this indefatigable couple shuffling down the broad leafy streets of Giffnock, dutifully keeping their distance from passers-by. I think of all they have walked together. I remember how two years earlier, when Ingrid was in hospital with an irregular heartbeat, she charmed the nurses by replying when they asked to listen to her heart, 'You can't have it. It belongs to Henry.'

'What do you want to talk about?' Ingrid asks me.

'Whatever you want to talk about,' I say. 'Your childhood. Your memories.'

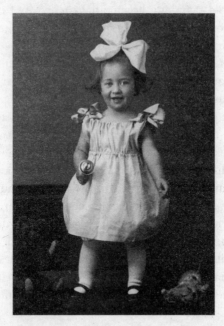

'Germany?' Ingrid replies slowly. 'I came here . . . then I can't remember what happened.' She pauses. 'It was so long ago. How did I come here?'

'You came by Kindertransport,' Henry replies. 'By train and boat.'

'Did I not come here because I had a job?' Ingrid asks him.

'No, no,' says Henry. 'You came here as a child. And the people who guaranteed for you sent you out to work. That's how you got a job. You would have liked to go to school but it didn't happen.'

'Henry, I'm not going back to anything, am I?' Ingrid asks after a while.

'No, no,' says Henry. 'You're staying here.'

Despite my only having sent it to him the previous day, Henry has already read my latest chapter, written after our encounter at Glasgow University. 'Funnily enough, my mother worked in a country club in the Catskills,' he says.

'She catered there and became the chef. A lot of German Jews who she knew from Nuremberg came as guests. She worked there for many years.'

That I have just written about the Catskills and neither known nor mentioned Lore working there after the war appalls me.

Here is the mother whose story I am struggling to tell.

'In all the languages I know it comes back to mummy, mum, mama, amma.'

My mother told me this one day in intensive care when the dialysis machine had been turned off, the monitor left blank and the lines removed from her small body. She said so many startling and prescient things in those days, each phrase as impossible to capture as the glint of light on water. Still, I tapped a few of them into text messages on my phone at her bedside and sent them to myself.

'We are mothers,' she said that same day. 'It is the hardest job.'

'Here you are,' says Hilary. While we are talking she has gone off camera and found, in Henry's files, a letter sent by Lore to her son on 24 April 1950. Springtime in the Catskills. It's on headed paper, sent from Ramble Hills Resort Club, Croton-on-Hudson, NY, complete with directions on how to get there from New York . . . 'SHARP RIGHT onto Quaker Ridge Road. Go ahead to the entrance of Ramble Hills (1 mile, just after the 2nd sign reading 'Slow Curve'.)'

The letter is two pages long, typed out in German, and signed 'Mutter' by hand. A few days later Hilary sends me a full translation. It is carried out by a distant relative called Kit, who is training to be an interpreter in Geneva but finds himself in Devon with his mother under lockdown. Kit is family, well sort of. His mother's partner, Anne, is the grand-daughter of Ingrid's uncle. When he learns about the book he asks to come on board and help with the major task of translating Lore's post-war letters. The letter, beautifully translated, is loving and upbeat; packed with news about mutual acquaintances, an inquiry as to whether Ingrid has received the copy of *Vogue* she sent, anecdotes about her 'familiar-style cooking' in the resort, films she has seen, guests she has met, and a memorable family gathering 'with Chianti and a good meal'. Lore expresses astonishment at how quickly she has become accustomed to being able to afford whatever she wants after so many years of privation. 'It's asparagus season at the moment,' she writes giddily, 'it's so cheap and you can do so much with it.' She muses about changing fashions and, in a line that almost exactly seventy years later, post-Brexit, in the midst of a global pandemic sounds like a sinister warning, observes that 'everything is going to Europe, no distance is far anymore, it's just a question of money.'

There is another translation of the letter, written years earlier by Henry. It is so abridged it amounts to just a few lines yet there is a weight to it, a truth even, that stands up to the original. Here are a mother's words distilled to their essence by her son after a war they both survived against the odds. He is picking out what matters to him. As our conversation draws to a close that morning Hilary reads out her father's translation of his mother's letter.

'The season has started. They like my cooking better than the previous chef's. They offered me more money but I asked for more help in the kitchen.'

'Typical!' Hilary laughs, and I laugh too because this lack of interest in money is also characteristic of my family.

'I feel we are coming from the same sort of place,' Henry says when I mention this. 'We are straightforward people.'

'Yes,' says Ingrid, 'but we still need looking after.'

Hilary continues to read the letter. 'Very long hours. I don't need money just to spend for doctor's bills. Bought new health [orthopaedic] shoes. Had a few days off and went to town [Brooklyn] to be with the family. I recognise some of the guests from Heilbronn and Nuremberg, all ex German Jewish refugees. My guarantors came to visit to make sure I am well and not in need of pocket money. How kind. Do you still have enough Alpecin hair tonic? I could send you some.' At this point Hilary and Henry burst into laughter and Ingrid and I, amused but estranged from the joke for different reasons, laugh along with them.

It is how Henry concludes his mother's letter that really touches me. His compressed translation closes with a variation on that most British of questions. 'How is your weather?' It makes me think of my own mother and how, after so much else has gone it is flowers that remain, pressed and dried in her book of memory. By the time she returned home from hospital, the crocuses in our local park had died back, reduced once more to flattened sprays of green leaves. Even spring perishes. But it is also true that life, in some other form, goes on. When I speak to my mother on the phone she insists I use a code word before she will agree to talk to me. The code words are all spring flowers and they change daily. Bluebell. Crocus. Magnolia. Daisy. Sometimes my sister will speak to her first and then text me afterwards. 'Just so you know sis the code word today is daffodil.'

And it is nature's capacity for self-renewal to which Lore turns, too, in the spring of 1950, after all she has been through, in a place I will not know belonged to her until after I write about it.

'We have beautiful sunshine, spring flowers, and the birds are singing,' she writes from the Ramble Hills Resort Club, deep in the Hudson Valley. 'What a yearly miracle how nature awakens.'

'She was very quiet, and very kind.'

In the final third of *Austerlitz*, Jacques travels to the Czech garrison town of Terezin to see the place to which his mother was deported in September of 1944. Theresienstadt ghetto and camp. The place from which we are left to infer that his mother was sent east. The place where up to 60,000 people, mostly over the age of seventy, were held at any one time, the majority of whom were sent to Auschwitz. The place where Henry's maternal grandmother, Helene Würzburger, died.

'On my way to Terezin,' Austerlitz begins, 'I could not imagine who or what I was.'

In another book this trip might constitute a reckoning, even some form of closure. In *Austerlitz*, as in life, it only further disorients him. As soon as Austerlitz gets off the train at Lovosice station, he is struck by how hidden, almost sunken in the landscape the town is, how empty and deserted are its streets. He stands outside an enormous junk shop, the Antikos Bazar, which is closed (and which now frequently haunts my dreams), and ponders the meaning of the mementoes stranded in the window. He lists them at length, arrested by these 'objects that for reasons one could never know had outlived their former owners and survived the process of destruction'. Everything in Terezin disturbs him. He finds the 'silent facades' of the houses 'extraordinarily oppressive' and follows up this observation with a series of photographs of closed gates and doorways, each one 'obstructing access to a darkness never yet penetrated'. At the Ghetto Museum, Austerlitz is overwhelmed by the history of the Holocaust, which he is beginning to understand is part of *his* history, too. 'I understood it all now,' he says, 'yet I did not understand it'. The mood of this section is akin to the disquiet that crawls about the skin at the start of a horror film.

Later in the novel, we encounter Austerlitz working as an assistant gardener in Romford. It is more than a year since his visit to Terezin. He has had a mental breakdown, been in a series of hospitals, and is now spending his evenings and weekends reading an existing book by the German scholar and Holocaust survivor H. G. Adler. Written immediately after the war about the Theresienstadt ghetto, it was the first scholarly monograph to describe conditions in a specific camp. It is at this point that one of the most famous passages of the novel begins. Twelve pages pass before a full stop is encountered as Austerlitz relays what he has learned from Adler's autobiographical study. In slow, inexorable prose that must be pushed through as if walking into wind blasting in the opposite direction, Austerlitz describes how the people in Theresienstadt had to make do 'with about two square metres of space in which to exist . . . until they were loaded into trucks and sent on east'. He lists the work they were forced to carry out, and the high rate of infection and death in the ghetto. He describes how the people deported from their homes were led to believe 'some tale about a pleasant resort in Bohemia called Theresienbad', filled with beautiful gardens and promenades, and how they thus arrived carrying luggage filled with 'all manner of personal items and mementoes'. He describes their mental state on arrival; how they were 'no longer in their right minds', 'frequently unable to remember their own names', and almost totally unable to speak or act. He records the skyrocketing deaths, rising to 'well above twenty thousand in the ten months between August 1942 and May 1943 alone', and how every single system at Theresienstadt was directed at the extinction of human life. He describes the notorious visit by the Red Cross in the summer of 1944, which spurred 'a vast cleaning-up programme' and even a film as the Nazis sought to use the visit as a propaganda exercise. He describes how the ghetto inmates were forced to turn Theresienstadt into a temporary spa town for retirees; setting up benches, planting more than a thousand rose bushes, and turning a former cinema used as 'a dumping ground for the oldest inmates' into a concert hall and theatre. He describes how the shops were temporarily stocked and a coffee house set up 'with sun umbrellas and folding chairs'. He describes how, during this grotesque masquerade, another 7,500 inmates were sent east, 'to thin out the population, so to speak'. He describes how, on the day of the visit itself, two Danes and one Swiss official were guided through the 'sham Eldorado' to see for themselves 'the friendly, happy folk who had been spared the horrors of war'. And he describes the film made, after which everyone shown playing football, singing and cultivating gardens to a soundtrack of Jewish folk music was ultimately sent east to their death. Finally, Austerlitz manages to obtain a cassette of the film and he watches it over and over again, slowed down so each frame is grossly elongated, in the desperate hope that he might discover his mother's face amongst the inmates.

Helene Würzburger and her husband have four children: a son, Fred, and three daughters, Lore, Fanny and Jule, all of whom will survive the Holocaust. By the time Henry is born, Helene's husband has died. She is a widow, living alone in Heilbronn. 'I used to visit her in her flat every year,' says Henry. 'She lived in part of what used to be the family brewery. I remember her as a lady in a dark outfit. She was very quiet, and very kind. She loved animals, I remember. She was a very nice lady. I liked her very much.'

Did Lore ever tell Henry how she found out what happened to her mother?

'No,' Henry says. 'But they were close. We went to Heilbronn at least once a year, until my mother couldn't travel there any more. I mean, her mother was put on a transport when she was nowhere near the town . . .'

Did Henry and Lore talk much about what happened to her?

'Not a lot,' he replies. 'She told me eventually, once she was in America, I think. She said her mother was transported to Theresienstadt. That's what made me decide to go there.'

And so, on 11 February 1993, Henry and Ingrid travel to Terezín to see the place where Helene Würzburger died. Lore, by this point, is no longer alive. They are supposed to stay with a young man who lives in a tower block in central Prague but the weather has frozen the pipes, there is no water, and so he directs Henry and Ingrid to a suburb of Prague, 'a bit like Pollokshields', where they stay in a large house with a French couple who speak no English. The next day they go by car to Terezin, 'forty miles due north, an unpleasant drive on a narrow road'. The air is mired in black fog. Snow is piled high on either side of the road.

'On the way, one of these goods trains passed with those horrible wagons,' Henry says. 'In deep snow. It was horrendous. This really blew my mind.'

Just as Austerlitz getting off the train at Lovosice is struck by a field 'poison green in colour', a petrochemicals plant 'half eaten away by rust', and sycamores and chestnuts with bark 'blackened by rain', Henry and Ingrid are disturbed by the atmosphere of the town. 'Everything was terrible to touch,' Henry says. 'Oily, dirty, horrible. I said, "Why is everything so greasy here?" Apparently they were making electricity from brown coal.'

Like Austerlitz, Henry and Ingrid go to the Ghetto Museum, where, Henry says, 'the whole story is shown in all its horror'. They go to the mass graves outside the walls, 'surmounted by a huge granite Menorah'. They go to the archives, where the names of the inmates of Theresienstadt are recorded meticulously, according to what Austerlitz describes as the Nazis' 'crazed administrative zeal'.

'There in this beautiful gothic handwriting . . . all written down, recorded, was her name,' says Henry. 'Helene Würzburger. She only lasted eleven days, thank God. That is my one consolation.'

'What are you talking about?' asks Ingrid. This is the question to which all others are becoming slowly, increasingly, boiled down by dementia.

'My grandmother,' Henry replies.

'Your grandmother,' repeats Ingrid softly, looking at her husband.

'That's the kind of place Baden-Baden was.'

On the screen before me is a photograph taken in Baden-Baden during the summer of 1938. One of Henry's most precious belongings. In the photo he is standing in a kitchen, dressed in a little white hat and an apron neatly tied at the waist. He is fourteen and nearly two hundred miles from home. He is a chef's apprentice at the Hotel Tannhäuser. One of his wiry arms extends to an aluminium pot on a stove, suggesting he is about to give the handle a good shake. He wears the unsmiling expression of teenage boys through the ages; an awkward jumble of aloofness, indifference and bare-faced vulnerability. A look that has grown more endearing to me over time. It occurs to me while in the company of this photo that becoming a mother of a son has allowed me to love teenage boys. As a girl and young woman, I was only afraid of them.

Beside Henry is his boss. Chef Johann Schneider, a man shorter than his apprentice though the height of his hat just about equalises them. His expression is serious too, if a touch more at ease. The effect of this photo on me, looking at it on my computer more than eighty years after it was taken, is an unexpected detachment. Though I know one man and the other will forever remain a stranger, both seem equally opaque to me. It is a peculiar truth that people, however well we know them in life, become more mysterious when we encounter them in photographs. It is as though the exposure of their external appearances plunges their interior lives deeper into a darkroom bath from which they can never emerge. The more we look, the less we know.

Schneider's left hand also reaches towards a much larger pot. Perhaps the two of them were told to pose like this, actively performing their societal roles like the young farmer, coal carrier and pastry cook in August Sander's portraits in *People of the 20th Century*. Portraits that by the sixth volume of Sander's compendium included 'The Persecuted': a portfolio of twelve studio portraits of German Jewish men and women, mostly taken in 1938, the same year as Henry's photo, and put together by Sander after the war ended. In these stark portraits the subjects are placed at an angle, their gaze directed away from the camera, their thoughts elsewhere. In Henry's photograph, he looks straight at the lens, the reflection on his glasses resolving into two discs of bright light eclipsing his gaze.

'I wouldn't say I'm happy,' Henry says of his expression. 'I look matter-of-fact. Concentrating, not smiling.'

Baden-Baden is the grandest of Germany's spas. It has welcomed the European elite, Jewish and otherwise, to its baths, hotels, casino and landscaped parks for more than a century. Even in the summer of 1938 life in the spa town the Romans called Aquae continues to oscillate between the opposing poles of taking the waters in the day and a seat at the gambling table by night. In belle époque Baden-Baden, even an unaccompanied Jewish teenager is protected by the droplet of civility and broad-mindedness that clings as definitively to the spa town as its hot springs. So for now Henry feels safe. Despite the signs hung in the shop windows saying 'Dogs and Jews undesirable'. Despite the fact that most of the guests in the town's two Jewish hotels have fled their homes and are awaiting emigration visas. Despite the fact that the synagogue in Nuremberg where Henry celebrated his bar mitzvah last year will be destroyed in a few weeks. Despite the fact that a Nuremberg law calling for Jewish men to take the additional name of Israel and Jewish women to take Sara is about to be enacted. And despite the fact that, in just over a year, less than a hundred miles away in the village of Grafeneck, the SS will turn a sixteenth-century castle used as a care home into an extermination facility. This will be the beginning of Aktion T4, the Nazi euthanasia programme in which around 250,000 physically or mentally disabled, incurably ill and elderly people will be systematically murdered during the Third Reich.

European spa towns are richly metaphorical and microcosmic places. They are suspended in the time in which they sprang up and the deeper imperial Roman past, to which they hark back with a nostalgia drafted in neoclassical colonnades and grand entrances enveloped in stone friezes. Spa towns speak of both the privilege of the cultural elite and, because they have always been regarded as curatives for illness and disease, the fragility of the human body. In literature the spa town is both a refuge from political life and a source of memory springing from the ground as the thermal waters bubble from the earth's crust. Time progresses more slowly in these worlds unto themselves, as in Thomas Mann's *The Magic Mountain*, where Hans Castorp intends to spend three weeks in the spa resort of Davos, Switzerland, but ends up staying seven years. 'They make pretty free with a human being's idea of time, up here,' his cousin tells him when he arrives. 'One's ideas get changed.' Another old spa town features in *Austerlitz*. Prompted by his nanny Vera, Austerlitz comes to realise he spent three 'almost blissful' weeks with his parents in Marienbad, also during the summer of 1938. And just as Baden-Baden remains to Henry an oasis, however eerie in retrospect, Marienbad is depicted as a kind of sanctuary from the creeping abnormality of life to Austerlitz. A place where the spa guests radiate an 'extraordinary peacefulness' and move 'at a curiously slow place through the grounds with their drinking glasses'.

Not that the European spa town has, historically, been a destination for people like me. I have only been to one in my life, and it was in southern Japan. I was nineteen when my friend and I jumped off a bullet train in the 'European-style' coastal resort of Shirahama, making a last-minute decision to bolt for the doors before they softly closed again and the Shinkansen sped on. Mostly I remember the blinding white sands for which the town was originally named and which had in more recent years been imported from Australia following a series of typhoons. It was a long, slow, quiet day. The beach was an empty crescent so snow-white it hurt my eyes. The sea was still as a lake and hot and clouded like soup. In a tiny onsen on the land's edge, bordered by giant concrete blocks, the only person we spoke to that day held an unglazed cup of boiling sulphurous water to my lips and ordered me in Japanese to 'Drink!'. I remember wondering if it was possible that the rough cup was made of the same stone as the place out of which the water came tumbling in a smelly surge. I remember how she thought me and my friend, a white Geordie with masses of curly light brown hair, were sisters, our differences smothered in this quiet place by our foreignness.

Back in the summer of 1938, the fate of Henry and hundreds of thousands of German and Austrian Jews has just been sealed in another spa town. On 6 July, perhaps even as he and Chef Schneider are extending their arms towards their pots in the kitchen of the Tannhäuser, the meeting of the Intergovernmental Committee for Political Refugees convenes in the glamorous spa town of Évian-les-Bains on the banks of Lake Geneva in France. A conference that the Swiss refuse to host in Geneva and that will only euphemistically refer to Jews. At the luxurious Hôtel Royal, the opening address is made by the head of the American delegation, Myron Taylor, not a politician himself but a businessman and personal friend of US president Franklin D. Roosevelt. He begins with a refusal. The number of refugees allowed into America will not be increasing from the existing 27,000 a year. The tone is set, and one by one the other delegates follow suit. By the final session nine days later only one country out of thirty-two, the Dominican Republic, has offered to take a substantial number of refugees. Not one agrees to temporarily relax its immigration rules. The justifications include a fear of civil unrest, economic hardship and increased anti-Semitism if large numbers of Jews are admitted. In this pristine sphere hovering over the glittering panorama of the lake, the international response to the impending humanitarian catastrophe is not to open borders but, even as the world watches, to barricade them shut.

At the Tannhäuser, located at the impressive-sounding Sonnenplatz 1, Henry continues to cook six and a half days a week, from 7 a.m. to 9.30 p.m. There are around fifty guests in the hotel and he has to provide two meals a day for them. Mostly he works in patisserie, down in the cellar.

There is a lot of tinning, mainly French beans and goose. There are no machines, and everything must be beaten by hand. Every now and then a Jewish supervisor comes to check on him. On a Saturday, according to shabbat rules, the cholent – a traditional Jewish stew – is dished up from the coal-fired stove it was cooked over the previous day. Henry sleeps on the top floor in his own room, next door to the chambermaid. The hotel proprietors are Theodor and Auguste Köhler-Stern, whose daughter has already emigrated to Palestine. 'Hands-on people,' says Henry. 'They were not the type who sat in an office. Whatever had to be done, they were there.'

On his half-day off, Henry strolls the Lichtentaler Allee, the famous tree-lined boulevard hugging the river Oos. He goes up into the hills and is mesmerised by the fountains springing with hot water. He hangs around the famous Kurhaus casino, a neoclassical behemoth fronted with smooth white columns and festooned inside with gold leaf. The only casino in the whole of Germany, which inspired Fyodor Dostoevsky's novel *The Gambler* and was declared by Marlene Dietrich the most beautiful in the world. 'A really pukka casino,' says Henry. 'We weren't allowed in but we saw the croupiers, all dressed up. I remember little things. In this hotel we had one lady in her sixties who had to have dinner at six o'clock because at seven a taxi came to take her to the casino every night. Wow.' He laughs. 'That's the kind of place Baden-Baden was.'

He does not go into the spas. The Nuremberg law forbidding Jews from parks, restaurants and swimming pools has existed for two years but some spas, however covertly, continue to admit Jews. 'I think we were permitted to go in, this was before Kristallnacht,' says Henry, then after a pause adds, 'but no, I would not have gone into a spa.' There is no trouble, as he puts it, but he suspects this is because no one knows he is Jewish. 'I mean, a boy walking along . . . who would know?' he says. 'Of course, I didn't have a kippah on.'

In September, preparing for the Jewish festival of Sukkot, Henry helps to build a temporary hut in the hotel. A simple structure strung with leaves and harvest fruit where guests can eat and sleep. 'It is to remind Jews of being driven out of the desert in Egypt on their way to the Promised Land,' Henry explains. 'What it reminds me of is something . . . not very nice.' He tells me an orthodox Jewish couple lived in the house next door to the Wugas in Nuremberg. 'They built a sukkah in their back yard and ate in there,' says Henry. 'A friend and I . . . well, we were not nice boys . . . the maid brought the food from the kitchen to the hut, and we put a wire across it so she would trip over.'

'Daddy!' says Gillian. 'That's horrible! That's the first time I've heard that story.'

'I know,' says Henry. 'This is what boys sometimes do. Really not nice.'

This memory stands apart from Henry's other stories, in which he tends to be cast as a boy unafraid to speak the truth. Something darker pulses beneath this one, a glimpse of the unconscious impulses of the child operating within the monumental workings of history. What was the liberal German boy forced to go to an orthodox Jewish school expressing when he laid that trip wire? Was he enacting the hatred and anti-Semitism he, too, was experiencing?

'Could be,' says Henry, 'but I think I was just being an impish fourteen-year-old.'

And then Chef Schneider is 'taken away'. All of a sudden the teenage apprentice finds himself in charge of the kitchen. 'I was alone,' says Henry. 'It was unbelievable. He was my main support. I remember well, it was quite traumatic when he left.'

We return to the photograph, which in and of itself is unexceptional. What elevates its power is the historical context swirling around it like the steam rising from Chef Schneider's pot. Once the photo is located in time, like a toddler's first steps placed in a family album between the baby sitting up, straight-backed and laughing, and the child triumphantly walking and holding her mother's hand, it gathers force. It has more to say about all of us and it says it with greater conviction. John Berger wrote of how photographs quote from appearances and the length of the quotation has nothing to do with exposure time but is calculated by meaning itself. The photo of an apprentice chef and his boss in a kitchen barely illuminated by the background of white tiles is unremarkable, highly specific, and quotes so briefly as to be almost indecipherable. Then you read the caption, and the meaning unfurls like a scroll. You understand the significance of what you are seeing. The image remains the same but its universal value has exponentially increased. The quotation, which describes middle-class German Jewish life in the run-up to the Second World War, has lengthened before our eyes.

For Henry, it quotes at length, instantly. Like the very first photographs taken a century earlier and kept, as Walter Benjamin wrote, in glass cases like pieces of jewellery, this photo is precious. It is a manifestation of his memory. 'It was not a historic moment,' he says, 'but it felt important to be photographed. And look, they gave me the original. It shows you . . . I treasured it and took it home. It is the only one from my time in Baden-Baden. Looking at it brings back tremendous memories.'

A curiosity about old photographs in particular is that they can seem to appear out of nowhere, as if they have taken themselves. Something stirs in them, wrote Sebald in *Austerlitz*, 'as if the pictures had a memory of their own and remembered us'. Unless it's the work of someone famous, we have to remind ourselves that every photograph has a photographer. Henry is convinced his photo was taken by Mr Köhler-Stern. 'He must have wanted to take a photograph of the young Jewish apprentice with his chef,' he says. 'I think he would have gone out of his way to do this.'

And when you look more closely a third person emerges, as if from deep water, in the background.

A woman standing in a darkened doorway, her torso hidden by Chef Schneider's extended arm, her presence suggesting that not only is this a moment worthy of being photographed, it is one worth witnessing too. She is smiling. Her eyes are white torches of light, like those of a nocturnal animal. She looks like she is holding a broom handle, or perhaps it's the door jamb.

Who is she?

'I think it must have been Mrs Köhler-Stern,' says Henry. 'The only other women I remember were the kitchen maids, but they were much younger. Yes, yes, it must be Mrs Köhler-Stern.'

A few weeks after Chef Schneider leaves, Henry just as abruptly decides he must go home to see his parents. He will forget what prompts the decision. A letter from his mother? Or worse, no letter? An exodus of guests from the Tannhäuser? Or an influx? A palpable change in the atmosphere of the spa town? Some sixth sense of danger? What he will remember is the conversation, which takes place in the kitchen.

The Köhler-Sterns are furious. They tell Henry he can't abandon his apprenticeship.

'You can't leave,' they tell him.

He will never forget them saying these three words. He refuses to back down. He is not asking their permission. He is telling them.

'It was a difficult parting,' he says. 'I was headstrong.'

For the first time, it occurs to all three of us that the Köhler-Sterns had no chef when Henry left. No wonder they refused to let him go.

Henry packs a small bag. He leaves most of his belongings behind in his room at the top of the Tannhäuser. He doesn't need much. He will be coming back soon. And yet, he takes the photograph given to him by the Köhler-Sterns. Probably he wants to show it to his parents, who must have given him permission to leave because the apprenticeship is unpaid, he has no money of his own, and they would have had to buy his train ticket. He will forget the journey home. He will forget whether his mother and father meet him off the train or, perhaps more likely considering the constant threat in the city now, whether the reunion takes place behind the softly closed front door of 15 Fürther Strasse. What he will remember is the date.

8 November 1938.

The day before the Reichspogromnacht.

'If I had not left I would have been taken away to Dachau with them.'

Exactly eighty-one years later, Henry returns to Baden-Baden for the first time since he left so abruptly in 1938. He has recently had a hip operation, is in pain, and is walking with a stick. He decides to go using a wheelchair to negotiate the airports, accompanied by Hilary. Gillian will stay at home with Ingrid. I will remain in Edinburgh, awaiting updates on my phone. I would never dream of asking to join them. It is a family affair, and a highly emotional trip for Henry. He will be returning to Baden-Baden having survived his operation and travelling without Ingrid beside him. My daughter is only one, I have no book deal, and though I have applied for a grant to help me write this book I have not yet heard back. I reason that there will be other chances. Now is not the time. Yet when the updates come, they bring tears to my eyes. Incentivised by regret, I start planning a trip to Berlin, where much of Henry's archive is held at the Jewish Museum. Perhaps I will go to Baden-Baden, Nuremberg, Heilbronn. I picture myself standing at the doors of 15 Fürther Strasse and Sonnenplatz 1. A mother blissfully, apprehensively alone, notebook in hand.

The day after the anniversary of the Reichspogromnacht I receive a message from Hilary.

'Wish you were here.'

Austerlitz also returns to his spa town, unaware at the

time that he went there as a boy. In the summer of 1972 he travels to Marienbad with his sort-of lover, a French academic called Marie de Verneuil, who happens to be researching an architectural history of European spas. It is a disturbing trip. In this frozen-in-time Bohemian spa town populated by sluggish staff in mouse-grey nylon coats and 'deathly still and deserted' state-owned spa hotels even the ice cream fails to melt. In the old pump room of the Auschowitz Springs, a name impossible to read without the ghost of another destination, one constructed not to cure but to kill, being evoked, Marie confronts Austerlitz and asks him why he has been 'like a pool of frozen water' since they arrived. Why does he open his mouth as if to speak but no sound comes out? Austerlitz cannot answer. Even here there is no cure for him. Instead the waters soften him further and weaken his resistance 'against the emergence of memory'.

Henry and Hilary fly to Frankfurt on 9 November 2019. They are put up by Baden-Baden's culture office in a Radisson hotel that was once a monastery. The following day is 10 November. Eighty-one years earlier, Henry was waking up in Nuremberg to a new dawn of terror. Today he and Hilary go on a three-mile horse and carriage ride along the Lichtentaler Allee. In a video Hilary sends me, Henry, dressed in flat cap, black scarf and dark glasses, cranes forward to look around at the promenade he strolled on his half-days off. The soundtrack is the rounded beat of hooves on the path. The trees lining the boulevard are aflame with late autumnal colour, throwing their confetti of leaves to the ground as the carriage passes slowly. The Allee is empty save for a lone cyclist pedalling in the opposite direction. The river Oos is a passive stripe of bright green.

Lunch is at the Kurhaus, the 'really pukka' casino where Henry once watched the croupiers. In the evening he speaks as a guest of honour at the commemoration of the Reichspogromnacht in the town hall, originally the Jesuit college. In German, wearing a kippah, he talks about the time he spent in Baden-Baden before the war, and his memories of the Tannhäuser. He recalls how one day the Lichtentaler Allee and iconic Brenners Park Hotel, which still presides over the avenue, were closed off by the police and he swears he heard the name 'Daladier' – the prime minister of France at the time – spoken on the streets.

'Was this during the Munich crisis when Czechoslovakia was "sold" to the Nazis?' he asks the audience. 'Were there meetings in Baden-Baden?'

There is no one there who can answer.

Afterwards, everyone heads down the hill to the town's Holocaust memorial. The candlelit walk is accompanied by a trio of musicians playing John Williams' main theme from *Schindler's List*. At the memorial there is an address by a rabbi and a minute's silence. A wreath is laid at the stone, which is carved with the words 'Das Geheimnis der Versöhnung liegt in der Erinnerung'. Back in Edinburgh I translate the phrase laboriously so each word emerges on its own, as it was once chiselled in stone.

The
Secret
of
Reconciliation
Lies
in
Memory

A famous photo was taken in Baden-Baden during the Reichspogromnacht. It is of a procession of around eighty Jewish men arrested during the twenty-four-hour orgy of violence and destruction. The men are being forced under Nazi guard to parade up a street. Theodor Köhler-Stern must be amongst them, and had he not left two days earlier Henry would be here too. In the foreground a car bearing an SS licence plate crawls alongside the display of public humiliation. Spectators line the street. In the middle distance a young boy runs alongside the men, a bystander in flight. Perhaps he is shouting anti-Semitic taunts as he goes. On a grassy bank a woman in a hat surveys the scene, her hands clasped in front of her. Beside her a man kneels to take a photo. After this captured instant, the men were marched to the synagogue on the street that runs off the Sonnenplatz. More crowds assembled and people jeered as they were forced to enter the synagogue without head coverings, sing Nazi songs and recite passages from *Mein Kampf*. They were beaten. Then the synagogue was set on fire and most of the men were deported to concentration camps.

'If I had not left I would have been taken away to Dachau with them,' says Henry.

After the Reichspogromnacht, the Jewish hotels, businesses and shops in Baden-Baden were forced to close. Across Germany, annexed Austria and areas of Czechoslovakia, those who survived Dachau, Buchenwald, Sachsenhausen and other concentration camps were permitted to return home some months later. The men who obtained release did so on the condition that they emigrate. Still, the Köhler-Sterns stayed in Baden-Baden.

Until the following year.

In October 1940, Baden-Baden's remaining Jews were deported to Gurs in southwestern France. Theodor and Auguste Köhler-Stern were amongst them.

In 1942 the couple were sent east and murdered in the gas chambers of Auschwitz.

After Henry left their hotel on 8 November 1938, he neither saw nor heard from the Köhler-Sterns again. He only learns what happened to them when I tell him after he returns from his second trip to Baden-Baden in the late autumn of 2019.

'I knew the Jews of Baden-Baden were taken away to Gurs,' he says. 'I did not know Mr and Mrs Köhler-Stern perished in Auschwitz. That they . . . well, I suspected.' He pauses. 'When I think back, I couldn't write to them to say I'm not coming back. It [the Reichspogromnacht] just happened. It was . . . immediate. It was horrendous. I assumed they were just taken away.'

Ten days after the Reichspogromnacht, on 20 November 1938, a final communication was sent to Henry from Baden-Baden. Not by the Köhler-Sterns, but by their ex head chef, Johann Schneider. A reference. A letter on a torn scrap of paper, beautifully handwritten at 6 Eichwaldstrasse, Baden-Baden, that would a few decades later help secure Henry's kosher licence from the religious authorities in Glasgow. Henry has no idea what Schneider was doing back in Baden-Baden nor what happened to him afterwards. He never heard from him again.

'Heinz is an intelligent young man and has already gained good knowledge and skills in cuisine and patisserie,'

wrote Schneider. 'He was very diligent, and I was pleased
with all his work. I issue this certificate as chef de cuisine
with 20 years' experience at the Köhler-Stern Hotel.'

'It was just a piece of torn-out paper signed by the
chef,' says Henry. 'But that piece of paper eventually
proved I was in Baden-Baden and I was accepted by the
authorities.'

Eighty-one years later, on Henry's final day in Baden-
Baden, he swims in the town's thermal waters for the
first and last time in his life. Before heading for the
airport they drive past Sonnenplatz 1. There on the corner
is the opulent building that was once the Tannhäuser.
The precise spot where Henry, during the summer of

1938, started to become what he would be for the rest of his life. A chef. Where he slept at the top of five elegant storeys, between which a lift trundled and up to fifty Jewish guests slept and ate and desperately tried to get out of their own country. The building is undergoing reconstruction and is completely obscured, covered in scaffolding and plastic sheeting. Even the pavement is sealed off. Henry recognises neither the street, which has long since been pedestrianised, nor the shops, which are all different. 'It did not mean anything to me,' he says. He does not get out of the car.

So neither Henry, Hilary, nor anyone else passing by, are able to see what lies embedded in the sealed-off pavement. Two small brass stones, laid diagonally side by side. Stolpersteine. The largest decentralised monument in the world. When you stumble upon one of these tiny plaques lodged in the ground by the German artist Gunter Demnig, and there are more than 70,000 of them laid all over the world, you have to crane your neck, bend over, perhaps even drop to your knees to read the words hammered into the brass.

Each stone commemorates a victim of the Holocaust outside their last known freely chosen address.

'My thoughts are always with you.'

On 3 June 2020, just after 3 a.m., my mother died. I sprang out of bed when I took the call from my father. I had been lying awake all night. My body was alert. I could see perfectly in the dark, like a nocturnal animal. My feet carried me to the window of our kitchen, which looks down our street, so that when my father said the actual words I was looking at a buddleia bush in a neighbour's garden, swaying in the winds that blow with northern conviction through Edinburgh all year round. I watched the skeletal waltz of the buddleia's branches. The long tapering blooms were like candles waving in the pale night sky. The moon was nowhere to be seen.

I thought, *I will never look at this buddleia again without thinking of my mother's death.*

It was the day before George Floyd's memorial service. The forty-six-year-old black American man was killed on 25 May in Minneapolis by a police officer who held his knee to his neck until he died. Floyd's dying words were 'I can't breathe', which according to transcripts later released to the public he repeated more than twenty times. By the time of my mother's death just over a week later these words had risen up into a howl of pain, a rallying cry and a mantra of centuries-old black oppression. Black Lives Matter protests swept the world, peaking just after my mother's death into one of the biggest movements in history. Everyone, everywhere, it seemed, was talking about what we grew up never talking about. Or, perhaps, finding a novel way to not talk about it. While I phoned a Hindu priest to ask for a local recommendation for funeral directors experienced in dealing with the deaths of Indians, in dressing the bodies of women in saris and drawing the kumkuma in the right place between the eyebrows, my social media feeds were flooded with a procession of black squares. It was the most tender and brutal postscript to my mother's death.

Four days before she died I travelled from Edinburgh to London to say goodbye to her at home. The decision was made on the spur of the moment after another call came from my father. The district nurse had visited. 'If her children want to come, now is the time,' she said. It was Friday. A major scandal had just broken in the country, which was still under national lockdown, as it was discovered the UK prime minister's most senior advisor, Dominic Cummings, had driven 260 miles with his wife and son to visit his parents. His wife had had Covid-19 symptoms at the time. Shortly afterwards Cummings, too, fell ill. There was no apology. Both he and the prime minister maintained that he had acted reasonably. The national mood was one of outrage and the deep pain caused by the irreparable injuries of injustice, racism and grief. The old wounds reopened. All of us who had followed the rules, who had not seen the people we loved who were dying, who had resisted all the normal impulses in abnormal times, were heartbroken. It was so personal. The contempt was absolute.

I bought a train ticket. A neighbour gave me spare masks and gloves. I wore them in the taxi to Waverley, which was like a station in a model railway set. Completely empty. Steeped in a narrow valley, between times. Crafted out of stone, glass and crisp morning light.

I wore them on the train, where the only other people I saw were the cleaners, all of them black men, who patrolled the carriages with hand sanitiser, wiping down the tables and arm rests on the hour. I wore them in the taxi from King's Cross, whizzing south across the city faster than ever before in my life, the windows wide open to the empty summer streets. I wore them when I arrived home, to the council flat overlooking the stretch of the Thames where the boat race finishes. I wore them when I briefly met the woman who was caring for my mother that day and stayed in another room, my old bedroom, with the door closed for reasons of safety more than privacy. I wore them until I pulled down the mask to eat one last meal with my parents. I wore them until I peeled off the gloves to hold my mother's hand one last time.

The same driver, from the cab company my parents used for years to make their regular trips through Richmond Park to the hospital for my mother's breast cancer treatment, took me back to King's Cross a few hours later. I wept out of the open window, into the warm afternoon of my home city, and the tears filled my mask. The driver said everyone at the cab company was devastated by the news about my mother. He told me his brother had died a few weeks earlier back home in Afghanistan and that he never got to see him to say goodbye. We said sorry for each other's losses; his just past, mine impending, both continuously present. We drove past the vertical ruin of Grenfell Tower, shrouded in white, anointed with a green heart and the words 'FOREVER IN OUR HEARTS'. We never spoke another word to each other, but when I returned to London exactly one week later for my mother's funeral, the same driver was waiting for me outside King's Cross Station.

The funeral was in a crematorium a few minutes' walk along the river. There is no stretch of the Thames I know better than this verdant half-mile of muddy bank overlooked by twisted willows and broad horse chestnuts, Georgian townhouses, luxury apartments with balconies so tiny all they can hold is a bicycle or yapping dog, a converted seventeenth-century tapestry works where designs by Raphael, Rubens and van Dyck were once weaved by a Flemish workforce on twelve looms, and the last major brewery on the banks of the Thames. Mortlake brewery has existed in one form or another on this site since the sixteenth century. It closed only recently, in 2015, taking with it my strongest souvenir of home. The rich malty smell of hops. As soon as I got off the train, for decades, the brewery just north of the station perfumed the air for miles in each direction. A scent so redolent in its association that whenever I smell it, I am instantly happy. On my way home.

There were five of us at the funeral. Masked, gloved and pitifully grateful for the privilege of attendance. The first song was a Hindu mantra played at many Indian funerals. The last was 'Happiness' by Ken Dodd. Afterwards we walked back home along the river. It was raining lightly, which my father said was a good sign, making everything smell a little more of itself. A straggly heron stood, one leg raised, in the precise spot on the bank beneath Chiswick Bridge where a heron often stands.

We threw a few nasturtium seeds into the earth, those cheerful, plucky plants with the parasol leaves that thrive in poor soil all through the winter. When I looked at the packet I noticed that this particular variety is known as the Empress of India.

Everything is about my mother.

The seeds.

The heron.

The river.

The earth.

The sky.

None of it can bring her back.

After her death, things fall apart as they should. The nights are long and flooded with fragments. Her voice, her face, her life, her death, her hands. With images, phrases, a certain expression, feeling, or vision, as though death has activated a playback of my past, plonked me down in front of it, and someone else is in charge of the remote control. Certain sentences are engraved, and not necessarily the ones I expect. Like the questions asked by the old-school funeral director with the cockney accent whom I will never meet in person.

Personal question, love, but we have to ask: did Mum have Covid?

Did Mum wear her sari over the left or right shoulder?

And my sister and I have to scour old photos, just to be sure.

Other things start falling into place. Revelations in life's marrow, and the tragedy is the one person whom I want to tell is no longer here. 'When his life had ended I began to wonder about that life, and also, in a new way, to be apprehensive about my own,' wrote James Baldwin in *Notes of a Native Son*, about the death of his father amid the Harlem race riots of 1943. Only after my mother is gone am I able to see her life in the round. Only now have I gained the degree of compassion that apparently required this unsurpassable distance, between the living and the dead, to be born. With grief comes the lifting of a blindness I never knew was there. I begin to see in the dark. And like Gloucester in *King Lear*, the seeing makes me stumble.

I want to say, *I understand. I get it now.*

It is too late.

I say it anyway.

My mother barely ate when she first came home from hospital. On the ward she survived on little sachets of honey stirred into a plastic cup of milk. 'I'm in the land of milk and honey!' she joked as I watched her mix the concoction with a spoon. Noisily. Vigorously. The way she stirs – or must I now say *stirred* – everything. When she got home, food, along with everything else, was a problem. As the nation was panic-buying toilet rolls and every bag of self-raising flour and basmati rice in the land, my mother was refusing to eat or drink. Everyone said it was normal at that stage. We had arrived at the point where not doing the things one needs to do to stay alive was normal.

And still, I could not go to her.

I contacted my friend, Suzanna, a chef who lives in Athens. The girl who once bunked off school with me to eat Anchor cream, straight from the nozzle, overlooking the view from Richmond Hill. She loves my mother's food, particularly, when we were growing up, her legendary masala dosas. A few hours later Zan came back to me. An Indian chef with whom she once worked wanted to cook a meal for my parents. Zan used to talk to him about my mother's cooking when they were cooking together at the River Cafe. He now runs a South Indian supper club in London, or did until the pandemic put a stop to it. He said he would cook the food and send it across the city in an Uber to my father, who could come down and collect it from the driver. When I contacted him to say thank you he told me that he, like my parents, is from Bangalore. He said he knew how much we Bangaloreans love our food. He refused payment. He said he was missing his own parents, back home in India. This was the least he could do. It was his pleasure. There was no need to thank him.

When the food arrived, my mother ate a little of every single dish. Palya, chapatis, kosambari, rice and saaru, homemade pickles, and kesari bhat for dessert. The food of my mother's childhood, and mine, made by a complete stranger from Bangalore. My parents eked out the meal, as is – was? – their way. It lasted for days. It was the most literal soul food, by which I mean it brought her back to life. Afterwards, my mother got up. She returned to the kitchen. She started cooking again. Stirring, vigorously, with Radio 4 playing at ear-bleed levels and the seeds she never stopped chucking into pots – a few chickpeas, tamarind prised straight from the block – sprouting on the window-sills around her. She even ate a little of the food she made. She lived for another eight weeks.

I was not there when my mother died. None of us were. I have not been to the hospice where she took her last breath though I continue to haunt its website. I have not seen the room in which the window was opened shortly afterwards, according to the hospice's policy to allow the departure of the soul, probably even as I was standing at the window of my kitchen, watching the night waltz of the buddleia. I could not see my mother in the last weeks of her life. By the time she returned home from her springtime near-death experience in intensive care the world was going into lockdown. Those four hundred miles were, for a time, as impassable as if they were five thousand miles. The distance between London and Bangalore. All I could do was keep my phone at my bedside all night long. Make every call count. Pray for them with the embarrassment of the irreligious.

Only afterwards will it occur to me that a faraway death is a common feature of immigrant experience. Alongside the shared stories of departures, journeys, arrivals, the painfully cold winters and the homesickness, the racism and the hunt for work, the recreated recipes with whatever ingredients are to hand, and the overwhelming trips back to the homeland you no longer recognise, are the stories of loss. The dreaded phone call that comes out of nowhere, often during the night because of the time difference, confirming what you feared from the moment you left.

The calls that my parents take during my youth, informing them of the deaths, imminent or foregone, of their parents in Bangalore.

The Red Cross letter that Henry receives during the war on 28 June 1944, from his mother in Nuremberg, informing him that his father is dead.

'My loving Heinz,

'Am sad and lonely, if only you were with me. Your good Father dead, heart attack. Stay well. My thoughts are always with you.

Mutter'

'The mere power that she had.'

'This is the most unbelievable document,' says Henry. He is sitting at his desk, upon which he has propped a small postcard. A flimsy piece of card, browned like a leaf by time, sent to him by his mother on 24 May 1946. A year after the war's end. From, of all places, Switzerland. Henry gives it to me carefully and I hold it in my hands as I would cradle the soft head of a newborn. It is as light as a feather.

'Now can you imagine Nuremberg in 1946?' he asks. 'How very difficult it was to move around? This was Germany under occupation. Defeated. Quartered into four zones. But my mother was determined to go and see her sister Jule. In Switzerland! In 1946! She was one tough lady.'

Postcards are like kites dispatched to the air. Harbingers of joy. The fact of their existence, the acts of acquiring and sending themselves often matter more than the contents, which tend towards the banal. The subtext of most post-cards is their attestation, however brief and coded, of love. Their universal message is, 'Look where I was when I thought of you!'

The only image on Lore's postcard is a stamp-sized photo of a town hall in Langenthal, Bern, which is just under a hundred miles from the Swiss–German frontier. A border that persisted throughout the Second World War and afterwards became part of the French zone. A postcard without an image is foreign to me, and at first I keep turning it over and over in my hand, unclear which side I'm supposed to treat as the front. Then again a reproduction of Swiss mountain scenery would have been a complete waste of space at such a time. A time when a fifty-five-year-old Jewish woman who had survived the Holocaust in Nuremberg was writing a triumphant message to her refugee son in Glasgow from a Swiss town she had managed to reach for one victorious day. Space is at a premium in all postcards, but in this one more than most.

'The mere power that she had,' says Henry softly. He makes a fist with his shaky hand.

'She was small but she was feisty,' says Gillian, guiding her own small and feisty mother into the room. 'You certainly wouldn't argue with her.'

'Henry!' Ingrid points at the postcard. 'That was your mother?'

242

'Yes,' says Henry.

'Determination,' replies Ingrid with a firm nod.

'To the end,' adds Gillian.

And so we travel back to the year before Lore sends her postcard.

2 May 1945.

The day after the announcement of Hitler's death.

The day a photographer scales the most symbolic building in Nazi Germany, lifts his camera to the wasteland of Berlin, and in a single image of a soldier raising the Russian flag on top of the Reichstag shows the world the war is over.

The day Henry's mother writes a letter revealing that she is alive.

'Today,' begins Sebald in 'Air War and Literature', an essay derived from lectures he delivered in Zurich in 1997, 'it is hard to form an even partly adequate idea of the extent of the devastation suffered by the cities of Germany in the last years of the Second World War, still harder to think about the horrors involved in that devastation.' Destruction of such magnitude, wrote Sebald, is beyond our grasp. No description, photo, or film can suffice. Explanation, paradoxically, only smooths further layers onto the silence. And yet to abandon the attempt is to sink into the deepest silence of all.

The whole of Germany is in ruins. Its cities have been reduced to indistinguishable seas of rubble. Out of these formless oceans of chaos, the blasted facades of buildings, crumbling walls, smashed statues, iron girders, arches and the occasional shock of a church spire project into spring skies. Maps no longer make sense. Darkness prevails. The power stations have been bombed out of action. There is no city where gas, electricity and water are functioning at the same time. More than seven million people are homeless. Everywhere the displaced are on the move, mostly heading from east to west, attempting to return home, get out, or reach one of the Allied DP camps set up in the occupied zones of Germany, Austria and Italy. Arriving in Cologne two months before Lore sends the letter announcing her survival, the American war correspondent Martha Gellhorn writes that it seems less like a city and more like 'one of the great morgues of the world'.

Nuremberg was flattened four months ago, on 2 January 1945, in one of the most concentrated single bombing raids of the war. In his Zurich lectures, Sebald wrote that the city could be seen in flames from as far away as Erlangen and Forchheim – respectively twelve and twenty-three miles away. Still, Lore has remained at 15 Fürther Strasse for almost the entirety of the war. Mostly she and Karl were in the cellar. Now she has lost everything, save a bed, two chairs, her linen, some clothes, the family china, which she hid with friends, and a handful of personal belongings she sent away to the Bavarian village of Pautzfeld, north of Nuremberg, for safekeeping. Amongst them is her son's Kiddush cup from his bar mitzvah in the long ago destroyed Grand Synagogue of Nuremberg. Her home has been bombed by the Allies. Her money has been taken by the Reich Finance Ministry. Her husband has been dead for a year. Her mother, though Lore probably does not know it yet, has died in Theresienstadt. She has no relatives left in Germany. Her only child is a thousand miles away in Glasgow. Now, from an undisclosed location outside Nuremberg, she writes in French – a language she has been learning alongside English in the desperate hope of escaping Germany – to her nephew Andre Kramer in Lyon.

'My dears!' she begins. 'Today, I want to tell you I've been saved!'

Seven days later, Andre sends a telegram from Lyon to Glasgow bearing the news.

A telegram Henry will refer to as the most important communication of his life.

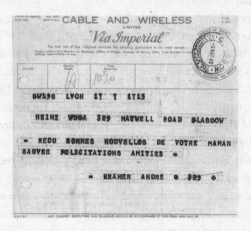

CABLE AND WIRELESS
LIMITED
"Via Imperial"

GW198 LYON 17 7 1715

HEINZ WUGA 329 MATWELL ROAD GLASGOW

= RECU BONNES NOUVELLES DE VOTRE MAMAN
SAUVEE FELICITATIONS AMITIES =

= KRAMER ANDRE = 329 =

How did a Jewish woman survive almost the entirety of the war in the heart of Nuremberg?

'It was because my father was not Jewish,' says Henry. 'He protected her. It was an "Aryan" household, so she managed.'

After Karl's death, Lore remained in the cellar of 15 Fürther Strasse until the war's final weeks, when some 'good neighbours' smuggled her out of the city and hid her in a small village. Henry believes it is somewhere near Bamberg. 'That way,' writes Lore in her brief first letter to Andre, 'the Gestapo could no longer find me.' In subsequent letters, which begin to increase in length and regularity as the year goes on, she occasionally touches lightly, swiftly, on those weeks in hiding. 'In the last few weeks, they took me into the countryside to save my life,' she writes in the summer of 1945. 'Because if we'd all stayed and not done this then we would also have been sent to the deathcamp.' On another occasion she writes: 'They took me in when I was truly on the brink, and I

245

spent 7 weeks unregistered and with no ration card. I was constantly terrified, but anything is better than dying at the hands of those Nazi scum.'

The neighbours who saved her life are the Rippels. A young woman called Fanny whom Henry used to 'cavort around' with when they were children, and her father, Mr Rippel, a postman. Like Henry's father, Fanny's mother died during the war. The Rippels, originally from Pautzfeld, are strict Roman Catholics. They are aided in their decision to hide Lore by a Catholic prelate, Monseigneur Dr Kroener, who works for Caritas, a confederation of Catholic charities which continued to operate under Nazi rule, rescuing hundreds of thousands of Jews by the war's end. 'They arranged it all,' says Henry. 'My mother was taken to a village where she pretended to be a refugee from the east. Not Jewish. And she survived.'

And so, with the permission of the American Military Commission, Lore returns home. She arrives to find Nuremberg unrecognisable and her apartment a blackened shell; 'burned down – because of the bombs'. It is uninhabitable. She is homeless. So she crosses the road, with the Rippels in tow, to 6a 11 Fürther Strasse, a small single-room flat in what she calls 'the pharmacy building'. It is directly opposite what remains of the Wugas' old bombed-out address. The third floor and rear buildings of number 17, the one next to their 'lovely large flat', she simply describes as 'gone'.

'When I think of all our lovely things, there is nothing left . . .' she writes. '[T]he country is too much of a wreck. Two wars, and I can see what's become of Germany, nothing but ruins.'

Number 6a 11 is neither empty nor hers for the taking. It is occupied by a woman. Lore drives her out. 'After a great odyssey I've managed to get this Nazi propaganda wife out of her apartment,' she writes. 'God helps those who help themselves. It certainly wasn't easy, but I, of course, was used to managing things myself.'

'Wow,' says Henry. 'She literally went to this Nazi woman across the road, said "I'm going in, and you're going out. You have done enough." She chased that woman out of the flat and moved in with the Rippels.'

'But where did that woman go?' asks Ingrid.

'I have no idea,' replies Henry, exasperated. 'My mother got rid of her!'

'She also had to have somewhere to live,' Ingrid insists.

'It did not worry her,' says Henry.

The newly acquired habit is for people to write their temporary addresses in chalk on the ruins of their old homes so their letters will, in theory, find them. Lore does this but still so many, especially the food parcels, go missing. Delays bend and twist time. The following summer, out of the blue, Lore will receive a wartime Red Cross letter sent by Henry two years earlier.

Every day she is confronted by what she has lost. 'Often, as I go downstairs, I see how my home is buried,' she writes the following spring, 'the place I spent so many happy years with father and son. All that is gone now, forever.' The might of her grief is matched only by her desperation to get out of Germany. To see her son. On the last day of August 1945, the same month the world's first atomic bombs are dropped on Hiroshima and Nagasaki, Lore asks: 'when will I finally achieve my one wish to see you, alive, to be fulfilled when it isn't even possible to receive a letter?'

Still, she continues to write. In twenty-seven letters mostly typed and sent from Nuremberg's railway post office over the course of a year, Lore alludes to what she has endured with extraordinary frankness, insight and restraint. 'Staying behind, totally alone, in a country where people had forgotten how to be decent human-beings,' she writes in the winter of 1945, 'with the spectre of death ever before your eyes just because you were born into a different cradle, one that was despised in the 3rd Reich.' She is acutely aware of the magnitude of her people's suffering: 'When you weave together the fate of each individual, it is an unmeasurable catastrophe.' History may still be making itself but already Lore understands that neither she nor the world will ever be the same again. 'We will never get past the anguish of these sinister times,' she writes. 'I know that I will never forget, because alone, I will never truly have a home again.'

At the same time, Lore remains grounded in pragmatism. Her letters are full of the granular detail of life in post-war Nuremberg. She chides Henry for worrying about her. She writes that she has no need of vitamins or medicine because her real disease is homesickness, not for a country but for her child, 'and there's no medicine for that', though she would appreciate some tea and cocoa. Her incredible fortitude is front and centre of the torrent of letters she taps out on her cherished typewriter, which survived the war alongside her in the cellar. 'I am perfectly able to earn my own living at any time,' she writes of being on her own. 'I have proved that throughout my life.'

The recurring motif of the letters, in which I immerse myself in the weeks following my own mother's death, is grief. Grief for the loss of her home, her country, her past, her future, and above all, her husband. The death of Karl, who stood by Lore when so many other mixed marriages ended in the abandonment of Jewish spouses, is simply insurmountable. She will never get over it. Her grief is 'a scar that will never heal'.

'He should have lived to see this after all the hard years,' she writes. 'I will never be able to overcome the hurt. Alone this is a life without meaning. He and I fought through so much together, he should have lived through this war.'

I understand, only now, how death breathes into Lore not just despair, but clarity, urgency, life.

'Life is so short,' she writes to her son, 'it seems like minutes so, dear children, make the most of every single hour. Spare each other heartache. Be happy and carefree.'

By this time Germany has been divided by the Allies into four temporary zones of occupation. Nuremberg is in the American quarter, covering 41,000 square miles and encompassing the whole of Bavaria. As winter approaches there is a ration cut and across the country, the health and food situation continues to deteriorate, the water supply is polluted, there are chronic medicine shortages and tuberculosis rates soar. Still Lore manages to keep fresh flowers on her bedside table, picked, perhaps, from the ruins as over time the rubble is reclaimed by nature. Next to them she places photos of her husband and son so she can see them first thing in the morning and last thing at night. She looks forward to parcels 'like a child at Christmas' and cries tears of joy when she opens them. She passes on gifts to those who remained loyal to her and turns away from those who were 'too cowardly to remember me before'. She has no money, and explains that after Karl's death she was forced to give up the stationery business, 'giving away the goods and inventory at cost prices, and I didn't see the money'. Instead the funds went into a secure account supervised by the Reich Finance Ministry and Lore was permitted 150RM for living costs, 'which of course was not sufficient because so many marks went on gifts to keep my head above water'. '[E]veryone,' she bitterly notes, 'had to be handsomely rewarded in order to help me in some way'.

20 November 1945. A freezing cold day where beneath tarnished skies the Nuremberg trials begin at the Palace of Justice. A dark pink sandstone building scarred with bullets and shell-holes, further along Fürther Strasse. For the next ten months this is where twenty-two high-ranking Nazis will be tried in a wood-panelled courtroom darkened by the permanently drawn heavy green curtains to allow filming. Hundreds of lawyers, judges and journalists from Europe and America descend on the medieval city to witness the making of history. All the world, it seems, is watching Nuremberg. It is the first time state leaders have been put on trial before an international court. The charges brought against them – crimes against humanity and genocide – are as newly invented as the freshly painted walls of the courtroom. There is a sense that the events playing out in this intimate room, however disproportionate to the unconscionable crimes on trial, are critical to the future of humanity.

And yet in the twenty letters written over the duration of the trials, on the same street where they are unfolding, Lore does not mention them once.

The letter *she* sends on the opening day of the trials is about a historic occasion too. The kind that plays out in the shadows. The past we all live with; recorded, if at all, not in court transcripts, sketches and newspaper reports but conversations, letters, photographs and, in our endlessly refreshed present, emails, text messages and social media feeds. Family history. It is in this extraordinary letter that Lore, returning to the previous year, describes for the first time the final moments of Henry's father's life.

'It was the morning of 29th April at half-past 5,' she writes. 'I heard father wheezing 3 times and thought – he can't breathe, because he had his chronic pharyngitis. I turned on the light and his eyes were already half closed. He didn't speak another word. I was on the brink of madness.' Lore called for the doctor but although he lived in the next house he didn't come for over an hour. By the time he arrived, though she stresses it would have made no difference if he had come earlier, it was too late.

Though Karl's death was unexpected, Lore sensed her husband was ill. He had 'made plans' as if he knew 'his end was near'. Yet he never said anything. 'I'm sure you still remember, dear Heinz, how he never wanted to be ill and didn't want to age,' she writes, 'but his "forever young" heart stopped beating so quickly. I try to believe that this separation is just temporary. I want to believe that you meet again after death. I believe it and I hope for it, but I don't know.'

I believe it, too.

I hope for it, too.

I don't know either.

After his death, Lore started trembling constantly. A relative came and helped her with the cremation. Then, 'as I didn't know if I would still be here tomorrow', she sent the urn filled with Karl's ashes to Graz to be interred in his parents' grave. She could not bear the thought of an unkept grave when she emigrated to Britain. Instead, Karl's siblings will tend it. Her deepest wish is that one day she and Henry will visit his grave together.

Now, as the Nuremberg trials open with a reading of the 24,000-word indictment against the defendants, Lore ends her letter with the plans she is making. She intends to hitch a ride in a lorry to see some old friends. At some point she will go to Heilbronn, which now is 'one big pile of rubble' with 'half the population . . . dead'.

Lore closes with a promise. 'As soon as I can I will go to the graves. I want to tidy them.'

January 1946. The start of the first post-war year. A saying is doing the rounds in Nuremberg. 'Each and every one we know, old and young, have no place to go,' writes Lore. It has been a brutal winter, and hunger levels are perilously high throughout the country. The attitude on the ground towards the Nuremberg trials, according to the German Jewish writer Peter de Mendelssohn, continues to be one of 'contemptuous indifference'. The city is blacked out at night and 'every building has burned down,' writes Lore. She is beginning to learn the fate of many of her acquaintances. 'The Muellers and their daughter didn't come back,' she writes. 'Most didn't.' The daughter of another friend, who is living nearby in the new town, came for a visit: '10 camps she was in, she has suffered terribly'. Lore has learned about the death of Henry's best friend Sigmund Mosbacher, killed in action in the last days of the war, and is heartbroken. Another old friend, Margot, who fled to England, 'has no parents left, either. They went to Riga and never returned. I know they're dead from an acquaintance.' At a local Jewish home where Lore volunteers there are two children from Belsen with their mother, 'and you can still see the suffering on their faces'.

In February, Fanny Rippel writes to her childhood friend Henry for the first time. 'Your letters speak of so much good fortune, happiness, and harmony,' she begins, 'which is of course the loveliest reward and greatest joy for your mother.' She refuses to allow Henry to thank her and her father for saving Lore's life. 'Your words of thanks weren't at all necessary. We will never be able to repay your mother for what she does for us, only God can reward her.' Henry's ears must be constantly burning, she continues, as the three of them spend all their time at 6a 11 Fürther Strasse talking about him and remembering 'wonderful past times in the garden, the courtyard, and at your house'. Fanny recalls with particular affection Henry's childhood trick of blowing up his tummy. 'How you used to make me laugh,' she writes.

Two years later the Rippels will be the sole reason for Henry and Ingrid's decision to return to Germany, briefly, to thank them in person.

'We were reluctant to go but this was important,' Henry says. 'The way we saw it, we didn't go to "Germany", we went to see the family who saved my mother's life. Our neighbours.'

He turns to his wife. 'Ingrid didn't want to go.'

'*That* wasn't home,' says Ingrid. 'Home was here. I didn't want to go back. To go to Dortmund where I grew up? No. Dortmund is not home.'

'But it's a different kind of country now,' says Henry. 'I admire them for how they deal with the Holocaust. They face it straight on.'

Did they talk about what they had all been through when they got together with the Rippels?

'You just didn't,' Henry says. 'We got on with our lives . . . but we never denied who we were. Some people said to me "I am no longer a refugee" and I said "Okay, that's your decision."'

'I've never denied I'm Jewish,' says Ingrid, 'and from the continent. But now I'm a Glaswegian.'

'If someone asks me where I'm from, I answer "I am from Glasgow",' says Henry. 'If they dig deeper, I say I'm a refugee. I was driven out by Hitler. I'm Scottish by adoption. I belong here.'

Did they want to talk about it, back then?

'No!' answer Henry and Ingrid at once, in a single voice.

In 1946, as the case for the prosecution rumbles on at the Palace of Justice, Lore's word remains 'worthless'. She is 'at odds' with the Finance Ministry, who continue to demand 'X-hundred' RMs in tax from her. 'I truly have nothing but losses to speak of from the Third Reich,' she writes, 'but that doesn't seem to be verifiable.' On 8 March, the day the defence begins its case, Lore writes that she is being 'left behind. Perhaps running for my life like that wasn't really worth it. A life of nothing is not worth living.' The following week, she marks a year since the bombs destroyed her home by taking two sleeping pills 'in celebration' to switch off her thoughts.

On 23 March, she meets a British soldier called Sergeant Walter Stern. The encounter clearly moves the young Jewish Englishman because he writes to Henry the very same day. 'I have had the pleasure today of meeting your mother,' he begins, 'and it is indeed a pleasure to meet somebody who, after so much suffering and fear and oppression, has preserved so courageous and wise and moderate an attitude'. Lore looks 'well and youthful', he assures Henry, and is on good terms with a number of neighbours, 'none of them former Nazis'. Unfortunately Lore's attempts to apply for emigration to Britain are so far thwarted because 'no British authorities have been set up in Germany as yet to deal with such applications'.

Spring comes to Nuremberg. The old town looks terrible, Fanny writes, 'and becomes a ghost town after closing time'. She lists a few of the familiar landmarks of her and Henry's childhood together that are gone: a local Bratwurstglöcklein, several churches including the iconic St Lorenz, whose towers 'are at least still there as an old landmark'. Fanny writes that you can easily count the people living in the centre of the blasted old town. On Fürther Strasse there are streetlights and the trams are running, but Lore rarely goes out in the evenings 'because it's so unsafe'. Letters continue to get lost in transit and Lore writes wistfully of the oranges and home baking described by Henry that never arrived. She does, however, receive a food parcel from her son containing a pipe and tobacco for Mr Rippel, and a fish, which the three of them devour for dinner, thinking 'lovingly of you with every bite'. 'He uses it enthusiastically,' Fanny writes to Henry of the pipe, 'making sure it smokes away, and proudly explaining where it came from.' As for Lore, like her son in Glasgow, she is 'always cooking'.

24 April. Lore has a plan. She wants to go to Switzerland to see her sister, even though she cannot get a return visa and without it she cannot enter the country. 'A real wish for me,' she writes, 'but who is interested in our heartache?' She goes to her first Seder in many years on Wielandstrasse with a few others and develops such crippling stomach cramps that after an hour she has to leave. 'Those sort of days make you remember even more,' she writes, 'and it makes the loneliness yet more painful.' She airs out the few items of Karl's clothes she has managed to keep for Henry: two pairs of grey trousers, a blue shirt, three 'very good' coats, underwear and two pairs of pyjamas. Tomorrow she has to pay yet another visit to the authorities. A gas and electricity bill has arrived for 15 Fürther Strasse, in which she has not lived for a year. 'The lodgers, who have since run for the hills, are the ones who used it and now I am to pay,' she writes, referring to the period when she went into hiding. She will go and explain but she is done with arguing. She wants only to be at peace.

Her Switzerland scheme continues apace. Though every zone of Germany is 'hermetically sealed' and it is exceptionally hard to even get a temporary pass for the French sector, which Lore will need to bypass to get to the border, she has somehow managed to procure one. This is nothing short of astonishing. Even the world-famous investigative journalist Rebecca West struggles to move between occupied zones when she arrives in Nuremberg four months after Lore's trip, to report on the end of the trials. West and a US correspondent land in Berlin only to be told to fly back to London as the British authorities have no idea how to get them three hundred miles south to Nuremberg. Nevertheless West, like Lore, finds a way.

'This is my current daring plan,' writes Lore on 14 May. 'I shall just go straight to the border and try to get a pass for one day. Someone over there will be merciful and telephone the Kramers and tell them to come to the border immediately.' It makes Lore tremble to think about it. The very idea is taking a toll on her nerves. Still, she will go, and the Rippels will help her. 'We are now doing everything we can to get her to Switzerland for a short while,' writes Fanny. 'We're hoping to try a border pass, and then your auntie will have to come to the border. Let's hope for the best.'

A few days later Sergeant Stern writes to Henry again, this time from St Albans in England. He has left Germany, and this letter paints a very different picture of Lore's health to his previous one. She has a cardiac disease, writes Stern, 'and during the time when she suffered persecution it must have been rather bad'. He thinks Lore should get a medical certificate, which will assist her application for emigration, 'as a "person with no relatives left in Germany, in need of care and attention on account of impaired health"'. Stern's concern is that Lore might decide to emigrate to the US, 'as German emigrants in her position to that country are already leaving Germany at this moment'. If she does, warns Stern, 'she would in all probability bar the road to Britain forever'. He has posted some items Lore gave him to hand on to Henry. An embroidered blanket for Ingrid, which he describes as a tablecloth. And 'your baptismal chalice'.

So this is how Henry's Kiddush cup is returned to him.

Stern also discusses the obstacles to Lore's forthcoming trip. In present-day Germany, Stern continues, 'a comparatively modest undertaking like this is fraught with difficulties'. He explains that ration coupons are not valid in different zones and there is no provision for travelling coupons so Lore will have to take her own food and drink for a trip that could take days. There is no counting on hotel accommodation and though train timetables exist they are 'not worth the paper on which they are stencilled (I don't think they have got into print yet)'. He concludes that 'your mother is fully alive to all the difficulties but is prepared to risk them in the hope of achieving a meeting with her sister'.

And she does.

Lore's next communication is the postcard I hold in my hands.

'You will be amazed to get this card,' Henry translates slowly. 'I really am in Switzerland! Overjoyed to talk to Auntie Jule for a day. Getting here was a long story indeed, I will tell you later. It is the land of milk and honey here! If only I didn't have to go back. Hopefully there will be post from you. I gave Mr Stern a swaddle blanket as a birthday present for you, dear Inge, and for you, dear Heinz, your cup. As a thank you I gave Mr Stern a doll for his little daughter. Warm wishes and kisses to you and regards, Inge, to your parents. Yours, Mother.'

The land of milk and honey.

The exact words my mother used to describe being in hospital.

Weeks before she died, she was lying in bed on the ward.

The last hospital room in which I saw her.

She had just come out of intensive care.

She was altered.

She was herself.

She was dying.

She was alive.

She was a miracle.

She stirred a sachet of honey into a plastic cup of milk. She said, 'I'm in the land of milk and honey!'

Days after Lore sends her postcard, Jule and her husband will emigrate to America. The couple have been through their own ordeal. They were deported on a transport from Heilbronn to Gurs, and survived the war by escaping to Switzerland. Now Jule has managed to see her sister. Now she will leave Europe for good.

One year after the Switzerland trip, Lore will finally emigrate to Scotland. For two years she will live in a flat close to Henry, Ingrid and Ingrid's parents on Maxwell Road in Glasgow. She will never be granted permanent residency by the Home Office. And for reasons too deep, inarticulable and even unknown to herself after all she has been through, Lore will not be able to settle in Britain. On 6 June 1949 she will leave to join Jule and her brother-in-law in New York, taking the time, of course, to pen a long letter to her son during the voyage across the Atlantic on the SS *Washington*. On the 'wonderful ship with very beautiful sitting rooms', Lore will rent a lounger so she can sunbathe on deck. In Le Havre, where the ship moors, she will be welcomed 'by glorious evening sunshine'. She will sleep in a 'lively' though 'rather puritanical' dormitory with ten women on the ground floor from all over the world. The women are Greek, Indian, Belgian, French and English. And as Lore will later put it in her future home in New York, 'international' is 'where life is best'.

In New York, Lore, Jule and her husband will live together for twenty-five years in an apartment on Ocean Avenue, Brooklyn. The flat is opposite Prospect Park, where Lore will refuse to sit on the benches 'with the other old people', preferring to take a train to the Rockefeller Center for a coffee, or go alone to the beach. Lore will become a chef in the Catskills and later work in a New York deli. She will become an American citizen. Every year she and her son will take it in turns to fly overseas and visit one another. Lore will send enormous parcels filled with matching clothes, knickerbockers, exotic American candies and Hershey bars to her granddaughters in Glasgow. With distance, the relationship between mother and son will knit together once more.

In 1976 Lore's sister Jule will die. Henry will go to Brooklyn to fetch his mother and take her home with him. Back to Glasgow. And so, for the final three years of Lore's life she will live with her son and his wife at 32 Dalkeith Avenue, out of which Henry and Ingrid will run the biggest kosher catering company in Glasgow from their kitchen. Lore will be present for Hilary's wedding, though by this point she will have 'a little dementia', and when her granddaughter walks in wearing her wedding dress she will say, 'Are you going somewhere nice?'

A year later, Lore will die, aged eighty-nine, in Glasgow's Victoria Infirmary of a heart attack.

She will be buried in the Jewish section of Henry and Ingrid's local cemetery.

Why did Lore leave Britain for America?

'It's very sad but true,' says Henry. 'She came here and we made her very welcome but we couldn't accommodate her in our flat. There wasn't any room for someone else. I think she felt a bit left out. She wanted to get work but it was difficult. She never got permanent residency. She worked for a friend who made stuffed animals for a while. She ate with us every night and we went to the cinema and the opera together.' Henry pauses. 'I can understand it . . . she didn't like the idea . . . I left her a fourteen-year-old boy and all of a sudden . . .'

Ingrid, who is listening intently, finishes Henry's sentence. '. . . he was a married man.'

'She liked Ingrid as a person but not as a wife,' says Henry. 'She secretly made connections with her sister in America and after two years she left. It was a shame.'

'I think she needed to be independent,' says Ingrid.

Despite Lore's promise in the postcard to tell Henry the long story of the trip later, there is no account of it. In her next letter she writes that '[m]y trip to Switzerland is still fresh in my mind like a fairy tale, you can achieve so much with an iron will. 10 horses couldn't have stopped me'. A month later she begins another letter with a complaint that 'you still don't have my account of the trip to Switzerland. It's been weeks now.' Eventually, she gives up: 'So you never received my account of the trip to Switzerland,' she writes in August, 'what a shame, but perhaps I'll soon be able to tell you in person.'

I scour the letters again, obsessed with this phantom account which neither Henry, Hilary, nor Kit, who is translating the letters for me, recall seeing. Kit is now in Geneva, working on the letters near the Red Cross headquarters through which Lore's precious wartime words once passed. 'It's funny to think of being in the same places, even the same buildings, where Lore's letters to Henry were dealt with,' he says. 'I feel like I got to know her as I was translating her letters. They are so expressive and open. She was a formidable person.'

The letter is gone.

Yet it exists for me now. I can even see Lore typing the words out at 6a 11 Fürther Strasse. I can picture the backdrop of trees screening the ruins during the baking summer of 1946 in Nuremberg. I can imagine the stench rising from the rubble bristling with flies. I can sense the relief uncoiling in Lore's belly for having achieved the impossible. Also the fear that sometimes, paradoxically, comes after the fact. I can see the keys striking the thin paper, one by one, letter by letter, setting out her elegant and decisive prose.

The first day of July 1946, a month that will be dominated by the summing up of the defence counsel at the Nuremberg trials. Lore's gaze is fixed on her future in Britain. Her 'whole life is waiting' for the arrival of her papers from Bonn, where she was required to apply for emigration. She has no passport, but she has managed to get a legitimation card and registration certificate photocopied and certified by a notary. Constantly, she witnesses people she knows leaving for America. When she finally gets a letter back from Bonn it is a request for more papers. Lore is running out of courage. 'Why, I ask myself, time and again, are they making it so difficult for those of us who already had such an ordeal in the Third Reich? Where are the laws of humanity? It is hardly a surprise that after 7 long years of missing your child, your only wish is to at last be reunited. Even more so with the lonely, joyless life I lead here. But the big wheel of world history seems to be mercilessly crushing that too.'

That same month Rebecca West arrives in 'the heart of the world's enemy' to report on the Nuremberg trials for the *New Yorker*. Now in its tenth month, the courtroom, she writes, 'is a citadel of boredom'. She likens the corruption emanating from the defendants in the dock to the smell of the old town that 'sometimes rises from the rubble where one of the thirty thousand missing Nurembergers has not fully reacted to time and the disinfectant spray'. She compares the hysterical atmosphere of the British section to 'that timeless institution, the Indian hill station', evoking the spirit of colonialism in occupied Germany a year before India gains independence.

The end of the war and the decolonisation of my parents' country yoked together, even at the time.

At night, writes West, lights burn in rooms 'that balance crazily on twisted towers rising from the plains of rubble'. In one such room on Fürther Strasse Lore remains, feeding thoughts and plans into her typewriter, and rarely going out during the baking heat of the day. Outside, the trees on Rosenaustrasse hide the ruins 'so there is some green after all'. One Sunday, Lore goes swimming in Langsee, a deep natural lake ringed with trees on the outskirts of Nuremberg where Henry and 'Mosch', his late best friend Mosbacher, used to go when they were young. 'I wasn't allowed to go for so many years,' writes Lore. 'All illegal. And I so love swimming.'

Occasionally she visits friends, but the main difference to her improving health is her liberation. 'At night, we can now go to bed without panic or shaking,' Lore writes, 'and the impact has been just immeasurable for me.' She asks after Peter, Henry and Ingrid's cat, bitterly noting that animals are more faithful than people. She recalls how 'dear Grandmother was known all over Heilbronn for being good to animals. Yet she died so alone and so sad.'

It is the first mention of her mother, Helene Würzburger, in her post-war letters.

The following month Lore confesses that 'thinking of Heilbronn scares me'.

Years will pass before Lore will be able to tell Henry what happened to her mother.

The justices come together to discuss a verdict. The days shorten, and the leaves begin to fall from the trees and blanket the rubble. Lore is starting to lose faith in the British government. She has received a request for papers from Bloomsbury House, the London hotel taken over by the Refugee Children's Movement during the war. Of course she cannot send them. Her papers are still in Bonn. The maddening levels of bureaucracy are causing her distress. 'All I want is some peace and quiet at last,' she writes. 'The past years have worn me down so much that I'll struggle to find a way forwards if I have to spend much longer here.'

Still, she writes her name on all her suitcases.

Makes long lists of contents.

Packs her remaining crockery and china for shipping.

Cleans out a large metal trunk.

18 September. The day after the judges at the Nuremberg trial decide to postpone the verdict for a week. Lore still has no visa but is hearing rumours that sixty people a month are being permitted to go to England. She is travelling regularly to 'the Joint' in Munich, the central Jewish agency assisting Holocaust survivors in Germany, Austria and Italy, and is looking into departure routes. Luggage restrictions are likely to be an issue, 'so I'll just do what we did in the bomb shelters – we wore as much as we possibly could to save the essentials. We could hardly move.' She has had a canvas duffle coat made and 'will stuff in whatever I can'. About one item in particular she is categorical: 'I will definitely bring my typewriter.'

Finally a response arrives from Bonn. Lore should receive an answer to her application for emigration 'in a number of weeks'. She gathers around ten cases. Two men help her pack her china. 'It's our most valuable service,' she writes. 'I just don't want to throw away everything that reminds me of the wonderful but so few years we spent together.'

21 September. The court is adjourned. Also suspended in time, Lore awaits a response from Bonn. She smokes an English cigarette while she writes to her son. 'It calms the nerves,' she confesses. 'A small comfort in my loneliness.'

1 October. The final day of the Nuremberg trials. A morning shrouded in fog, like the metaphorical opening of *Bleak House*. Reporting on the closing sessions, West sees at once the inadequacy of the verdict and its historic achievement. 'The law tries to keep up with life,' she writes. 'It never quite succeeds but it is never very far behind.' The afternoon session, during which twelve of the twenty-two defendants are condemned to death, seven receive prison sentences, and three are acquitted, lasts just forty-seven minutes. 'Then the court rose, rose up into the air, rose as if it were going to fly out of the window.'

23 October. Lore's verdict comes at last. Her application for a visa to enter Britain has been accepted. She is 'walking around in a dream'. The joy she feels is 'indescribable'. She will take every single item she has salvaged with her 'because afterwards', she notes in a clear-eyed imagining of her future refugee status, 'I will be poor and won't be able to make money.' Her possessions matter more with the passing of time and, she predicts, with the crossing of borders. 'You so need what little you have left,' she writes. Whatever happens, her typewriter will accompany her. 'It has become', she writes, 'my best friend.'

The letter is a single page of type that holds the weight of the moment Lore has been anticipating for years. It pulses with optimism. With faith in an unknown future in which a mother will be reunited with her son. A future where she will continue to sail forward, horizon-bound, the distance from the island of her past growing ever wider. 'I want to try and become a new person in this new country,' she writes. 'Here, you can forget nothing. In fact, we will never be able to forget, but we can perhaps at least try to move on. You will help me to do so, I'm sure.'

Yet on the flip side of the paper, the past bleeds through once again.

In a completely different tone, Lore addresses her son about a separate matter. His father. 'Dear Heinz, a few more words directed to you,' she begins. 'And this is sincere and well intentioned, because why shouldn't I speak to you about how I feel.'

'Let me explain what happened,' says Henry. 'It's so sad. As you know, my father was not Jewish. I am what the Germans called "ein mischling". A mixture.'

And so in Glasgow, one week after ten Nazi criminals are hanged in the bomb-blasted gymnasium of Nuremberg's prison, Henry is advised by people including his cousin Grete not to mention that his father wasn't Jewish. 'In the Jewish community, if you were not fully Jewish you were sort of pushed aside. My cousin said "Don't mention it here. You will only be sidelined." Unfortunately, that's how it is. So I was told not to talk about my father. And for thirty years, it simply was not talked about . . . that my father was not Jewish. Eventually I said "That's it, I'm going to state it now." And I do. It's public knowledge. But I didn't then.'

'You had a bar mitzvah, which means you are fully Jewish,' says Hilary. 'You were brought up Jewish. You *are* Jewish. And the fact is, if your father *had* been Jewish your mother and father would probably not have got out.'

'That's true,' says Henry. He pauses. 'I am fully Jewish.'

Back in 1946, Henry tells his mother that he has been instructed not to mention his father was not Jewish. Perhaps he seeks her reassurance. Perhaps he seeks to protect her. To prepare her for all the tiny negotiations and unacknowledged acts of assimilation and defiance that await in the new country. His country. Perhaps he doesn't fully understand how his words, however well-meant, might curdle when read by a Jewish woman who has seen what she has seen.

'She didn't understand,' he says. 'She was deeply hurt.'

And in a single breathtaking paragraph Lore pours her hurt onto the page.

'You say I should speak to no-one about father. My dear Heinz, do you realise how much that hurt? If your dead father, who suffered so endlessly for us, knew that was how you saw things. We, who suffered so unspeakably because of senseless racial hatred, have every reason to look beyond all prejudice. The inner value of man does not depend on the cradle in which he is born. Do the right thing and fear no-one. That was the principle in the house of your parents. For my whole life, we have never lived by judging others and I stand far above such opinions. It is simply wrong to go through life in secrecy "just" because of others. And those who care can stay away because I can do without such people. If, out there, people are concerned with such things, they have not grasped our tragedy. I hope that, with me, you will honour father. He loved you through everything and, for me, the wound of his loss can and will never heal. Do not let the reunion we have so longed for be tarnished. We want to be free, open people. Help me to find a way to forget all the pain and humiliation I have been through.'

'Your mother showed love from the saucepan.'

In the morning the news wallops you afresh.
    She is dead.

You gasp out loud while your daughter sleeps beside you. You put your hand on her rising and falling chest, and watch it turn into your mother's hand. The tears roll from the corners of your eyes and fill your ears. The days empty of all meaning. The exposure, softness and exhaustion remind you of those first weeks after the births of your children, which until now you thought were incomparable. They are not. Turns out there is a precedent for death, and it is called birth. Flowers arrive, the most enormous *living* bunches of peonies, roses, and a ficus ginseng that looks like a little womanly tree. Stupefied by loss, you cannot wait to phone and tell her you've got a tree that reminds you of her bum.

Then you remember.

She is dead.

The grief is a button, located somewhere around your heart, and pressing it is the most sublime torture. Sometimes *it* presses you, when you are cooking, walking, getting out of the bath, tickling your child's chin, watching *Gardeners' World*, waking, falling asleep, or breathing. You cannot make sense of other people's words. They are useless. You cannot hear the words other people use to describe her enough. They are the next best thing.

You make a list of them.

Warm.
Kind.
Non-judgemental.
Unusual.
Mischievous.
Clever.
Citizen of the world.
Doctor.
Gardener.
Singular.
Cook.

An old family friend who is Jewish sends a card with an image of the view from Richmond Hill in winter. She writes that 'your mother showed love from the saucepan'.

Like Lore, you think.
Like Henry.
Like you.

Now the button is pressed by saucepans. And the buddleia beyond the kitchen window when it sways with a certain rhythm. The grief is so young and strong it can withstand time itself until you realise entire weeks have passed. It has been a month. The grief is ageing alongside you, invisible like a ghost.

'It wasn't all chicken soup and chopped liver.'

It is the early 1950s and Henry is a top chef in Glasgow. His ascent through the kitchens of the city's hotels and restaurants is steep, and fast. By the time he leaves the Corn Exchange on Gordon Street in 1944, he is chef de partie. At the art deco Beresford Hotel, built between the wars for visitors to the Empire Exhibition, he cooks under a Japanese head chef as Glasgow's first skyscraper, as it's known, turns into a rest and recreation stop for American soldiers. He cooks in the Royal Hotel on Sauchiehall Street. He cooks in Rogano, whose redesign has been modelled on the most famous cruise ship in the world, the *Queen Mary*, the Cunard liner constructed at John Brown's shipyard on Clydebank. During the war, as the *Queen Mary*'s long sleek exteriors and bright red funnels are painted camouflage grey and she ferries tens of thousands of servicemen at a time from New York, Bombay, Suez, Florida, Sydney, and Singapore, Rogano's heyday begins. The glossy pearl in the centre of the blackened town keeps its own stretch of river for salmon. It brings in lobsters from Brora for its famous thermidor, and oysters from Portpatrick. It becomes the most famous restaurant in town.

Practically everyone working in the trade in Glasgow is foreign and Henry experiences no anti-Semitism. But during the early years of the war one incident takes place. 'There was a woman, a sous chef, a big Protestant lady from Ayr, a good friend of mine, and she said to me "I ken ye carry floo'ers",' says Henry.

'Men in Scotland didn't carry flowers,' explains Ingrid.

'This woman said "Will ye tak a bunch hame to yer wife?" Well, I was very lucky to not be beaten up on the way home. It was the twelfth of July and she had given me a bunch of orange lilies. Do you know what that means?'

And so Henry sits in a tram car holding the orange flowers, with everyone staring at him.

'I had no idea why,' he says. 'The next morning this chef said to me "How did you get on?" I said it was not the right thing to do, and she replied "Oh well, I knew nothing would happen." And that's how I realised the problem between Catholics and Protestants in Glasgow.'

After the war, Henry is headhunted for his biggest job yet. Sous chef at the Grand Hotel, another Glasgow institution famed for its cocktails and lavish wedding receptions. Within a few years he is head of one of the top kitchens in the city, commanding 'an entire brigade of cooks'. He introduces kosher functions. The boy who learned his trade at a Jewish hotel in Baden-Baden becomes a head chef.

The Grand lies in the beating heart of Charing Cross. In another ten years this beloved Victorian landmark will be demolished to make way for an inner-city ring road. The blueprint for this destruction is originally proposed at the end of the Second World War. In the decades that follow, as the past becomes something to be walked away from as quickly as possible without looking back, humanity will develop an accompanying zeal for tearing down old buildings, and the plans for the first urban motorway of its kind in Europe will be hailed as a great modern achievement. By the time I live in Charing Cross in the early years of the next century this once imposing gateway to the city centre will be known, mostly, as a place of lost history. A place where Glasgow's heart has been cut out by the M8 slicing through it like a blade. A place where you mostly find yourself waiting impatiently to cross the road at a set of traffic lights.

In the early summer of 1953, while Ingrid is pregnant with their first child, Henry leaves Glasgow for France's gourmet capital. He spends three heady months in Lyon cooking under two famous chefs, Joannes Nandron and Roger Roucou. He practises his French. He learns his wines. He helps prepare a six-course tasting menu printed on silk handkerchiefs. And then he returns home in time for Ingrid to give birth to a girl on 10 September 1953. They call her Hilary.

When Henry goes back to the Grand, bringing to his dishes a certain Lyonnaise flair, he finds his heart is no longer in it. Perhaps it is becoming a father that leads him to hand in his notice. Perhaps he can no longer face the long hours. Instead he sells bird cages for a while, linseed and other pet supplies, to shops in villages and towns all over the country. He switches to frozen food supplies. He sees the whole of Scotland, in all weathers, from his van. He enters an uncharacteristically directionless phase of his life.

Yet Henry's new career is already here, taking care of itself like a stew puttering in a pot. Friends keep asking him to cater their functions. A bar mitzvah here, a wedding there. Word gets round about this cook's modern continental food and the offers start flooding in.

And so Henry becomes a private Jewish caterer.

He needs a kosher licence. At first when he goes to see the rabbi he is told there are enough Jewish caterers in Glasgow. Henry, as ever, stands his ground. Finally, after several attempts, using his reference from the Tannhäuser in Baden-Baden, he gets his licence from the Beth Din.

Four years after the birth of their second baby, Gillian, on 2 June 1957, the Wugas move into a large Victorian villa on Dalkeith Avenue in Dumbreck. Their family home, in which they will live for the next thirty years until they retire to Giffnock. They choose the house for its large kitchen and storeroom. 'It was in rather a poor state,' says Henry. 'No central heating, terrible windows and wiring. It took years to make it into our home.' The house has a grand porch, two large public rooms, a wide staircase leading to five bedrooms and a bathroom, two kitchens and, in a separate washhouse, stone sinks, a coal cellar and butler's pantry. In the basement Henry and Ingrid discover a vast cellar that can store up to 120 bottles of wine. They buy four thousand pieces of Wedgwood crockery – red for meat and green for milk – and Viners silver-plated cutlery in two designs. It's an enormous gamble to spend what little they have on the best equipment but it pays off. Ingrid begins to help with the baking. Wuga Catering, which will become known as the top kosher catering company in Glasgow, is born.

'It was all word of mouth,' says Henry. 'We were new, we were different. It wasn't all chicken soup and chopped liver. We were European in spirit. We brought continental cakes, afternoon tea, crudités, and instead of having everything out on the table we came around with trolleys filled with gateaux. Our nut cake was very famous.'

'It's made with ground hazelnuts,' says Ingrid.

They employ five staff – 'Protestant and Catholic women,' says Hilary, 'prepping side by side in our kitchen' – and during busy functions up to twenty people cook across the two kitchens on Dalkeith Avenue. In the beginning, when a client fails to pay up, Henry takes them to court, and Giffnock's Jewish community is shocked. This is not how they do things. But from this moment on there will be no trouble. Some of the Wugas' events will cater for just ten people, others for up to four hundred. They will develop such a tight bond with the community that over the next thirty years Henry will not once take a deposit. It will be complicated dealing with the religious authorities, whose rules are strict and whose values don't necessarily align with Henry's progressive faith. 'The strange thing is I have never been orthodox yet I became a kosher caterer,' he says. 'It just happened because I was a good cook. Look, we have never denied our Jewishness. On the contrary we practise it, but I do not hold with strict orthodoxy. It helped that I worked in Baden-Baden and went to a Jewish school, but as a family we were liberal. Well, the licence was granted and we had to keep to the rules. A supervisor had access to our kitchens at all times.' Henry and Ingrid join the orthodox Pollokshields shul and only after they retire will they become members of the Glasgow Reform Synagogue. 'I simply could not have had a kosher licence being a reform Jew,' says Henry. 'Often it was difficult but I live here, so I had to deal with it.'

On the first day I go to Giffnock for lunch, I will see the ghost of Wuga Catering in action when Henry wheels their 1960s trolley into the room. I will see it in the display of elegant dishes presented on well-cared-for china. In the sliced boiled eggs with Marie Rose sauce. In the continental warmth of plates loaded with food in the cold light of our post-Brexit days. I will fall in love with the Wugas, and their food, at the same time.

After my mother's death, my sister, father and I will grieve for her by cooking in our separate kitchens in London and Edinburgh, unable to come together during lockdown. In those first thickened weeks after her death, when I will feel as if I am moving through milk rather than air, my father will send us shaky videos of his first attempts at making dosas. My sister and I will cobble together a list of our mother's recipes, many of which were never written down. And I will produce pot after pot of saaru, eking out the memory of my mother with every last teaspoon of her rasam powder, a closely guarded blend of lentils, chillies, curry leaves and spices as varied as the South Indian families that make it, that she would roast on the hallowed days of the first forty years of my life, making our home, for an entire twenty-four hours, smell like Bangalore. Her other home. The dry roasted spices always, like the memory of them now, drew tears from my eyes. After her death I will begin to ration the powder, mixing the last jar she gave me with a shop-bought version to make it go further and further, until it is gone, too.

More than a year before her death I start to take photos of the food my mother made me standing at the gas cooker, floored by cancer, determined with every turn of the knob to keep a spark of herself alive. To keep cooking.

On 30 May 2019, I take a photo of her dosas. I stand on the wobbly chair in my mother's kitchen filled with steam to get an aerial shot of a plate that has been around almost as long as me. On it lie two dosas folded in half and neatly stacked. There are three accompaniments in a row: mango pickle, a puddle of homemade thuppa, and a little bronze settlement of chutney powder. I will come down off the chair and eat it all, ravenously, with my hand while my mother stands at the cooker, pouring the next ladleful of batter into the blackened pan, swirling the dosa with the underside of the ladle, round and round.

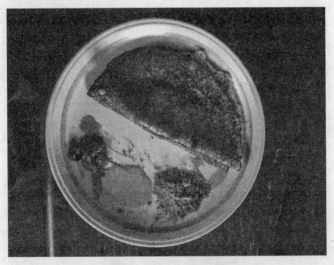

On 28 December 2019, I take a photo of her lime pickle. I cannot know it yet but this is the last time I will visit her at home before she goes into hospital, and coronavirus comes into all our lives. By this stage, my mother is obsessed with pickling. With the act of preservation towards the end

of her life. She is eating less of her own food, and more of the soft, bland, sugary cuisine of the very young or very sick. Yoghurt, ice cream, the tiniest piece of toast spread with the most miserly layer of hummus. Western food. For the first time in her life my mother cannot eat her own food. She cannot eat *rice*. I find this concept of a South Indian woman unable to eat rice indigestible. So this pickle goes way beyond a condiment. It is a life raft to which we are all clinging. My mother's latest craze is to throw everything but the kitchen sink in her concoctions, which now cover two-thirds of the dining table. This one contains whole garlic cloves yellowed like teeth by turmeric, preserved lemon, green chillies, capers and olives. It is the most multi-cultural pickle on the planet. An immigrant's pickle. The pickle of a Londoner.

'A man filled with empathy.'

21 November 2008 is the seventieth anniversary of the Kindertransport. Henry and Ingrid are in London for the reunion. During the long day of keynote addresses, celebrations, panel discussions, a visit by the Prince of Wales, lunch and a klezmer concert, they are introduced to the chief archivist at the Jewish Museum in Berlin. A Canadian Jewish scholar called Aubrey Pomerance. He is instantly charmed by this effervescent couple from Glasgow and when he returns to the UK the following March he goes to visit them in Giffnock. Henry and Ingrid tell Aubrey their life stories. Henry opens the wooden cabinet in the sitting room and shows Aubrey items from his growing archive.

By the summer of that year Henry and Ingrid are in Berlin at Aubrey's invitation, giving their first workshop to a group of German school children in Europe's biggest Jewish museum. Housed in Daniel Libeskind's lightning bolt of a building, its design is inspired by an exploded Star of David and filled with empty voids slicing through it from basement to roof. It is inside this shimmering zinc-clad monument to remembrance, off which seems to bounce all the heat and light of Berlin, that Henry and Ingrid start talking about their pasts not just in public but in Germany for the very first time.

'It was an absolute joy to have them,' says Aubrey. 'They

have such a warmth and openness. Henry, in particular, is a very gregarious fellow. Every single person who meets him is charmed by him. He has this twinkle in his eye, as well as a real knack for talking. He is someone who is able to see all sides of his own story. He is a man filled with empathy.'

Over the following decade, as the fleeing of more than a million refugees into Europe becomes the worst humanitarian crisis since the Second World War, Henry and Ingrid keep going back to Berlin. Every year they give workshops to children and young people from all over Germany. Henry gifts his archive to the Jewish Museum, where a few of his most 'iconic' pieces, as Aubrey calls them, are displayed in carefully lit glass cases. The rest of Henry's original letters, photos and documents are transferred to the building opposite the museum, a pair of tilted cubes situated on the site of an old flower market. High-quality photocopies are made for Henry to keep at home in Giffnock, but there are a few originals with which he refuses to part. Around a dozen letters sent before and after the war. The wartime Red Cross letter from his mother informing him that his father was dead. The postcard she sent him after the war from a small town in Switzerland. The cloth yellow star Lore was forced to wear during the war. The 'white card' he had to show when he docked at Harwich and alighted on British soil.

'We decided that all of it would end up in a bin bag at some time or another . . .' says Henry, sweeping a hand across the neat stacks of documents covering his desk. 'I mean there comes a time when grandchildren and so on don't want to know any more. So everything is safeguarded in Berlin.'

'What will go in a bin bag?' asks Ingrid, appalled at the thought.

So this is how Henry and Ingrid start talking in their ninth decade about their lives. This is why they start going back to Germany every year. This is how they become Holocaust educators. And this is how their lives begin to change at home in Scotland too. They start visiting schools, colleges and universities all over the country. They start giving lectures at memorial events. They start doing interviews with the press, which is how they meet me.

In October 2019, Henry flies to Berlin with Gillian, her son and Hilary's son, while Ingrid, whose dementia has made her contribution to the workshops impossible, stays at home with Hilary. Henry's Berlin trip is timely. The scale of the Windrush scandal has been fully exposed. A year earlier, as the UK celebrated the eightieth anniversary of the Kindertransport, it was revealed that Britain had admitted just twenty unaccompanied child refugees into the country in two years. Meanwhile the global refugee crisis, though rarely headline news, goes on. And shortly after Henry's visit a global pandemic will sweep the planet, the Jewish Museum will close for five months, and it will be clear that he will never go to Germany again.

Henry's final talk takes place in the Jewish Museum. 'All the students were born in Germany but none of their parents were German,' he says of his audience. 'All immigrants. Their parents were from Turkey, Lebanon, Syria, Vietnam, Afghanistan. That made an immediate connection between us.'

During Henry's presentation, one of the students keeps edging closer and closer to him. A young man with dark skin and hair, a moustache and beard in mid-growth. He is dressed in black apart from his spotless white trainers. At some point, he notices Henry's water glass is empty. He ventures further forward until they are standing right next to one another. Wordlessly, the boy lifts a jug and fills the glass for the elderly man. As Henry talks, sips, and clears his throat, the water in the glass gradually goes down. Each time it nears the bottom of the glass, the boy steps forward. Refills it. Stands back.

'He was fifteen,' says Aubrey. 'The same age as Henry was when he came on the Kindertransport. He was born in Iraq but from an Afghani family. He came to Germany unregistered in 2015 along with hundreds of thousands of refugees.'

When Henry gets home from Berlin, he phones me and tells the story.

'I think because I came at the same age he felt we had something in common,' he says. 'Who knows the journey he must have faced.'

'My Ingrid'

As I am living between a triptych of times – my grief-stricken pandemic present, post-war Nuremberg, and Henry and Ingrid's catering years in Glasgow – Ingrid gets an infection. She goes into hospital and within days begins to deteriorate. Her kidneys fail, just like my mother's did. She sleeps most of the time, is most contented listening to BBC Radio 3, goes days without eating and drinking, then rallies, cracks a joke, takes a little soup and water. Gillian visits every day. Hilary travels up from London on the train. Henry, shielding, stays at home. Autumn feels unusually spectacular, the colours intensified by loss, every fallen leaf a perfect metaphor. Covid-19 restrictions tighten and become ever more locally focused and complicated. The four countries making up the United Kingdom seem ever more estranged. The world braces for a second wave.

A few weeks later Ingrid is moved to a nursing home in Giffnock.

And a few days after that, on the morning of 17 October 2020, at the age of ninety-six, Ingrid dies peacefully in her sleep.

She is buried in the Jewish section of Cathcart Cemetery in Glasgow, high on a hill, bordering Linn Park. An enormous park bisected by a river, the White Cart Water, which is laid out by Field Marshall Colin Campbell of the 'Sugar

Campbells'. He acquires the land in 1820, just as the Campbell's sugar plantations in the West Indies and Demerara are reaching their peak. It is Campbell, whose family owns a West India shipping line, who names the land The Lynn – after its waterfall – and builds a mansion house for use as his summer residence. He plants much of the existing woodland and gardens. And in 1833, when slavery on British plantations is abolished, the Campbells – amongst the top ten sugar traders in the country – receive £50,000 in compensation for the loss of 1,200 enslaved African men, women and children across six plantations. Seven years later he sells the estate. And history, which is to say life, goes on.

A century later, it is here in the winter of 1945 that Henry introduces Ingrid to skiing. There is a particularly beautiful photograph of the two of them in the first snow they ever encountered in Glasgow. They hired two pairs of wooden skis and poles and took a tramcar to Linn Park in their plus-fours. They skied across the brilliant white landscape while the locals looked on, amused at the sight of this dapper couple – him in his knitted headband, her with a silk scarf at her throat – skiing through a city park in the first winter after the war. At some point on this exhilarating winter day, by which point Henry knew his mother had survived the war in Nuremberg, he and his wife stood side by side on a white slope. They had been married a year. Their skis were crusted with fresh snow. They held their poles in their hands. Their bodies fell into similar poses. And someone, either friend or stranger, took their photograph.

'I am writing this in January 2020,' begins Henry in an essay he titles 'My Ingrid' and works on slowly over the course of what will turn out to be his wife's last year on earth. 'Now that we have been together for 75 years it is about time to look at our life from an elderly gentleman's view.' He writes about Ingrid's arrival on the Kinder-transport. How they met at the house on the hill in the spring of 1941. He recalls their 'wartime wedding' in the winter of 1944, Ingrid's formidable skill with a needle and thread and her ongoing ability, at the age of ninety-six, to thread a needle. He recalls their many cycling and skiing adventures around Scotland and Europe, and Ingrid's favourite piste in Verbier, which she ski-bobbed when she was seventy-seven years old, breaking her leg and still making it to the bottom of the slope.

'WHAT A GIRL INGRID,' Henry writes, ascending into capitals as he has the habit of doing when particularly moved. 'ALWAYS CAME BACK. NEVER GAVE UP.'

Henry moves on to their joyous years of parenting Hilary and Gillian. The kosher catering business they ran for thirty years, and Ingrid's lifelong devotion to classical music, which he describes as 'the best part of our life'. And their renowned voluntary work, not just as Holocaust educators, but as ski instructors with Blesma, which took them all over Europe after their retirement.

'Now in our late nineties we try to escape the virus,' Henry concludes. 'Happy to be safe at home.'

When someone we love dies the archeology of grief is born. It is not something that can be learned in advance. Only after the person is gone, and the past has become fixed, can the dig begin. The excavating of one's mind for moments, no matter how trivial. The discovery of something, anything, that might preserve the one we have lost a little longer. The gentle brushing away of the history to reveal the details, which were so incidental at the time but are freighted, now, simply for being the last ones. For becoming history.

I summon Ingrid's preference for a half cup of tea. How she often insisted the other half went to Henry. How she believed it was up to the community to make foreigners welcome. 'It is not for me to knock on your door and say I'm coming in for a cup of tea,' she would say. 'It is for you to invite me.'

I summon my mother, who insisted on sampling everything on my father's plate, and insisting he try everything on hers. How she would cook a proper hot meal for anyone who came through our door. How friends of mine who were struggling always ended up staying with us. How kind she was.

As our families are reconfigured in the tempest of grief, I start to understand how similar we are. I do not want this epiphany, now.

It is too late.

It is never too late.

The last time I saw Ingrid was on the first day of July. It was almost a month after my mother's death, and three months before her own. We were just emerging from national lockdown and the world seemed vast and emptied of meaning. Henry and Ingrid were living with Gillian in Edinburgh, and I was first invited for Ingrid's ninety-sixth birthday, which I had to cancel because my son had a dental emergency, and then again a week later for a socially distanced visit to their garden. It was the first time I had gone anywhere beyond the immediate circumference of home since my mother's funeral. In those days I kept finding myself in places without knowing why I was there. Grief-walking. Stumbling between different zones of time. I lost my keys, amazingly found them lying in the grass of our local park, then promptly lost them again, this time for good. At the end of the visit, Gillian pressed a succulent into my hand that she had just dug up from her garden and potted for me. I put it at my feet in the taxi, got distracted talking to the driver about how much he had struggled during lockdown without any financial support from the government, and forgot to pick it up when I got out.

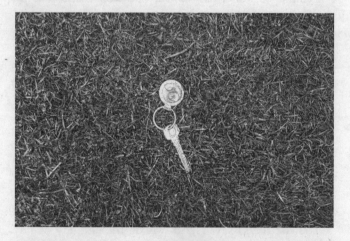

For the first time I enter Gillian's house not through the front door, but round the back. A light rain is hovering in the air, what Scots call a smirr, and the grass instantly soaks my boots. I have never been in the back garden before, despite looking out onto it from the conservatory during many past visits. I wander around on my own, the ghost of my mother beside me admiring the planting. Every leaf and bloom cuts to the heart of my grief. I know it will be this way for a long time. I cannot bear the thought of it being otherwise. Beyond the garden wall lies the open expanse of the Pentlands, where the skies are writing today's journal entry in light and shadow across the hills. All this space and time, and my mother, who would have loved nothing more than a nose around this garden pressed against Scottish lowland hills, is nowhere to be found in it.

'Why are you sitting out there?' asks Ingrid when I perch outside the doorway under an umbrella and heater, with a blanket over my knees. It makes absolutely no sense to her that I am out in the rain while she and Henry are positioned inside the door of the conservatory with tartan rugs on their laps as if gathered round a fire. Over the course of the next hour, she will keep asking me if I am warm enough, and why we are sitting here with the door open. And, over and over again, reminding me of my son in the persistence and pertinence of her questions, she will keep asking me what happened to my mother.

'Who passed away?'

'Where did your mother live?'

'Who liked gardening?'

'Who died?'

We talk about losing parents who are far away. We talk about Henry's father's death in Nuremberg in the spring of 1944.

'Were we together by that time?' asks Ingrid.

'Yes, we were,' says Henry, 'which helped.'

Henry and Ingrid have been living with Gillian for a month. Every day they go for a short walk around the block, Henry using his stick and Ingrid her walker. Henry says he is getting lazy, having everything done for him, but is cherishing the length of quiet time spent together. Until, that is, he opens a newspaper and then he gets 'depressed'. Soon he and Ingrid will return home and a carer will move in with them full-time.

'She is not coming to live with us!' insists Ingrid.

'Yes, she is,' says Henry. 'Ingrid doesn't understand why we need someone to look after us. She says we can look after ourselves.' He turns to her. 'You don't realise, Ingrid, you're now ninety-six and you are allowed to have someone looking after you.'

The most precious finding of the grief dig is this.

We are talking about this book, which I have been struggling to write since my mother's death.

'What's it about?' asks Ingrid. 'Your family?'

Yes. And yours.

'What do you want to write about us?' Ingrid asks.

So much.

'There is nothing interesting,' she shrugs. 'We are just man and wife.'

And she reaches across her tartan blanket, takes Henry's hand, and they smile at each other.

'Our buddleia'

After you're gone I wake up most nights at 3 a.m. It happens like clockwork, as if I were a child shaken at the shoulder by her mother to get up for school. Except you woke me gently, often with a giant cup of coffee made *on the pan* as we called it, which only decades later did I understand was an Indian thing. Instant coffee granules, full cream milk and sugar heated on the stove until it bubbled up and formed a thin brown skin.

3 a.m. Entry into the hour when you took your last breaths. When you exited this world, which until you were gone I honestly thought was the only one.

My eyes snap open like camera shutters. First recorded thought: you are dead. Never: you were alive. Some time passes, the fraught and unconsecutive time of the night. Eventually, after an invisible fight with myself I get up and go to the kitchen window where I flew when I heard the news. When my father's words appeared to leap out of the smudged black glass of my phone and slip like a burglar through a window into my head, where they lie still, fresh and unabsorbable.

I look at the buddleia. It is backlit by one of the environmentally friendly streetlamps installed by the council since you died. At first I thought their light was too cold, too twenty-first-century blue, but I have got used to them. Some things, I can accept.

Your buddleia. Spotlit like a starlet. Also sometimes, on a clear night, actually starlit. It is a sturdy but impressionable bush, our buddleia, swaying with even the softest breath of wind. Its droopy leaves shimmer and its purple torches wave respectfully, their honey scent drawing bees and childhood memories of long sun-washed summers with you. Except now their smell reminds me of the night side of life, too.

I look at the sky. Recently I stupidly told your granddaughter, who is talking, really talking, now, that this might be where you live. Now I sometimes see her looking up with a puzzled, almost reproachful expression on her little face, scouring the air filled with light and cloud for actual you.

Your grandson doesn't understand the word 'died'. He calls it 'dived'.

The truth is, I do sometimes wonder if you have dived up there. The absurd has become plausible and I believe all sorts of things now. Grief has prised open my mind. How I would love to tell you that for the first time in my life I feel like a Hindu.

I look back to our buddleia, to this earth you have departed, where I must find a way to live. I look for you in the sky with my eyes that are also yours. Then I go back to bed.

Just in case you're wondering.

This is what the year will look like after you're gone.

'We are not like other Indians.'

On 30 May 1942, as Henry and Ingrid are falling in love in the house on the hill on Sauchiehall Street, my father is born in Tumkur. A town about forty miles from the city of Bangalore, which is itself high on a plateau in British-occupied India.

The following year, on 23 September, as Henry's political consciousness emerges in what was not so long ago the second city of the empire, my mother is born in Basavanagudi, one of the oldest areas of Bangalore, in the house of her grandmother.

Two years later, the Second World War comes to an official end in Europe.

And two years after that, 'at the stroke of the midnight hour' on 14 August 1947, India gains independence. This follows almost a century of British Crown rule, and a further century of British company rule from a small office explicitly set up for the exploitation of trade with India, Southeast and East Asia. A private and unregulated company operating out of East India House, a fine neoclassical building in the heart of the city to which my father will emigrate twenty years after independence. London. My city.

'When the world sleeps,' says Jawaharlal Nehru in his famous speech to the Indian assembly, 'India will awake to life and freedom. A moment comes, which comes but rarely in history, when we step out from the old to the new, when an age ends, and when the soul of a nation, long suppressed, finds utterance . . . the past is over and it is the future that beckons to us now.'

More than seventy years into that future, these historical moments begin to swirl and resettle like blizzard snow. For the first time in my life I see them together, side by side. Connected. The past not over after all but beckoning to us like the future. It happens even as this book is starting to write itself, the sentences unfurling perfectly in the pitch-black of my head. A spell only ever broken by the attempt to carry them, no matter how carefully, over to the page.

By night I have recurring dreams about trains. Running for a train, missing a train, catching the wrong train, catching the right train and realising, as it pulls away, that I have left my luggage on the platform. Watching a train leave the station with someone I love on it. By day I read *Austerlitz* obsessively. The book is a faithful dog following me around wherever I go, sitting beside me on the sofa – sometimes under the actual dog – while I write. Every time I flick through it, *Austerlitz* seems to fan open, a book bewitched, on the exact right page. I am at that magical-dangerous stage of writing when the whole world is a channel running into the tributaries of Henry's life, my life, our lives. This breaking news is about the book, this falling blossom, this piece of music, this bowl of gazpacho, this life. Still, I don't quite understand what it all means. Henry and I are unlikely friends. There is nothing binding us beyond our selves. We just get on. That is the point. The charm of our story lies in our difference.

Meanwhile, in the summer of 2019, I am preparing to chair an event with the Cambridge professor Priyamvada Gopal in Norwich, where, with perfect alignment, Sebald lived, taught, wrote, and died. Claire, our daughter and I go by train to Norwich, which involves travelling directly to Peterborough, and then in a classic Sebaldian manoeuvre, taking probably the slowest train of my life to Norwich that seems to travel backwards for most of the journey. Before the event itself, Gopal, a first-generation immigrant from Delhi, and I sit around the back of a Spiegeltent erected in an unchanged Victorian park, drinking tea and talking about the rise in nationalism, populism and racism at home and abroad. I tell her about my life. My pre-repossession childhood in a leafy, affluent and predominantly white borough of London, my white female partner, our children. I tell her about my parents. How they let my sister and I study what we wanted, love who we love, become who we are. How we were never taught to speak their language, or observe their Hindu faith. How, like Henry, Ingrid, and so many German Jews of their generation, they are assimilators. Products of their time, which I am beginning to understand is the same time, flowing with the single current of history. How, above all else, they are themselves. Gopal shakes her head, over and over again, and says 'your parents sound like very unusual Indians'. I beam with pride.

Afterwards Claire goes north to our son, who stayed in Edinburgh with his aunt, and I travel south to London with our daughter, to go home and see my parents. We arrive into Liverpool Street Station, where Henry and Ingrid pulled in on separate Kindertransports almost exactly eighty years earlier. My daughter is fast asleep in her buggy, sweat matting her soft hair to her head, her cheeks flushed by the heat and exertion that arriving into London induces, whether young or old, asleep or awake. As soon as we pass through the turnstile into the belly of the Victorian station her eyes open.

London, her mother's homeland, wakes her up with its essential sounds of footsteps criss-crossing in every direction, the scrape and roll of luggage on wheels, talk bellowed into phones, and the repeating monotone of train announcements. The slightly queasy smell of coffee hangs in the air. We are cocooned in the gloomy light cast by high

Victorian glass roofs scribbled with decades of grime. London light. I am filled with what Muriel Spark called an 'in-pouring' of love for my home. The feeling of being amongst my own. With people who are coming and going. People who might be from anywhere.

I want to go outside and sit for a while beside Frank Meisler's sculpture commemorating the Kindertransport. I want to go for a drink in the bar of the old Great Eastern Hotel, where Austerlitz and Sebald's narrator have one of their profound chance encounters. I want to go back into the station and loiter on the platforms like a trainspotter. I want to climb the stairs and wander the walkways so I can get closer to the brick arches and iron tracery atop the slender columns. I want to find the ladies' waiting room, a large disused space in a 'remote part of the station', which, according to Austerlitz, is entered through swing doors and a heavy curtain, and laid with a monochrome diamond-patterned stone floor. The place where Austerlitz first glimpses his past. Where, as the new station is 'literally rising from the ruins of the old Liverpool Street' in the 1980s, he sees a vision of a boy sitting alone on a bench, his legs 'in white knee-length socks' dangling above the floor, holding a small rucksack on his lap. Himself.

None of this is possible. My daughter is by now disorientated, hungry, wanting to be unstrapped from her buggy and carried. Climbing stairs, in such a situation, seems as preposterous an exit strategy as leaving by paraglide. It is a condition of early motherhood to want things you cannot have. Even simple things become the most impossible abstractions. Even the wanting itself must be squeezed shut. Besides, at that precise moment I see my sister descending on an escalator to meet us, and my heart travels in the opposite direction. The fantasy evaporates. We hug on the concourse, two mothers still with a mother of their own bathed in homelight. We fuss over the baby. We leave. I think *next time*.

We head west, crossing the Thames to the side I know best. South of the river.

Home.

While I am there I ask my mother if I can interview her about her life. She says yes. The breast cancer is a fifth member of our family now, an unbearable patriarch controlling everything and everyone, in command even of time. We know we must make the most of every moment. We are all, in our own heads, living in this pressurised endtime, recording what's left. After my mother's death the following summer I will not be able to listen to the hour-long recording. The file will sit on my dictaphone, as it still does today, burdening me with its precious existence.

During this visit I tell my parents what Gopal said about them.

'It's true,' my father says. 'We are not like other Indians.'

And my mother nods and adds, 'And we didn't bring you up like Indians either.'

But in my memory her tone is different to mine. Textured, like sand. She sounds proud, but also protective, uncertain, guilty, resigned, a little sad.

Insurgent Empire, Gopal's latest book, is a profoundly hopeful and long neglected history of anti-colonial resistance and dissent. It contains a section on how inexorably the Second World War set in motion and accelerated the process of decolonisation in India. A war in which 2.3 million British Indian soldiers fought, the largest volunteer army on the planet, and more than 89,000 of them died. A war that happened in tandem with the increasing struggle for India's freedom from British rule. A war that turned the entire subcontinent into a garrison. A war that forced Henry and Ingrid to flee to Britain. A war that quickened the pace of the march towards independence and thus, however indirectly, produced the first memories of my parents.

The word 'independence' everywhere.

The sound of celebrations outside, flowing through the streets.

Prayers in school.

The feeling of being on holiday.

'Habits once formed are difficult to get rid of,' wrote the influential journalist, anti-colonialist and Pan Africanist George Padmore in 1930s London. 'That is why we maintain that Colonies are the breeding ground for the type of fascist mentality which is being let loose in Europe today . . . The fight against fascism cannot be separated from the right of all colonial peoples and subject races to Self-Determination. For any people who help to keep another people in slavery are at the same time forging their own chains.'

It is a lightbulb moment, coming late in my life, and the life of this book.

For the first time I see the ideological and historical connections between slavery, colonialism and fascism. Not that they are equivalent, but that they are chapters in the same story. Our story. I learn how vociferously, and often, Hitler expressed his admiration for Britain's subjugation of India. How he intended that eastern Europe would become Germany's India. How the Jim Crow laws in the American South served as a precedent for the Nuremberg laws. I see the race hatred underpinning the greatest crimes in human history. And I see the common ground. Between refugee and immigrant experience. Between then and now. Between Henry, Ingrid and my parents. Between Henry and I.

The four of them met only once, during the Edinburgh International Festival, which was founded in the stunned years after the Second World War when, as Arendt wrote, refugees were instructed to forget, and 'we forgot quicker than anybody ever could imagine'. At the time, the homes of long established arts festivals in Salzburg and Munich had been colonised by the Nazis then bombed by the Allies.

296

The founders of the Edinburgh International Festival hoped to reconcile the world through the balm of the arts, which sounds ridiculously idealistic, but also makes complete sense.

So, around seventy years later, this is the utopian backdrop to the only meeting between Rama, Shylaja, Henry and Ingrid. My parents, and my adopted Jewish grandparents. It's a chance encounter, wedged between shows and sprints back to the office to file reviews. Afterwards I will not be able to recall a single word that was exchanged. I will not think much of it for years. Until, after two of the four characters in this scene have died, it begins to preoccupy me. It becomes a favourite film clip, which I keep rewatching. As Austerlitz keeps finding himself back at Liverpool Street where he is plagued by a heartache 'caused by the vortex of past time', I keep returning to this chance meeting in a music hall in Edinburgh that was once a chapel. Keep trying to breathe it, and them, back to life.

They make a dapper foursome, this Jewish refugee couple in their eighties, and this Indian immigrant couple in their sixties. If I didn't know them, I would want to know more. They are so different, so the same. So proud. So metropolitan. So foreign. So British. It is the interval. People are milling around, leaving coats, bags and programmes on seats to go and get a drink. They come together right in front of the stage, upon which a glossy black grand piano sits. The formality of the occasion is a little hysteria-inducing and Shylaja, my mother, is giggly. Probably slightly in awe of the elderly gentleman with the bow tie. The irrepressible combination of his grin and deportment are working on her like a spell. In the two gentlemen I see a meeting of minds, outlooks, and a kind of reciprocal approval, however projected by me. In the two women I find kindness, warmth, mischief, themselves. All four, in their own very different ways, are people with 'a talent for happiness' as the writer Judith Kerr once described her father to me. Only now do I see how inextricable this trait is from their refugee and immigrant experience. How the forging of existence in a foreign country and the lifelong generation of identity it requires depends upon a certain aptitude for happiness. 'We wanted to rebuild our lives, that was all,' wrote Arendt in 'We Refugees'. 'In order to rebuild one's life one has to be strong and an optimist. So we are very optimistic.'

This is how these four wildly different British people ended up here in Edinburgh's Queen's Hall, watching a recital one summer morning during the tumultuous second decade of the twenty-first century. This is how they ended up in the same country to which each of them fled or emigrated a mere three decades apart. They came for reasons continents apart. They came for reasons as bound together as the ocean floor.

History brought them here.

And the shadow it casts is as long as time.

'One of your first words was "home".'

When I was one, we nearly went back to India for good. It was a transitional time for my family, and the country. I was born in 1979, delivered directly into the cold blast of the Winter of Discontent. Two months after my birth, Britain's first female prime minister, Margaret Thatcher, was sworn into office. Which I grudgingly suppose makes me one of Thatcher's children, too. My father was unhappy in his job at the time and was supporting us. My mother had stopped working as a doctor. She wanted to be around for her children and was looking after my sister, and now me, full time. A year later, with a one-year-old, four-year-old, escalating mortgage payments and very little money, my parents found themselves at a fork in the road. An intersection that many first-generation immigrants probably find themselves approaching at various points in their lives. Should they go back? Repeat history? Should they educate their daughters in India? We were still, just, at the age when such decisions could be made by parents overwhelmed by the responsibilities, precariousness and exhaustion of life. And so my mother and father made one. We would go back to India. For a few months. Indefinitely. Perhaps for ever.

In India, we lived in my grandparents' house in Rajajinagar, a residential district of Bangalore. Our house in Twickenham was sublet, though it took months. My sister was enrolled in a local school and I stayed at home, a baby in arms, my cheeks no doubt pinched a hundred times daily by a flock of relatives. It was the only time I ever spent with my grandfather, a doctor famed for his kind and often freely given treatment. The man with the uncashed cheques tucked in books. He died unexpectedly three years later in a motorbike accident. And it was in India that I started to walk, where my feet would have been set for the first time on the cool red oxide floors of that house, to which I have returned a number of times over the years. I know nothing first-hand about this vague other-life when I almost became an Indian through and through. An Indian like my parents. Even though it is a part of my own past, it's as inaccessible to me as Henry's childhood.

For my parents it was a homecoming of sorts. In some ways it must have been a sunlit time. A return home. A serendipitous period, for which my mother would be eternally thankful after her father's death, which broke her heart like nothing else in her life. But it was also stressful.

300

My parents had no income. The challenge of looking after two small children in the house of my mother's parents, in a country they had officially left, must have been considerable. They had mortgage payments to keep up in a country riven by unrest, strikes and soaring inflation rates. Their other home had become a burden too.

So what happened?

Forty years later, I ask them. It is a few days after a sorrow-laden Christmas. My last proper visit to see my parents before my mother's death. We are reeling from the news we knew was coming as inevitably as the new year. On Christmas Eve my mother had an appointment with her oncologist confirming the cancer treatment was no longer working. We had come to the end of the road.

Now we are beyond it, walking an off-route path through the wilderness of this disease. Chatting one evening while my daughter sleeps next door in my old bed.

My father says it was a combination of factors. The person letting our house – 'some big pharmaceuticals man' – gave a month's notice and took off. We had no money to make the mortgage payments. My father had no choice but to go back. Also there was the sense that it had been an experiment, they had dutifully performed it, and now the results were in. We were immigrants after all. British. It was time to go home to London. My father returned first, in October 1980, and my mother, sister and I followed at the start of the next year.

My mother says it was my sister. She just couldn't settle in Bangalore. She kept crying for her best friend. For her old life in suburban Twickenham. She kept saying, every single day, that she wanted to 'go home'.

'Come to think of it,' says my mother, 'you started talking in India. I think one of your first words was "home".'

We keep talking. I consider sneaking into my daughter's bedroom to get my dictaphone. I cannot bear to forget a single thing about this moment. But nor do I want to change any of the variables. So I remain rooted to the armchair, in my pyjamas, talking to my mother over on the big sofa and my father in his chair with the shiny worn arms. The television is blaring and as usual we are chatting loudly, across, over and through it. The room is filled with noise, histories told and untold, and the easiness of familial love.

Soon my parents will start arguing over some detail of the past and I will roll my eyes at my mother. She will smile knowingly back at me. I will say, slightly theatrically, that I've had enough. I will get ready for bed, wandering in and out of the room to interrupt them while I brush my teeth, talking through the foam in my mouth. Afterwards I will lie next door beside my slumbering daughter, drifting off to sleep for the very last time to the celestial sound of my mother and father talking, talking, always talking.

'I should really interview you guys about this,' I say as I walk out of the sitting room.

My mother's voice follows me out of the door.

'Ask me anything,' she says.

'Just don't leave it too long.'

'I won't be ninety-seven,
I'll be Henry Wuga.'

On a rare sunny day in December 2020, as the first year of the pandemic draws to a subdued close, Henry and I meet at Cathcart Cemetery to visit Ingrid's grave. The date, twice rearranged due to restrictions, falls on what would have been the forty-sixth anniversary of my parents' wedding. We are still, Henry and I, living in the season of grief, when time is kept according to the incalculable geometry of loss. Dates come at you fast and frequent in this perennial winter. Each one is an epitaph inscribed on the heart. I want to keep feeling, after all, and keeping the dead close keeps the living alive. I am beginning to understand that remembrance aches like new love. I am beginning to understand that this is my home, now.

Two months since Ingrid's death.

Six months since my mother's death.

The iron gates of the Jewish section, adorned with two Stars of David, are padlocked. Behind the slender black bars is the plain red-brick prayer hall where services and eulogies are held, and just beyond the first rows of headstones can be glimpsed. The entrance lies at the foot of a road, steep in gradient and rural in spirit, bisecting the old and new sections of the forty-three-acre cemetery.

The Jewish section, which is on the new side, opened in 1927, three years after Henry's birth. But the first Jewish burial in Glasgow took place almost a century earlier, a few miles north, behind the cathedral. In the shadow of the Bridge of Sighs, newly constructed to carry funeral processions over a burn where the city's founder and patron saint is said to have fished for salmon, the body of a Jewish jeweller called Joseph Levi was buried on 12 September 1832. He died of cholera. The very first burial in what would soon become the city's most famous Victorian garden cemetery, a northern hilltop homage to Pere Lachaise in Paris called the Glasgow Necropolis, was of a Jew.

The Jewish section of Cathcart Cemetery – the younger, less flashy Victorian cousin of the Necropolis – contains, at the time of writing, 1,344 burials. It is one of four active Jewish burial grounds in Glasgow, and one of the most diverse. Just over the hill lies the cemetery's Muslim section. So here, on either side of a peaceful hill in Scotland's largest city, Jews and Muslims are laid to rest in eternal conversation.

The Jewish section is generally closed, aside from when the gardener comes on Wednesdays. But a little way up the road there is an opening in the wall, an unofficial entrance used by dog walkers, joggers and locals cutting through the cemetery on their way to Linn Park, where Henry and Ingrid went skiing after the war's end. Not many cemeteries are throughways. So life and death are in daily communion here, just as the Victorians originally envisaged the role of garden cemeteries – and death – in the community. The living picnicking amongst the tombstones. A friend of mine who can see the cemetery from the upstairs window of his house and walks his son to school through its gardens every day tells me that during the first national lockdown Cathcart Cemetery became unusually busy. Locals trying to socially distance on their daily sanctioned walk spilled over from Linn Park into the forty-three acres. It was a matter of pragmatism, but he also wonders if during the pandemic the cemetery began to function as a kind of 'vaccination against despair'.

A local trustee of the Jewish section comes to unlock the gates for us. Henry is already standing outside with Gillian. He is wearing a red jacket with a Ski Bob Association logo and a beige woolly beret. It is the first time I have seen him since Ingrid's death. He looks well. Intact. Himself. We say hello but keep our distance. We are all wearing masks.

Once inside, Henry leads me down one of the first rows of gravestones.

'I know it is one of these,' he mutters. 'The last time I found it right away.'

The paths between the rows are narrow, necessitating that we walk in ceremonial single file. The softened edges of some of the older stones are decorated with a thin tracery of moss, the engravings dark and streaked. Despite its age, however, this is a well-tended cemetery. The black granite of the newer stones glitters in the rounded amber light of winter. The predominant sound is the crunch of our shoes on gravel and my own amplified breath inside my mask. Henry pushes his walker, searching for what he wants to show me. At first we end up in the wrong row. Henry is struggling to read the names, which involves looking directly into the sun as it returns intermittently from the clouds. His glasses keep steaming up behind his mask.

Eventually we find it.

Four graves, all in the same row.

Lore Wuga, Henry's mother.

Etta Hurwich, Henry's guarantor.

Erna and Ascher Wolff, Ingrid's parents.

'How unusual,' murmurs Henry. 'My guarantor, my parents-in-law, my mother . . . all in the same row.'

Henry and Gillian place a small white pebble on each grave. A Jewish tradition, Gillian explains, 'like maintenance, to show that somebody has remembered, that someone has been here'. Until she and Hilary came to the cemetery two months ago for their mother's funeral, neither of them knew that more than a century of their history happens to be archived along a single row of gravestones. That the two women who saved Henry's life were laid to rest virtually side by side.

At Lore's grave, I ask for Henry and Gillian's permission to place a pebble of my own. As I bend down I realise, for the first time, that Henry's mother died in the same month and year that I was born. March 1979.

Lore Wuga, whom I never met.

Lore Wuga, whose post-war letters were a cold sea I plunged into to shock myself back to life after my mother's death.

Lore Wuga, whom I found myself suddenly able to write about when I could do very little else.

Lore Wuga, whose courage, humanity, strength and integrity helped me grieve the death of my mother more than anything else on this earth.

Lore Wuga, Henry's mother.

We move on.

'Did you and your mother ever go to Graz to visit your father's grave?'

'No,' says Henry. 'It never happened. Impossible. My mother, as you know, found it too difficult here and went to America. She never managed it.'

'Have you been?'

'Yes. The problem is, the grave is no longer there. You can only rent it for so many years.'

We begin the short climb up the hill, on a wider path towards Ingrid's grave. Henry lifts his walker over the occasional stone step, then pushes it forwards again. He is very quiet.

Afterwards we will leave the cemetery and cross the road so Henry can perch on his walker in the sun. We will take off our masks and talk, two metres apart, beside a row of semi-detached houses, in front of a garden in which large plastic figures of a penguin and Santa have been placed on the grass. Whether we want it or not, Christmas is coming.

'You won't know this,' says Henry, 'because the fact is, my mother is buried here, but she didn't want to be buried. She wanted to be cremated.'

Henry will explain that by the time Lore died, on 26 March 1979, twenty days after my mother gave birth to me, Wuga Catering was well established as the top Jewish catering company in Glasgow. Cremation is forbidden for orthodox and conservative Jews, and so Henry, stricken with grief and forced to make a quick decision, found himself in an impossible position. 'It was horrible,' he says. 'I simply couldn't do it as a Jewish caterer. People would have . . . the community would not have accepted it.'

I imagine Henry in the 1970s, a middle-aged liberal Jew running a kosher business, trying to do right by everyone. A refugee always treading the thin line between inside and outside. A father with a young family to support. A son who has just lost his mother. A person trapped, as we often are in the middle of our lives, between our duties as a parent and a child. I know this constricted and fragile place. I am living in it.

'I couldn't go with her wishes,' says Henry. 'It was very difficult. She had to be buried. I just had to face these things as they arose.'

Henry doesn't know why his mother wanted to be cremated. Perhaps it was an emotional decision that arose from a general feeling of statelessness. A final act of unbelonging. Perhaps it was an expression of how Lore felt towards a community that had, so unforgivably to her after the horrors of the war, instructed her son not to mention his father wasn't Jewish. A resistance to orthodoxy in any form. Or perhaps it was Lore's way of returning to her beloved husband. Karl, whose body she somehow managed to get cremated and whose ashes she somehow managed to send from Nuremberg to Graz during the height of the war.

The soldier who returned from the First World War, never spoke about it, and signed 'dissenter' under 'religion' in the family book. The husband who stood by his Jewish wife in Nazi Germany to the very end. The man whose grave she was never able to visit.

Before I leave, we will take a few photographs of each other. I will ask Henry how he is coping without Ingrid, and he will reply, 'Very well.' And Henry will ask me how my father is coping without my mother. And I will reply, 'Very well.' Henry will tell me he made his first apple pie without Ingrid, the master baker, at his side. And that last night he cooked lamb cutlets for his supper.

'But I suppose I am old now,' he concedes.

'You're going to be ninety-seven in February!' laughs Gillian.

And Henry will reply, flashing me one of his grins, 'I won't be ninety-seven, I'll be Henry Wuga.'

Back in the cemetery, we walk up the hill.

It is as though we are ascending through time, from the past to the present.

On the day of Ingrid's funeral, the family trod this very path. It was autumn, and the ground was sheeted with wet slippery leaves. Still, Henry refused to use the walker.

'I walked up with my two sticks behind the coffin,' he says. 'They didn't think I would make it, but I did.'

'It was important for you to walk up by yourself.'

'Yes,' he replies softly.

We turn left along a row of graves. There are fewer plots here on the brow of the hill. There is more space, more exposure to the elements. To the air. The sun. Life, as we the living know it.

Ingrid's grave is filled in with earth, the occasional stone and twig. There is no headstone as yet. I have never seen anything like this. My heart knocks rudely in my chest. At the top of the grave is a small handwritten sign on a rectangle of black wood, the white letters huddled close together. It says 'Mrs I Wuga'. It is Jewish custom to have three distinct mourning periods after a death, lasting seven days, one month, and a year. The stone-setting has to happen between the month and the year. So this is how Ingrid's grave will look for some time. Raw. Brutal. Beautiful.

We stand in silence. As if it were pre-arranged along with the unlocking of the gates, the sun comes out. For a moment, the hill is rinsed with soft golden light.

'The sun came out on the day of the funeral,' says Gillian. 'And here was Mummy at the top of the hill, nothing overlooking her.'

'I know,' says Henry.

'She will never be in the shade,' says Gillian.

We stand a moment longer. The sensation of grieving into a mask, soaking it with sorrow, of not being able to rub my eyes or nose, of only being able to see the mourning eyes of others, is acutely familiar to me. The wind picks up, nudging the clouds back over the sun. The top of the hill is just a few steps away. From my standpoint at Ingrid's grave I can see Alexander 'Greek' Thomson's Grecian temple to domestic life in Glasgow, Holmwood House, the grounds of which extend from the other side of the cemetery wall. I can see the bare winter trees partially screening Linn Park, its woodlands and gardens dreamed up by a family of slave traders. In the distant north, though I do not turn to look at them, lie the undulating Campsie Hills. I know all this, but still there is the sense that if I were to go a little further, to the bare cap of the hill, there would be more to see. I want to walk up there now. To stand alone on the sun-washed summit and see what lies ahead. But time is pressing on. I have to get home for my children. Life, as ever, floods back.

Henry is already turning his walker around.

'Daddy, do you want to sit down?' Gillian asks.

'No,' Henry replies. 'I want to go.'

And so we turn back and head down the hill.

'This train journey will forever be in my mind.'

'You are going on a train to Glasgow.'

This is what Henry's mother tells him.

'Of course I had no idea where Glasgow was,' says Henry. 'But I knew I had to go away. It did not worry me. I had been away before. I knew I had to face this. It didn't come as a surprise to me to be at that train station.' Still, the magnitude of what Henry is hearing overshadows his comprehension. He thinks adjustments can be made. He thinks there is an element of choice. 'I will tell you one thing which was a bit silly, but I was a child,' he says. 'I had a cousin in France and so I said to my mother, "Why must I go on that train? Why can't I go via Paris and spend a week with my cousin before going on to Glasgow?"' Henry laughs. He shakes his head. 'I didn't quite realise that was not possible. How naive one can be.'

Lore packs a small leather case, filling it almost exclusively with clothes. Perhaps she does this alone, or with Karl. Henry has no recollection of it.

'I had a good think about it,' he says, 'and I didn't bring very much. First of all, they were all examined, yes? So we knew not to bring anything valuable.' He pauses. 'You brought what you wanted beside you. I can't recall what that was.'

Later Lore will send on a large trunk to Glasgow filled with all his favourite belongings. His walking boots, libretti,

312

a black leather-bound file with the initials 'HW' on it, his Zeiss Ikon Baby Box camera and a small selection of the photos Henry took before he left Germany. In time this pragmatic expression of maternal love will have the side effect of muddying Henry's memory. He will forget what was in the original case.

3 May 1939. Lore, Karl and Henry walk east along Fürther Strasse to Nuremberg Central Station, an immense neo-baroque building capped with a dome, entered through a towering arch and decorated with fine mosaics, all of which will be bombed by the Allies in six years, and then replicated stone by stone. Henry's memory of the goodbye, which takes place on the station platform amongst dozens of other families enduring the same ordeal, is fragmented. Like Vera, Austerlitz's nanny, recounting Jacques' separation from his parents at Wilsonova station, all that will remain is 'an indistinct, rather blurred picture of the moment of farewell'. The 'fluttering of white handkerchiefs like a flock of doves taking off into the air' as the parents on the platform wave their children off. The impression that the train, rather than leaving the station, simply rolls a little way before 'sinking into the ground'. Over the years Henry's memory will be intercepted by the flurry of reports, documents, and images of farewells between parents and their children taking place on railway platforms throughout Nazi-occupied Europe in the months leading up to the war. All he will hold on to is that it was 'tearful and difficult'. What will stay with him is the sound of the 'howling and shouting' of the younger children on the platform.

Henry gets on the train.

He can see his parents standing and waving on the platform.

The train pulls out of the station.

It will be another seven years before he sees his mother. He will never see his father again.

'It was a lottery,' says Henry. 'You would have one hundred children in a town wanting to go and there was only room for thirty. There must have been tremendous trauma for parents. "Why can't you take my child?"' He shakes his head, lost for words. 'You can only imagine.'

You can only imagine.

At some point, probably after the births of his daughters in Glasgow, Henry must have made the imaginative leap from child to parent in this foundational memory. All parents know this automatic transfer of perspective. How effortlessly the shift signalling the transition from one station of life to the next happens. How smoothly the railroad switch diverts the train of thought onto a new track. How one day, not long after giving birth, you might be pushing a buggy along the street when you see a mother waving off her daughter at the school gate. But this time, instead of occupying the child's gaze as you have always done, braving the storm of her courage, pain and indignation, feeling the weight of her rucksack, and picturing the little line of hooks beneath names where she will soon hang up her coat, you have become the mother. You are the one putting on the cheerful face. It is your arm extending involuntarily into the air, waving frantically in a performance enacted for both your sakes. It is your insides rearranging themselves as your child, an actual part of you walking around outside your body like an organ on legs, disappears into the building. And so Henry, at some undesignated point long after the goodbye on the platform of Nuremberg Central Station, must change tracks. The memory reel replays just as it has always done, but now he will see the brave teenage boy standing in his shorts on the platform with his little case and a label round his neck through the eyes of his parents. He will feel their agony instead of his own. His heart will multiply, beat and break in the bodies of his parents.

In Hamburg, two months later, it is Ingrid who is saying goodbye to her parents on a railway platform. It is 3 July, high summer, and she has just turned fifteen. In her case is a copy of *Grimm's Fairy Tales*, her school uniform, and, in one of the pockets, three pfennigs. Her guarantors, when she meets them, will unpack her case and take them, but eventually Ingrid will get the pfennigs back. One will end up on the wall of her grandson's flat, and the other two will wind up back in Liverpool Street Station, where Ingrid is due to arrive in just over a day. In 2003, they will form part of the first sculpture commemorating the Kindertransport, *Für Das Kind*, in which a bronze figure of a girl stands on a stone plinth, looking at a glass case filled with items carried by the thousands of children who arrived into Liverpool Street. The case will contain toys, books, clothes, photographs, drawings, sculptures, and Ingrid's pfennigs. The sculpture, by Flor Kent, who in sixty years will persuade Ingrid to give her the pfennigs at a major reunion of the Kindertransportees, will be situated in a piazza outside the station. But over time the sun bearing down on the glass and the unstable conditions inside it will fade the belongings. The sculpture will be dismantled. The artefacts will be returned to the Imperial War Museum. And in July 2011, the same month I meet the Wugas, the bronze sculpture and plaque will be moved to the ground floor of Liverpool Street Station, near the entrance to the Underground.

On the station platform in Hamburg children are crying 'bitterly'. Ingrid sees a father unable to part with his daughter lifting her out through the train window at the last minute. She watches her parents run alongside the slowly departing train, waving and waving. 'I will never forget saying goodbye to my parents,' says Ingrid. 'You wave goodbye until you can't . . .' She trails off, starts up again. 'You wave and wave until the train is so far away you can't see your parents any more. It's just horrific. You don't know what will happen or what lies ahead for you.'

From Nuremberg, Henry's train bears northwest for the German–Dutch frontier. The journey takes most of the day. He does not recall speaking to anyone. Each compartment is under Nazi guard. Trauma has neatly and efficiently swept all but a few traces of the memory away. 'Really I cannot . . . I remember the horror,' he says. 'Look, it was all right for me. I had been away from home in Baden-Baden, I was older, but many of these kids were six and seven years old. They had never left their mums and dads. I tell this story a lot. It never gets . . . it was the howling of the children. Carriages full of screaming children. Horrendous.'

When Henry's train reaches the border the Nazi guards get off, and the atmosphere on board changes instantly. It is palpable, this rush that comes with the abrupt exit of the people who have persecuted them for so long. On the frontier, they hover briefly between times. Behind is the homeland forever lost to them. Ahead lies the unknown. Foreign places and tongues. The future. Henry experiences this metamorphosis as an almighty release. 'The pressure lifted,' says Henry. 'Even the little ones felt it.'

Groups of Dutch women volunteers come onboard. And here, Henry's memory returns in a flood of colour and sensation, preserved by the balm of hospitality. For the first time in years, he experiences how he is treated by strangers outside Nazi Germany. With kindness. 'We were received by these smiling ladies handing out chocolate, apples and sandwiches,' he says. 'White bread and red apples. Being children, this was what you remembered. We didn't have sliced loaves like that in Germany, it was always rye bread. We were made welcome, and the difference was unbeliev-able. After all that crying on the train . . . The minute someone was kind to you, you felt better.'

The train bears west through Holland for the coast. Dusk falls across flat lands. The children arrive at the southwest corner of this strange new country apparently run, in a mirror image of the classic German fairy tale, by kind women proffering shiny red apples.

'I had never seen the sea before,' says Henry. 'I had never been on a boat.'

By the time they arrive at the land's edge, it is dark. The channel is an inked black expanse merging with the rim of the night sky. Henry boards a ferry. He falls asleep instantly.

The next morning he awakes in a new country. Britain. The country which will be his lifelong home. The boat docks in the maritime town of Harwich on the Essex coast, with its Victorian pier, pair of lighthouses, and fort which will soon be put into military service when war breaks out. The children see none of this potted British history studded on the mantle of the coast. Immigration officers come on board the ferry to check and stamp their 'white cards'. Only then are the children permitted to walk down the gangway. Those without guarantors to meet them in London are taken to the nearby seaside town of Dovercourt, where a Butlin's camp is being used as a kind of clearing station for the 'unguaranteed' children until further arrangements can be made.

The rest of the children, Henry amongst them, board a train for Liverpool Street Station.

4 May. Henry arrives in London. His first sight of the capital is a vast subterranean station built upon multiple layers of history. Time is stacked vertically in all ancient cities, but even by London's standards Liverpool Street is history on steroids. The station, whose main concourse is sunk some twenty feet beneath street level, is built on the site of the first Bethlehem Hospital. Founded as a priory in 1247 to care for the poor and needy, it eventually becomes known as Bedlam, Europe's first asylum for the insane. In

1415 it is described by London's Lord Mayor as 'an abode for those who have fallen out of wit'.

All this suffering, and more, is sensed by Austerlitz, whose night wanderings in the city inevitably seem to terminate at Liverpool Street. 'Whenever I was in the station,' he observes, 'I kept almost obsessively trying to imagine the location in that huge space of the rooms where the asylum inmates were confined, and I often wondered whether the pain and suffering accumulated on this site over the centuries had ever really ebbed away'. Even before Austerlitz realises Liverpool Street Station is part of his own history, suffering and salvation, he is disturbed by the ghosts he senses as he passes through the station halls and up and down the flights of steps.

Death continues to abound on the site. In 1569, propelled by the growing Empire, increasing immigration and a severe plague, the flooded medieval marshland known as Moorfields is turned into London's first municipal graveyard. Over the next 170 years up to 25,000 bodies are buried in the New Churchyard as London's parish graveyards become over-crowded, and the dead, like the living, must move with the times. This is how the non-parochial burial ground becomes the final resting place of Londoners unattached to any church. People who lived on the margins are, in the end, buried on the margins. Radicals. Religious dissenters. Non-conformists. Migrants. People like Karl and Lore Wuga. People like Henry and Ingrid. People like my parents. People like me.

Until the 1980s, when Liverpool Street Station is modern-ised into the brightened and concealed station I grow up with, it continues to be known as 'the dark cathedral'. A labyrinthine Victorian station mired in soot and suffering. This is the station Henry, Austerlitz, and, of course, Sebald, inhabit. A station described by Austerlitz as 'one of the darkest and most sinister places in London', and 'a kind of entrance to the underworld'.

A decade after Sebald's death, history is unearthed again

in Bishopsgate during the biggest archeological dig in London's history. Construction work to lay the city's latest Underground line across seventy-three miles of the metropolis begins in 2011, the year I meet the Wugas, and takes six years. The biggest and most historically important work happens around Liverpool Street. Here, sixty archeologists contracted from the Museum of London work on the Crossrail dig in two shifts, excavating around three thousand skeletons from the site. The bones are piled on top of one another, generations of Londoners mingling in the ground. The archeologists burrow through four time zones; past the Victorian and Georgian eras, the New Churchyard years, the period of the Moorfield marshes, and finally, six metres below street level, they wind up in Roman times, where they find horseshoes pleasingly known as hippo sandals, fragments of doors, and the remains of an engineered road into Londinium. During the dig, visitors are permitted to visit the site on their lunch break to watch, through a window, the archaeologists hunched over on their knees, digging, turning and scraping the ground. After the dig, an exhibition is staged displaying some of the objects excavated along the route. Bones from Black Death victims. Crosse & Blackwell marmalade and pickle jars. The jawbone of a medieval mouse. Sebald would have loved it.

When Henry enters Liverpool Street Station he senses this unseen history, like the rumble of a tube train running somewhere deep underfoot. It seems to him 'a black hole'. The children are taken 'into a cellar or cavern of some sort', deeper underground, closer than they can know to their human ancestors. Here, in this underworld, they wait to be collected. Most children are picked up by their guarantors, a process which takes hours. Others have no one. 'People volunteered to take a child and then came to the station to pick one,' says Henry. 'I tell you, I saw children sitting there while people walked past and said "No, I don't like him or her." I saw siblings separated because someone didn't want to take a younger sister, or an older boy. It was a cattle market. It was quite traumatic.' Henry is to go to Glasgow the following morning, along with two younger children; a boy and a girl. Because of this he has to wait in the bowels of the dark cathedral all day, watching the lives of children being determined around him, over and over again.

On 4 July, a shopkeeper called Mr Overton comes to collect Ingrid from Liverpool Street Station. A date that Ingrid, in the future, will refer to as her very own Independence Day. Alan Overton is a kind and rather formal Christadelphian volunteer, and a key figure in the Movement for the Care of Children from Germany. He has already assisted scores of Kindertransport children arriving into the country. Every week he comes to Liverpool Street to meet the boat trains. He places advertisements in newspapers calling for more homes to be found. He turns his own home into a transit house. He establishes a hostel for refugee boys in Rugby. He begins to receive a tide of letters from the continent as he becomes known as a man willing to help the Jewish children of Nazi Germany, Austria and Czechoslovakia. Many of the letters are simply addressed to 'Overton, Rugby, England'.

Ingrid and Mr Overton walk through the city to a west end Lyons' Corner House, a huge bustling art deco restaurant across a number of floors. The Lyons' Corner Houses, of which there are a few in London, have become the favoured meeting places of Jewish refugees. Jewish-owned, though not kosher, they are said to harbour so many German Jewish professionals that refugees joke that the Central Berlin District Court has transferred, wholesale, to Lyons' Corner House, Piccadilly Circus. 'It was quite something,' says Ingrid. 'Very proper.' They sit down, and Mr Overton tells Ingrid she can order whatever she likes. She asks for tea, which she finds to her astonishment is taken with milk. She watches Mr Overton break bread with his hands instead of cutting it with a knife. She sees him cut a potato with a knife instead of breaking it with a fork. These, like his kindnesses, are small acts, but they stand for something vast and unsayable, and she will never forget them. After the meal is over Mr Overton slides a penny across the table towards her. 'He said "You may need that",' Ingrid recalls with a chuckle. 'I didn't want any money but eventually I realised it was to put in the slot so I could go to the loo. He was just too polite to say it.'

Back in May, Henry and the two other children are taken to a hostel. The following morning they are collected by a volunteer and taken to Euston Station where they board a Royal Scot train for Glasgow. The volunteer hands them over to the train guard, who takes them first to a compartment, and then to the dining car for refreshments. Henry's young mind, so freighted with all it has been forced to bear, is blown. There are waiters with white gloves serving tea from silver teapots. One of the children he is with, a girl much younger than him, refuses the tea and asks for a hot chocolate. Unbelievably, a hot chocolate is produced. 'It was beautifully upholstered,' Henry says. 'A bit of luxury. I had never seen a dining room on a train before. I mean, in Germany we travelled third class on wooden benches. Oh, we were well looked after on that train. It was unbelievable to me. This train journey will forever be in my mind.'

The Kindertransports will continue for just three more months. The last train will leave Berlin on 1 September, the same day Hitler invades Poland and the Second World War officially begins. Afterwards, leaving Nazi-occupied Europe will become virtually impossible. In less than three years, on 20 January 1942, as Henry and Ingrid are falling in love at the house on the hill in Sauchiehall Street, a meeting attended by fifteen SS officers will be held in a mansion along Lake Wannsee on the outskirts of Berlin. The single item on the meeting's agenda, the euphemistic minutes of which will survive the war, will be the 'final solution of the Jewish question'. Six million Jews will die in the Holocaust, more than one and a half million of whom will be children. The vast majority of the Kindertransport children will be orphaned by the genocide. They will not go back to the homelands they left because neither their homes nor the people who made them will exist. Almost all of the Kindertransport children, as they will be known for the rest of their lives, will remain in Britain.

The Royal Scot heads north, nosing up the western side of the country. Henry is carried, on a track laid a century ago, through landscapes encircling the cities of Birmingham, Manchester and Liverpool. He is carried past the bright green and forever rained upon hills of the Lake District. He is carried across another border, into Scotland. Towards his future. To the life that he cannot yet know has been saved. To Glasgow, the city to which he will belong for the rest of his days.

The countryside begins to level out as it invariably does on the approach into a city. The organic blur of grass and sky is replaced, first randomly and then at pace, by the angular greys and browns of warehouses, the blackened stone of factories and houses, smoke unfurling from chimneys, and the sudden green flashes of parks and trees. There is the dreamlike sensation of moving in and out of tunnels, between dark and light. The particular thrill that accompanies any advance into a great post-industrial city on a train. The crossing of the invisible threshold into humanity in its most condensed and clamorous form. A place where life is potent, fluid, tough, possible.

The track ascends.

The train seems to glide through the air, level with the upper parts of buildings and trees.

It merges with the vista.

With the city itself.

The Royal Scot chugs across a wide railway bridge poised over the Clyde. The river, once bristling with ships, that made the city of Glasgow. The river that was deepened to make way for the rapid expansion of the tobacco and sugar trade, so that Scotland could sail ever more ships to Africa to get ever more slaves, then on to the West Indies and America, so ever bigger ships bringing slave-traded sugar and tobacco could dock back in Glasgow. The river that in less than two years will become the target of intense German bombing because of the concentration of historic Clydeside shipbuilding. The river out of which history will continue to silently spring.

The train slows down.

It is swallowed by the open mouth of Glasgow Central Station.

It comes to a stop on platform one where, Henry hopes, his cousin Grete Gummers will be waiting for him.

He stands up.

Grips his case.

The door opens.

Henry gets off the train.

Hinterlands

Here are the hinterlands that made *Homelands*. I'm indebted to each and every one.

Books

- *Austerlitz* by W.G. Sebald (Penguin 2011, translated by Anthea Bell, first published 2001) – for literally everything, from how to infuse another person's life with truth and dignity to what lies beneath Liverpool Street Station. My aloof German dead white male spirit guide. Who knew?

- *The Emigrants* by W.G. Sebald (Vintage 2002, translated by Michael Hulse, first published 1993) – for Dr Henry Selwyn, Paul Bereyter, Ambros Adelwarth and Max Ferber, and the real Jewish émigrés who inspired them.

- *Notes of a Native Son* by James Baldwin (Penguin Classics 2017, first published 1958) – for his 'special attitude', which birthed mine. For his delicious (radical) irony, brain and style. Because he was born in 1924. The same year as my Henry.

- *Blind Spot* by Teju Cole (Faber and Faber 2016) – especially for his photos of, and meditations on, Berlin, Nuremberg, Wannsee and Bombay. For seeing cities as places where history has happened, even if all that remains is a Burger King. For feeling the lingering presence of death in spring. For knowing that 'in a dark time, the eye begins to see'. For being a person who goes places with his universal mind, particular black body and camera.

- *The Years* by Annie Ernaux (Fitzcarraldo Editions 2019, translated by Alison L. Strayer, first published 2008) – for the observation that 'our memory is outside us, in a rainy breath of time'. For the sheer bravura of writing an autobiography without using the word 'I'. For reading history (in such riven times!) as collective experience. For every fucking generous sentence.

- 'We Refugees' by Hannah Arendt (*The Jewish Writings*, Schocken Books 1943) – because she saw and wrote the reality in which we live. For pondering, in the midst of the Second World War, why immigrants are optimists. A handful of words that more than seventy years later built a bridge between Henry and me . . . and changed everything.

- *The Holocaust* by Laurence Rees (Penguin 2017) – for the devastating granular detail, month by month, year by year, so I could position my Henry in the epic landscape of history. It was necessary. It broke my heart not to look away.

- *and our faces, my heart, brief as photos* by John Berger (Bloomsbury 2005, first published 1984) – for that title! For writing a book with two parts: Time, Space. For helping me try to accept my mother's death (still haven't).

- *Understanding a Photograph* by John Berger (Penguin Classics 2013, originally published 1967–2013) – for saying the deepest things in the simplest ways. Like: 'All photographs are of the past.' For blowing the door of my mind open and making me believe in this world once more, as only Berger can.

- *A Fortunate Man: The Story of a Country Doctor* by John Berger and Jean Mohr (Canongate Books 2016, first published 1967) – for the kind, wise, deep focus on one ordinary man. For doctors (as the daughter of one). For the concept (Berger-sized) of a landscape as 'a curtain behind which [its inhabitants'] struggles, achievements, and accidents take place'. Hence landmarks: biographical as well as geographic. Wow.

- *A Seventh Man* by John Berger and Jean Mohr (Verso 2010, first published 1975) – for humanising migrant workers (in the 1970s!). For the simple idea of making 'a little book of life stories, a sequence of lived moments – such as one finds in a family photo album'. Which is exactly what I've tried to do.

- *Slouching Towards Bethlehem* by Joan Didion (Fourth Estate 2017, first published 1968) – always, but specifically in this case for 'Goodbye To All That', because it helped me understand, as only Didion can, that any 'goodbye to all that' is inevitably a 'hello to all this'. And for its profound first sentence, which inspired mine.

- *The Cost of Living* by Deborah Levy (Penguin 2019, first published 2018) – for the idea of living autobiography. For all the women of courage and insight who live and write it.

- *Jewish Refugees from Germany and Austria in Britain 1933–1970* by Anthony Grenville (Vallentine Mitchell 2010) – for the facts, specificity, insider perspective, and what's often overlooked: the everyday lives of Jewish refugees in Britain in the decades after the war.

- *One-way Street and Other Writings* by Walter Benjamin (Penguin 2009, first published between 1921 and 1936) – because he wrote: 'the work of memory collapses time', which rebuilt *Homelands* and (sort of) me after my mother died. For prompting me to think about how memory and forgetting live side by side in us like objects in a room. For making me want to read Proust (still haven't).

- *On the Natural History of Destruction* by W.G. Sebald (Penguin 2004, translated by Anthea Bell, first published 1999) – for his account of the aerial bombing of Germany by the Allies in the last years of the Second World War. For writing, calmly and responsibly, about that which has been silenced. For showing me how little I knew (see also Priyamvada Gopal and David Olusoga).

- *Taking a Long Look: Essays on Culture, Literature, and Feminism in Our Time* by Vivian Gornick (Verso 2021, published from 1970s to 2017) – for her thoughts on Arendt's concept of 'worldlessness' – i.e. being outside history. Thanks to Gornick, I now understand why Arendt believed we cannot absent ourselves from the world in which we find ourselves. I believe Henry thinks this, too. So do I.

- *The Bitter Taste of Victory: Life, Love, and Art in the Ruins of the Reich* by Lara Feigel (Bloomsbury 2016) – for being foundational: the book you need to build your own that has actually been written! For taking me into the ruins of post-Second World War Germany, accompanied by the likes of Martha Gellhorn – what a card! – and the inimitable Rebecca West. For allowing me to see (sort of) through the eyes of Lore Wuga.

- *If This Is A Man* by Primo Levi (Abacus 1987, first published 1958) – to do my best (forgive me, I wanted to look away) to imagine what moral stamina and the preservation of human identity actually means and requires.

- *Night* by Elie Wiesel (Penguin 2008, first published 1956) – because he was fifteen when he was sent to Auschwitz, the same age as my Henry was when he got out of Nazi Germany on a Kindertransport. No book broke my heart more.

- *Into The Arms of Strangers: Stories of the Kindertransport* by Mark Jonathan Harris and Deborah Oppenheimer (Bloomsbury 2017, first published 2000) – for David Cesarani's brilliant introduction. For the stories.

- *Kristallnacht: Prelude to Destruction* by Martin Gilbert (Harper Perennial 2007, first published 2006) – for the meticulous detail and eyewitness accounts. To understand the night of horror that prefigured the Holocaust and prompted the great (however flawed) British humanitarian gesture that was the Kindertransport.

- *The Magic Mountain* by Thomas Mann (Vintage 1996, first published 1924) – for the strange, intoxicating, outside-of-time vibe of spa towns. For the snow, malaise and pandemic aptness. Because it came out the year my Henry was born.

- *The Hare with Amber Eyes: A Hidden Inheritance* by Edmund de Waal (Vintage 2011, first published 2010) – to see a master at work. (See also *East West Street* by

Philippe Sands). To see how I might find a way into a story that, unlike de Waal's, was not remotely mine.

- *Surfacing* by Kathleen Jamie (Sort of Books 2019) – for the archaeology of memory, and how to write about others and their cultures, lands and histories with compassion, and a certain lightness of touch that is actually the manifestation of depth and moral integrity. Because her essays are the river's confluence, and I adore her (as a person, too).

- *On Photography* by Susan Sontag (Penguin Modern Classics 2008, first published 1977) – for seeing photographs as memento mori. Spooky, and true.

- *Insurgent Empire: Anticolonial Resistance and British Dissent* by Priyamvada Gopal (Verso 2019) – for inducing me, a British Indian child of the 1980s, to realise I knew little about post-colonialism and nothing about anti-colonialism. Thus, for teaching me the history I didn't know happened. For linking, so vitally, the end of the Second World War and the death of the British Empire. For being her kickass, professorial, take-no-shit, forever-tweeting-truth-to-power, fabulously Indian queen self (therefore slightly channelling my aunties). For liking the sound of my parents (good taste).

- *Brit(ish): On Race, Identity and Belonging* by Afua Hirsch (Jonathan Cape 2018) – for going there. For courage, handed from one south-west Londoner to another. If she can do it, etc.

- *The Survivor* by Primo Levi (Penguin Modern Classics 2018, poems first published 1988) – for the lines in 'Shemà', written on 10 January 1946: 'Ponder that this happened: / I consign these words to you.'

- *Look We Have Coming to Dover!* by Daljit Nagra (Faber and Faber 2007) – for speaking in one's own voice (whatever that means). For Indian (also quite Jewish) humour and chutzpah.

- *Reunion* by Fred Uhlman (Vintage 2015, first published 1971) – to understand the mindset of liberal, metropolitan, assimilated German Jews in the (pre) Nazi era. Because Uhlman was also interned on the Isle of Man. Because I saw Ali Smith talking about *Reunion* with Ali Smith levels of enthusiasm (and she's always right).

- *Address Unknown* by Kathrine Kressmann Taylor (Serpent's Tail 2019, first published 1938) – for the importance of letters, especially wartime ones, for what they carry and withhold. For the art of concision, because I always intend to write a 'slim volume' (maybe next time).

- *The Train Was on Time* by Heinrich Böll (Penguin 2019, first published 1949) – to try to understand Germany, and the German psyche, after the war. For trains, especially as metaphors for journeying through life, with the final stop being . . . the end of the line.

- *Lost in Translation: A Life in a New Language* by Eva Hoffman (Vintage 1998, first published 1989) – for memoir at its most pure and direct. And because my beloved bought it for me when I had lost my way in my own *Homelands*.

- *The Refugees* by Viet Thanh Nguyen (Corsair 2018) – for that beautiful line about stories being our (refugees', immigrants' and their descendants') belongings.

- *East West Street* by Philippe Sands (Weidenfeld &

Nicolson 2017, first published in 2016) – for legal and historical context on the Nuremberg Trials. To see how memoir, at its height, is done by someone on the inside of the story. Someone unlike me.

- *Axiomatic* by Maria Tumarkin (Fitzcarraldo Editions 2019, first published 2018) – because there are always other, weirder, equally valid ways of writing about history/trauma/others/oneself.

- *Two Lives* by Vikram Seth (Abacus 2006, first published 2005) – because (unbelievable!) it's a memoir linking the Holocaust, Second World War and India. For the chapter (3.33) ruminating on how events in Germany shaped the century and sealed India's fate (independence, at last). To immerse myself in a certain kind of (good, grateful, upstanding) Indian first-generation immigrant sensibility. (Seth is a decade younger than my parents.)

- *Two Lives: Gertrude and Alice* by Janet Malcolm (Yale University Press 2007) – for originality, cool intelligence and the journalistic endeavour to investigate 'how . . . the pair of elderly Jewish lesbians survived the Nazis?' Also for the pleasure of reading two completely different books called *Two Lives*. (Four Lives?)

- *Minor Monuments: Essays* by Ian Maleney (Tramp Press 2019) – for unexpected connections between memory loss (dementia, Alzheimer's) and music. Also our need to record things for posterity (whatever that means).

- *A Literature of Restitution: Critical Essays on W.G. Sebald* edited by Jeannette Baxter, Valerie Henitiuk, Ben Hutchinson (Manchester University Press 2013) – for essays on the moral power of *Austerlitz* being its structural limitation/remove: remaining always a witness to a witness. Also train stations as thresholds. For Anthea Bell's foreword, in which she recalls being 'bowled over' by the typed manuscript of *Austerlitz* she received from Sebald (who still had 'grave doubts'). And how she read it – his magnum opus, his last book – in a single day in her garden 'one warm summer's day' in June.

- *Face of Our Time: Sixty Portraits of Twentieth-Century Germans* by August Sander, introduced by Alfred Döblin (Schirmer Art Books 2003, translated by Michael Robertson, first published 1929) – to understand the context swirling around the photo taken of Henry and Chef Schneider in the kitchens of the Hotel Tannhäuser, Baden-Baden, in the summer of 1938. For the societal record. For the faces.

- *Mister Cleghorn's Seal* by Judith Kerr (HarperCollins Children's Books 2015) – for the dedication – 'To my father, who once kept a seal on the balcony' – which happens to be true. For the privilege of interviewing Kerr, in her south-west London home in the summer of 2016 (she lived near my parents), and how much she reminded me of Henry and Ingrid (love of life in spite/because of what happened. Also mischief, laughter and that way of arranging biscuits on good plates). Because she described her father, the theatre critic and writer Alfred Kerr, as having 'a talent for happiness'.

- *Frank Auerbach: Speaking and Painting* by Catherine Lampert (Thames and Hudson 2015) – because he inspired the character of Max Ferber in Sebald's *The Emigrants*. For painting as action (all those layers!). For his background, about which he rarely speaks (obviously he turned down my request for an interview).

- *Doctor Faustus* by Thomas Mann (Everyman's Library 1992, translated by H.T. Lowe-Porter, first published 1947) – for music and myth and the times, as seen *in* the times (he wrote it in exile from Nazi Germany). Because, in all honesty, I felt I had to (bloody hard work, still only halfway through).

- *The Cut Out Girl: A Story of War and Family, Lost and Found* by Bart van Es (Penguin 2019) – for that arresting opening line about it being Hitler who made Lien Jewish.

- *Intimations* by Zadie Smith (Penguin 2020) – for so accurately describing our contemporary virus of contempt. For writing with such clarity in the midst of said virus, as I myself was trying to do. For her final essay, 'Intimations', a list of 'Debts and Lessons', which inspired the chapter called 'Hinterlands' you are reading right now.

Audio

- The German folk song 'Die Gedanken Sind Frei' – because Ingrid continued to sing it when so much else had fallen away from her memory. Because it's about freedom of thought.

- *Die Meistersinger von Nürnberg* by Richard Wagner – because my Henry risked all to see it, in Nuremberg, during the Nazi era (my god! also, silly boy).

- *Richard Wagner: Power, Sex and Revolution*, presented by Paul Mason, BBC Radio 4, April 2013 – particularly episode two, which wades into the dark territory of nationalism and (just say it, folks!) anti-Semitism in *Die Meistersinger*.

- *The House on the Hill*, BBC Radio Scotland, 1989 – for the amazing tales, told by refugees including my Henry and Ingrid, of the house on Sauchiehall Street during the war. For the descriptions of the food. For the squeal-out-loud thrill of hearing Henry and Ingrid's supple young 1980s voices speaking to me in my grief-stricken sitting room during lockdown.

- 'Judith Kerr', *Desert Island Discs*, BBC Radio 4, 5 March 2004 – for her musical choices ('Willkommen' from *Cabaret* and Beethoven's Symphony No.7 in A Major, Op 92!). Because she spoke so beautifully about living well on behalf of all the children murdered in the Holocaust who did not get the chance. Which helped me answer the question – how can Henry and Ingrid be so happy?

- 'Into My Arms' by Nick Cave and the Bad Seeds (1997, *The Boatman's Call*) – does every book have an ear worm? I have no idea, but this one does. The most glorious song, a prayer for the broken-hearted agnostic, which for all the reasons echoed in my head throughout the writing and researching of *Homelands*.

TV and film

- *The Last Survivors*, BBC Two, 27 January 2021, directed by Arthur Cary – because Cary gave survivors, and their descendants, space and time to speak about their lives in the round. Because his beautiful, spare, dignified documentary was the greatest antidote to complacency in a world that seems to be forgetting.

- *Whatever Happened to Susi?*, BBC, 1991 – because it was the documentary that inspired Sebald to create the character of Jacques Austerlitz. Because I found it lurking on YouTube. Because Susi Bechhofer should be remembered too.

- *Lost*, created by Damon Lindelof, Jeffrey Lieber and J.J. Abrams, ABC, 2004–2010 – one of the greatest TV series of the century (fact), for its dizzying application of the flash-forward, which hugely influenced my decision to (somehow) make a century of history unfold at the same time. Also, for the same reason, Muriel Spark (bizarrely never mentioned in the same breath as J.J. Abrams), who used the literary device of the flash-forward with such bite, wit and dark intent.

- Richard Linklater's *Before* trilogy, especially *Before Sunrise* (1995) and *Before Sunset* (2004), because it is about how cities/places vibrate with the energy of the people who have been (and loved) in them. For the frames lingering on the places – a cafe, park bench, cemetery – where Jesse and Celine were. For the double bill my beloved and I watched in a tiny cinema in the CCA as we were falling in love, metres away from Henry and Ingrid's house on the hill.

- *Black and British: A Forgotten History*, presented by David Olusoga, BBC Two, 9 November 2016, and 'British Empire: Heroes and Villains', presented by David Olusoga, *Timewatch Guide*, BBC Four, 1 February 2017 – for showing the ways in which the British Empire has been (mis)represented to us, thus shining a light on the holes in my own education. For teaching me that remembrance is a political act. And history is never done.

- *Unremembered – Britain's Forgotten War Heroes*, presented by David Lammy, Channel 4, 9 November 2019 – for

336

revealing the neglected history of the unmarked, unnamed burial of hundreds of thousands of black African bodies killed in the First World War. For showing the undeniable links between racism, colonialism and historical revisionism.

Journalism

- Amelia Gentleman's essential and tireless reporting on the Windrush scandal, *Guardian*, April 2018 to present – because she revealed the true scale, injustice and tragedy of what was being carried out in plain sight by our government. Because she showed us what living in a hostile environment really means for so many.

- *The Marginalian* (formerly known as *Brain Pickings*) by Maria Popova – for her extraordinary capacity for synthesis. In particular, her writings on James Baldwin and Hannah Arendt ('Between the World and Us'), which illuminated the world that lies between Henry and me, and thus showed me the way.

- *The New Yorker* – for Rebecca West's astounding reporting on the Nuremberg Trials. For a trio of pieces on W.G. Sebald ('Why You Should Read W.G. Sebald' by Mark O'Connell, 14 December 2011, 'W.G. Sebald, Humorist' by James Wood, 29 May 2017, and 'W.G. Sebald and *The Emigrants*' by André Aciman, 25 August 2016) that helped me understand his oblique genius. For 'Bedlam's Big Dig' by Sam Knight, 9 April 2015, which brought to the surface/present the deep layers of history unearthed by the Crossrail dig around Liverpool Street Station.

- 'Hidden Treasure on Sauchiehall Street', *The Herald*, 21 February 2001, which reported on the incredible discovery of a Georgian villa during the refurbishment of the CCA in Glasgow.

- My interview with Judith Kerr (*The Scotsman*, 21 August 2016). See *books*.

- My interview with Russell Hoban (*The Scotsman*, 3 November 2010) – because when I met him in a cafe near his West London home he said to me, 'If you look at ten people crossing the road each one has something in his or her head that has nothing to do with crossing the road'. And then we watched people crossing the road outside the cafe in silence. Because at the end of the interview, which remains one of the great encounters of my life, he recited the whole of A.E. Housman's 76-line poem, 'Terence, This Is Stupid Stuff' for me. Because he was the son of Ukrainian Jewish immigrants. Because he (too briefly) became my friend. Because he died the following year, and I went to his funeral, and it was at the same crematorium where my mother's funeral would be nine years later.

Acknowledgements

From the moment I met Henry and Ingrid, it was as though I walked over the threshold of their door into a new chapter of my own life. Right then and there, on that June day in 2011, this book started writing itself in some unplumbed and, then, inaccessible room inside me. Over the years I continued to interview 'the magnificent Wugas', as they became known in my home, as a journalist. But it took seven summers before I began in earnest (way too earnest, it turned out), trying to write the book that needed to be written though I had no idea how to write it. It took time. So many individuals and organisations helped along the way, in as many ways as it is possible to help a person write a book.

So, here goes.

Thank you . . .

To The National Archives (TNA), whose public records, materials and online blogs were so essential to the researching and writing of *Homelands*. Particularly: the Aliens Department Internees Index in First and Second World War records; the internment card for Annamaria Wuga issued at a wartime tribunal on December 14, 1939, which I downloaded from findmypast.com and which, incredibly, Henry had never seen before; resources on the Kindertransport; and information on Papers of the Royal Botanic Gardens, Kew, During the Second World War. It was TNA that sent Henry his files, requested through FOAs first in 2008, then in 2019. And in many ways it was the files that sparked the book. It was also through TNA that I tracked down and interviewed Roger Kershaw, Head of Strategic Operations and Volunteers in the Collections Expertise and Engagement department of TNA, and a bit of a rock star to me as the author of such brilliant TNA blogs as 'Collar the lot! Britain's policy of internment during the Second World War' (2 July 2015), 'Internment of enemy aliens in 1940: The fate of Italians resident in a Britain at war' (10 June 2020), and 'Empire Windrush – 70 years on' (21 June 2018). Our conversation about what made Henry's internment unusual – he was so young! He was a Jewish refugee labelled a Category A dangerous enemy alien! He was held for ten months in Peveril! – confirmed and clarified so much.

To Aubrey Pomerance, chief archivist at the Jewish Museum in Berlin, which holds Henry's extensive archive. Through interviewing Aubrey about Henry and Ingrid, I came to understand how and why Henry became a Holocaust educator in the latter decades of his life.

To Dr Anthony Grenville, the British-born son of refugees from Vienna and editor of the *Association of Jewish Refugees Journal* from 2005–2016. He interviewed Henry at great length on 4 October 2004 for Refugee Voices (AJR Refugee Voices Testimony interview RV74 with Henry Wuga), the AJR's testimony archive, which permitted me to reference the wonderful transcript.

To the Warth Mills Project, which sought out Henry in 2018 and told him he was the last known survivor of Warth Mills. Through this fantastic project I learnt about the terrible and previously buried history of one of the largest, certainly most brutal, Second World War internment camps in Britain, as well as the tragic sinking of the SS *Arandora Star*, on which Henry could so easily have been a passenger.

To Gathering The Voices Scotland, a Glasgow-based project committed to telling the stories of Jewish refugees who escaped Nazi persecution through audio and video testimonies and making them freely available online. Gathering The Voices interviewed Henry and Ingrid at length, recording their testimonies at a much earlier stage than me. These far-ranging transcripts were vital to the writing of *Homelands*, particularly the months and years after Henry and Ingrid arrived in Scotland.

To the National Records of Scotland, held at General Register House in Edinburgh, particularly senior court archivist James McCormack, who searched for records regarding Henry's High Court appearance in June 1940. He was the one who explained to me that the wartime tribunals were classified as hearings before a judge rather than criminal trials under Scots Law, and the charges against Henry would have been under emergency powers instituted by the British Government. In other words there were no official records, and he found nothing.

To the National Library of Scotland, who directed me to a wealth of available e-resources in the midst of a pandemic, which allowed me to trawl the many mentions of Henry through the decades in the Scottish newspapers. Thankfully for all of us, he loves a bit of press.

To Royal Museums Greenwich for the maritime history of the *Empire Windrush* ship. And the Pathé news footage from 22 June 1948, which described the 1,027 passengers as they are so rarely portrayed in the mainstream more than seventy years later: as 'ex-servicemen who know England' and 'served this country well. In Jamaica they couldn't find work. Discouraged but full of hope, they sailed for Britain, citizens of the British Empire coming to the Mother Country with good intent.'

To the elderly couple who now live at Rossie House in Forgandenny, Perth and Kinross, where Henry was briefly evacuated when war broke out. They kindly invited us to visit, before the pandemic made it impossible.

To Barnes and Mortlake History Society, particularly their addictive interactive map of where precisely, around the streets where my parents live(d), the bombs fell during the Second World War.

To the Royal Collection Trust for the fascinating history of Mortlake's tapestry industry. Oh, how I fell down the rabbit hole!

To English Heritage for the long, star-studded history of my beloved view from Richmond Hill (top-notch Wikipedia entry, too). The research was so enveloping this nearly ended up being a joint biography of Henry Wuga and . . . a view.

To Canmore, Scotland's National Record of the Historic Environment, for detail on two places where Henry was interned: Maryhill Barracks in Glasgow and Donaldson's in Edinburgh, where he ended up cooking a meal for a couple of hundred incoming internees with German sailors as his kitchen hands.

To Airfields of Britain Conservation Trust for information on the Scone Airfield in Perth where Henry could hear RAF pilots training with de Havilland Tiger Moths.

To Manx National Heritage and the National Library and Archives at the Manx Museum, Douglas, Isle of Man, for explaining that only a partial listing exists for Second World War internees on the Isle of Man as the men's cards were destroyed after the war. Also, for directing me to the invaluable library where I read every newspaper published on the Isle of Man during the ten months of Henry's internment. To Manx Museum curator Yvonne Cresswell, who sent me a watercolour of Peveril, where Henry was held, by internee Herbert Kaden and – just wow! – an image of twelve chess pieces sculpted out of scrap wood by another internee, Hans Schwarz, the faces of which are thought to have been modelled on fellow internees and guards at

Peveril. Oh, and everyone looked for a record of Henry's enigmatic German-speaking metallurgist whom he remains convinced was an MI5 agent. Nothing was found.

To the Abbotsford Trust, for history on the world-famous flibbertigibbet of a house where Henry cooked a wedding banquet for Sir Walter Scott's descendants during the war.

To BLESMA, The Limbless Veterans, for heartwarming stories about the decades of volunteering work Henry and Ingrid did as ski instructors with the charity.

To The Kindertransport Association, for history on the rescue effort.

To the online interactive archive Lost Glasgow, for colour (as we journalists call it) on the post-war period in which Henry cooked his way through the hotels and restaurants of the city. Particularly good on the Corn Exchange on Gordon Street and the Grand Hotel in Charing Cross.

To the Imperial War Museum, for individual Kindertransport stories (and objects).

To Historic Hansard for Commons debates on 'Refugees', 10 July 1940 (HC Deb 10 July 1940 vol 362 cc1208-306), during which the independent MP Eleanor Rathbone spoke an astonishing twenty times. Also 'Racial, Religious and Political Minorities', 21 November 1938 (HC Deb 21 November 1938 vol 341 cc1428-83) during which Home Secretary Sir Samuel Hoare set out the urgent case for permitting a number of unaccompanied Jewish refugee children into the country. The rescue effort that would come to be known as the Kindertransport.

To the Scottish Jewish Archives Centre, in particular its director, Harvey Kaplan, who generously gave me all the information the centre had on the poorly documented wartime refugee centre at 358 Sauchiehall Street where Henry and Ingrid met. One article he sent me in what was then *The Glasgow Herald* ('Refugees remember a fading episode from Glasgow's past', 7 September 1988) was particularly instrumental. This is such a rich and neglected seam of Scottish history; someone should write a play about it. In the meantime, I wish the new, much-needed and welcome Scottish Holocaust-era Study Centre every success.

To BBC Radio Scotland, for sending me the audio file of *The House on the Hill*, a wonderful 1989 documentary on which Henry and Ingrid appear talking about the refugee centre at 358 Sauchiehall Street.

To the Scottish artist Bet Low, who died in 2007. Her vivid account of cultural, political and social life on Sauchiehall Street during the war ('Clinging to the Radiators', *Scottish Review*, 1996) was the key to writing 'It all goes back to the house on the hill'. Low wrote about fire-watching on the roof of the Glasgow School of Art during the war, just as Henry and Ingrid were on the roof of the house below. She recalled renting a tiny flat in the tenement opposite 'the last remaining villa house in Sauchiehall Street', in other words Henry and Ingrid's house on the hill, where 'three great women of the kitchen, Ailsa, Rosa and Gita . . . would help me to survive in the next few years'. She wrote about the free bowls of soup the women refugees gave her as she painted through the night in her 'thick wartime coat' while mice galloped around the room. And she wrote about the break-up of the refugee centre a few years later. 'For a brief period,' she concluded, 'Glasgow was cosmopolitan. It seemed to us that the city was alive. But in the bleak 1950s, it was as if nothing had happened at all'. Henry and Low never met but I showed him her account of a past he, too, recalls so vividly. It blew his mind.

To Glasgow University Archives & Special Collections, for sending me a scan of an elusive painting Bet Low made in 1946 of the house on the hill when it became the Unity Theatre. It took ages to track it down. The painting was bought by my old university in 1983 and is currently part of the Scottish Theatre Archive collection. Finally, it arrived in my inbox: a narrow, dark-toned oil painting in a tradi-tional gold frame depicting the thin slice of the street where the last villa once stood (now the Dental Hospital). Here was 358 Sauchiehall Street exactly as Henry and Ingrid remembered it. What a thing to see.

To Jewish New Yorker and researcher Aryeh Levi, whose ancestors ran the Central, an elegant kosher hotel a few doors down from the Hotel Tannhäuser in 1930s Baden-Baden. Levi gave an excellent talk about his family's hotel in pre-war era Baden-Baden at the town hall commemora-tion of the Reichspogromnacht at which Henry was guest of honour. (I watched it on Youtube.) It closed with an impassioned plea to the audience, which included Henry and Hilary in the front row, not to allow the natural beauty of Baden-Baden to conceal its past. This provided essential backdrop to my two-part chapter on Baden-Baden, as did the wonderful back-and-forth Aryeh and I shared on email about Baden-Baden, the specific atmosphere of belle époque spa towns, the Jewish hotel trade between the wars, his great-great-grandfather Philip Lieblich who, like the Köhler-Sterns, stayed in the spa town for as long as he could, and much else besides.

To translator Kit Sainsbury, whose mother's partner, Anne, is the granddaughter of Ingrid's uncle. He offered to translate the extraordinary pre- and post-war letters of Lore Wuga, Henry's indefatigable mother. And what a job he did. Never have I been privy to such extraordinary, beautifully written and detailed primary material as a jour-nalist. And I wouldn't have been able to read a word of it without Kit.

To Friends of Cathcart Cemetery for the history, the will to preserve it that so often lives and dies with local commu-nity groups, and their wonderful virtual map recording names, graves and lives often unsung.

To author, journalist and ex-colleague of mine Peter Ross

for his evocative account of Cathcart Cemetery in his life-affirming elegy to Britain's graveyards, *A Tomb With A View* (Headline). And for the chat/semi-interview on the phone in lockdown in which we talked, naturally, about death, the Wugas, writing and the particular loveliness and low-key grandeur of Cathcart Cemetery, which he cuts through daily on the school run.

To Peggy Hughes, programme director for Writer's Centre, Norwich, and friend, who advised me so gently and rightly at early stages of the book. And because she was the one who invited me to chair Priyamvada Gopal at Norfolk and Norwich Festival.

To Stuart Kelly, writer, ex-colleague and friend, who said to me after my mother died 'make it for her'.

To the writer Ali Smith, whom I first interviewed in 2005 for *The Big Issue in Scotland*. Fourteen years later we shared a stage at Glasgow Women's Library, and she offered herself up as an early reader of *Homelands*. I know, lucky me. It's true that she gave me the most intense feedback at the worst of times. It's true that she told me three things that became the pillars holding up *Homelands*: put everything you can in the present, keep it simple, keep going. It's true that it nearly killed me. It's true that I am beyond grateful for it.

To Zan, best friend since forever (age four). For our magical shared childhood, soft hearts, love of food, dogs, our mums, Richmond Park and her kindness then and now. Because she loves the Ramaswamys and when my mother was dying, took it upon herself to organise (from Athens!) a south Indian meal cooked by an Indian friend of hers who is a chef to be sent to my parents in London. A meal that turned out to be a piece of magic.

To Avi, the Bangalorean chef and complete stranger who cooked the magical meal and sent it to my parents in an Uber during lockdown. Simply because we were suffering,

346

and he could do something to help. 'We Bangaloreans love our food,' he said. That meal brought my mother back to life. I hope one day I get to thank him in person.

To Jenny Brown, agent, booster in human (always smiling) form, and yet another inspiring mother in my life who has a way of holding a writer's hand – in this case, mine – so lightly and cheerfully that they don't even realise they're being nurtured. And who also, like so many of the best, possesses 'a talent for happiness'.

To Canongate, my dream publisher, and in particular my dream editor, Francis Bickmore, for perfectly understanding this strange book and, therefore, me. It was Francis who took me and my baby daughter out for coffee years ago and asked me what I was working on. Which sparked the realisation that I was, and had been for years, working on this.

To Creative Scotland, for awarding me Open Project Funding in the years when I was a part-time working mother of small children turning down paid commissions to tinker away at this . . . thing. The funding bought me time and confidence: both of which must be generated in excess to turn a thing into a book. I could not have got going without this grant.

To our childminder, Sharon, who looked after my daughter through this book (and my son through the last one). When a parent of very young children – especially a mother, and even more so when a child has additional needs – writes a book, others must come on board in order for her to finish the damn thing. Sharon is our others. Thank you, also, to local pals Emma and James, who gave me their basement flat to write in over a grim and frazzled Christmas, and Dawn, who offered the study of her late husband, Keith, who died a fortnight before my mother, and left a signed copy of a James Baldwin novel on his desk. Which meant that, for a time, I got to write beside Baldwin's signature.

To Hilary and Gillian, Henry and Ingrid's daughters, who worked tirelessly to track down this document and that photo, answered every single email within hours, set up Dropboxes for letters (Hilary), ferried Henry's archive across the Central Belt (Gillian), were present at every interview to make tea, entertain my daughter and look after their mum and dad (Hilary and Gillian), were delighted for their lives to be endlessly trawled over, and welcomed me into the fold.

To Ingrid Wuga, a mother, like my own, to model oneself on, for the interviews, mischief and warmth, whose questions were always pertinent, and who never stopped delighting in life, music and her family.

To my beloved, Claire, the rock on which this whole enterprise (the book, but more importantly life) balances. For being my (almost always) gentle but never soft-soapy first reader, for weathering the grief storm with me (not over yet), and doing her best to keep our children away most mornings of lockdown so I could write (it didn't work, but I appreciate the effort). Also our children, who hinder the actual writing but help in more fundamental ways. This includes our dog, Daphne, as sturdy a sofa companion as *Austerlitz* (though any comparisons with Sebald end there).

To my parents, who gave me everything and nothing, which is exactly as it should be. My loving, kind and unusual mother, who loved to be written about, and told me the last time I saw her that she knew this book would be wonderful. (Oh, the faith of a good mother. How am I supposed to live/write without it?) My dapper, right-minded, special-outlook-possessing, metropolitan, increasingly sweet father, who is so like Henry, and whom I realise, with each passing year, I am so like too. And my dear sister, who accepts this weird compulsion of mine to write about my (our) life, and is the one person on earth who understands what the loss of our mother really means (everything).

Thank you, above all, to Henry Wuga, for answering a decade of questions with patience, integrity and generosity. For reading every word I wrote with great enthusiasm. For his archive, special outlook, bow ties, cooking, love of music, babies, mountains, truth and life. For his kindness to me before and after my mother's death. For gifting me his story. For friendship.

Credits, Permissions, References

All quotes from *Austerlitz* by W.G. Sebald reference the 2011 Penguin special tenth anniversary edition translated by Anthea Bell with an introduction by James Wood. Page vii – excerpt from *Austerlitz* by W.G. Sebald, translated by Anthea Bell, translation copyright © 2001 by Anthea Bell. Used by permission of Random House, an imprint and division of Penguin Random House LLC. All rights reserved.

All quotes from *The Emigrants* by W.G. Sebald reference the Vintage 2002 edition translated by Michael Hulse.

All quotes from *On the Natural History of Destruction* by W.G. Sebald reference the Penguin 2004 edition translated by Anthea Bell.

Page 9 – document from Henry's file HO 405/60809. The National Archives, ref. HO396/202.

Page 15 – '. . . to create here in Britain . . .' Interview with Theresa May by James Kirkup and Robert Winnett, *The Telegraph*, 25 May 2012.

Page 18 – photograph of a section of the River Thames. Chitra Ramaswamy.

Page 62 – photograph of the view from Richmond Hill. Chitra Ramaswamy.

Page 66 – photograph of Lore and Karl in the years after the First World War. Henry Wuga.

Page 68 – photograph of Henry as a teenager in Nuremberg. Henry Wuga.

Page 71 – Henry's *Die Meistersinger* libretto. Henry Wuga.

Page 75 – 'In the dark times . . .' by Bertolt Brecht, Motto to the *Svendborg Poems*, 1939.

Page 77 – photograph of Henry and Ingrid at home in Giffnock. Copyright © Robert Perry.

Page 82 – 'spectres of the past', 'Unfortunately there is to this day . . .' 'Spectres of the past: Angela Merkel sounds alarm over antisemitism' by Kate Connolly, *Guardian*, 28 May 2019.

Page 85 – photograph of the glass roof of Glasgow Central. Chitra Ramaswamy.

Page 88 – photograph of Ingrid as a teenager. Henry Wuga.

Page 97 – photograph of Henry as a baby on Karl's lap. Henry Wuga.

Page 98 – Henry's and Ingrid's German passports issued by the Nazis. Henry Wuga.

Page 100 – photograph of Henry and Ingrid in their flat

on Maxwell Road, Glasgow. Henry Wuga.

Page 104 – photograph of Chitra's son watching the trains from the bridge over the tracks accessed from Princes Street Gardens, Edinburgh. Chitra Ramaswamy.

Page 107 – card issued to Annamaria Wuga regarding her exemption from internment. The National Archives, ref. HO396/202 (accessed via findmypast.co.uk).

Page 111 – photograph of four photos Henry took with his Zeiss Ikon Baby Box camera including the one (top left) of the Grand Synagogue of Nuremberg. Chitra Ramaswamy.

Page 113 – 'Yes. Even before 1933 . . .' The Avalon Project: Documents in Law, History and Diplomacy, Nuremberg Trial Proceedings Vol. 12, 116th day, April 29, 1946, morning session.

Page 113 – 'to my shame' 'Terrible really, just one of those things.' AJR Refugee Voices Testimony interview RV74 Anthony Grenville with Henry Wuga.

Page 115 – photograph of the cobblestones at John's Place, Edinburgh. Chitra Ramaswamy.

Page 119 – studio portrait of Lore, Henry and Karl in late 1930s Nuremberg. Henry Wuga/Jewish Museum Berlin.

Page 120 – 'This was before he knew . . .' 'The Last Word' by Maya Jaggi, *Guardian*, 21 December 2001.

Page 122 – photograph of Rama's hand lying across his panche as he holds Chitra's son. Chitra Ramaswamy.

Page 135 – photograph of Henry and Lore walking arm in arm in late 1930s Nuremberg. Henry Wuga.

Page 138 – photograph of the row of buildings opposite the entrance to Glasgow Central where the Corn Exchange once stood. Chitra Ramaswamy.

Page 139 – letter Robert Douglas sent to Henry on 28 August 1944. Henry Wuga.

Page 140 – studio portrait of Karl. Henry Wuga.

Page 141 – photograph of Henry and Ingrid on their wedding day. Henry Wuga.

Page 144 – photograph of a stretch of Scotland's Moray coast. Chitra Ramaswamy.

Page 146 – photograph of the house on the hill at 358 Sauchiehall Street, Glasgow. Copyright © the collections of the Scottish Jewish Archives Centre.

Page 149 – photograph of Henry and Ingrid talking at the house on the hill. Henry Wuga.

Page 151 – photograph of Henry and Ingrid on one of their weekend rambles with fellow refugees from the house on the hill. Henry Wuga.

Page 165 – *Rocks at Carrick* by David Sassoon (1888– 1978). Copyright © The Stewartry Museum, Dumfries & Galloway Council.

Page 168 – report about Henry by the procurator fiscal, Kircudbright, from Henry's file HO 405/60809. The

National Archives, ref. HO396/202.

Page 172 – 'The future of Jewish life . . .' 'Antisemitism "calling into question future of Jewish life in Europe"', *Guardian*, 1 May 2019.

Page 173 – 'Where was everybody? . . .' '"Thou shalt not be indifferent": from Auschwitz's gate of hell, a last, desperate warning' by Jonathan Freedland, *Guardian*, 27 January 2020.

Page 176 – photograph of Henry at Glasgow University. Chitra Ramaswamy.

Page 177 – photograph of Henry's hand holding the cloth yellow star Lore was forced to wear during the war. Chitra Ramaswamy.

Page 183 – photograph of Henry's class at the Jewish school in Fürth. Henry Wuga/Jewish Museum Berlin.

Page 184 – 'to resort hotels as Bergdorf Goodman is to department stores . . .' 'From the American Scene: The Green Pastures of Grossinger's' by Morris Freedman, *Commentary* magazine, July 1954.

Page 186 – photograph of the children at their desks in Henry's class at the Jewish school. Henry Wuga.

Page 190 – photograph of Non Viet Hai, Glasgow. Chitra Ramaswamy.

Page 191 – photograph of Shylaja and Rama in the garden they made behind their flat, London. Mani Ramaswamy.

Page 203 – 'I don't think history repeats itself . . .' 'Philippe Sands: "When the virus crisis is over, nationalism could be rampant"' by Rachel Cooke, *Observer New Review*, 26 April 2020.

Page 205 – studio portrait of Ingrid as a toddler. Henry Wuga.

Page 208 – photograph of budding magnolia in south-west London. Chitra Ramaswamy.

Page 213 – photograph of Helene Würzburger. Henry Wuga.

Page 215 – photograph of Henry cooking in the kitchens of the Hotel Tannhäuser, Baden-Baden, summer of 1938. Henry Wuga/Jewish Museum Berlin.

Page 220 – photographs of the synagogue and River Oos, Baden-Baden, taken by Henry with his Zeiss Ikon Baby Box camera. Henry Wuga.

Page 228 – photograph of the Jewish men paraded through the streets of Baden-Baden by the Nazis during the Reichspogromnacht. Copyright © bpk.

Page 230 – reference Johann Schneider sent to Henry on November 20, 1938. Henry Wuga.

Page 231 – photograph of the Stolpersteine for Theodor and August Köhler-Stern. Copyright © Stadtmuseum/-archiv Baden-Baden.

Page 232 – photograph of the buddleia outside Chitra's kitchen window. Chitra Ramaswamy.

Page 234 – photograph of Waverley Station, Edinburgh. Chitra Ramaswamy.

Page 236 – photograph of a heron on the River Thames at Chiswick Bridge. Chitra Ramaswamy.

Page 240 – Red Cross letter Lore sent to Henry informing him of Karl's death. Henry Wuga.

Page 242 – postcard Lore sent to Henry from Switzerland on 24 May 1946. Henry Wuga.

Page 245 – telegram Andre Kramer sent to Henry on 9 May 1945, informing him Lore was alive. Henry Wuga.

Page 249 – photograph of Lore in Nuremberg after the war. Henry Wuga.

Page 259 – photograph of Lore, Henry, Ingrid, Hilary and Gillian outside 32 Dalkeith Avenue, Glasgow. Henry Wuga.

Page 262 – 'the heart of the world's enemy', 'is a citadel of boredom', 'sometimes rises from the rubble . . .', 'that timeless institution . . .', 'that balance crazily . . .' 'Extraordinary Exile' by Rebecca West, *The New Yorker*, 30 August 1946.

Page 264 – 'The law tries to keep up with life . . .' 'Last Dramatic Scenes' by Rebecca West, *Daily Telegraph*, 1 October 1946

Page 264 – 'Then the court rose . . .' 'The Birch Leaves Falling' by Rebecca West, *The New Yorker*, 26 October 1946.

Page 268 – photograph of a postcard sent to Chitra by a friend after her mother's death. Chitra Ramaswamy.

Page 271 – vintage postcard of the Grand Hotel in Charing Cross, Glasgow. Sourced from glasgowhistory.com.

Page 273 – photograph of Henry catering a Jewish Burns supper. Henry Wuga.

Page 275 – photograph of a jar of Shylaja's rasam powder. Mani Ramaswamy.

Page 276 – photograph of Shylaja's dosas. Chitra Ramaswamy.

Page 280 – front and back of the 'white card' Henry had to show when he docked at Harwich in May 1939. Henry Wuga.

Page 284 – photograph of Henry and Ingrid skiing in Linn Park, Glasgow in the winter of 1945. Henry Wuga.

Page 286 – photograph of Chitra's house keys found on Leith Links. Chitra Ramaswamy.

Page 288 – studio portrait of Henry and Ingrid. Copyright © Robert Burns.

Page 296 – 'Habits once formed are difficult to get rid of . . .' *How Britain Rules Africa* by George Padmore, London, Wishart Books Ltd (1936).

Page 297 – photograph of The Queen's Hall, Edinburgh. Chitra Ramaswamy.

Page 300 – photograph of Shylaja, Chitra, Mani and a cousin in Bangalore. A.S. Ramaswamy.

Page 302 – photograph of Shylaja, Chitra and Rama walking in Richmond Park, London. Mani Ramaswamy.

Page 304 – photograph of the gates of the Jewish section of Cathcart Cemetery, Glasgow. Chitra Ramaswamy.

Page 307 – photograph of Chitra and Henry outside Cathcart Cemetery, Glasgow. Gillian Field.

Page 323 – photograph of the railway bridge over the River Clyde, Glasgow. Chitra Ramaswamy.